WITHDRAWN
UTSA LIBRARIES

Cetshwayo Ka Mpande

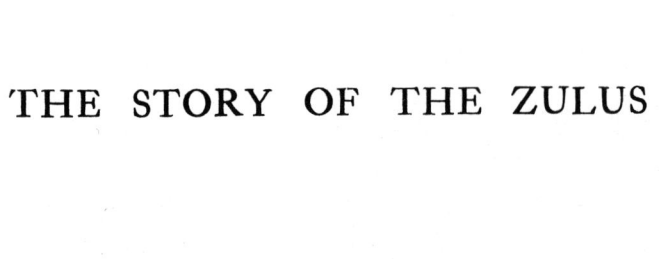
THE STORY OF THE ZULUS

THE STORY OF THE ZULUS

BY

J. Y. GIBSON
FOR SOME YEARS A MAGISTRATE IN ZULULAND

WITH 11 ILLUSTRATIONS

NEW EDITION, REVISED AND EXTENDED

NEGRO UNIVERSITIES PRESS
NEW YORK

Originally published in 1911
by Longmans, Green and Co., London

Reprinted in 1970 by
Negro Universities Press
A Division of Greenwood Press, Inc.
Westport, Connecticut

SBN 8371-3592-3

Printed in United States of America

PREFACE TO NEW EDITION

THE writing of this book was brought about rather by the influence of the author's circumstances than by any aspiration or desire on his part to appear before the public in the character of a writer. During his childhood, which was spent in Natal, one of the chief topics of conversation there, of both the black and the white races, was the Zulus. His mind was filled with thrilling tales of what they had done and were doing, all rendered the more romantic by a surrounding element of haze. In after years, when he chanced to be closely associated with the people and the affairs of their country, he was led by a natural process to inquire into the actual facts. The task was one to which it was necessary to devote a good deal of time and patience. There were many Zulus living who possessed the information which was required, but, scattered as they were over a wide extent of country, there was difficulty, first in learning of and then in meeting them. Eventually, however, the material was got together which was embodied in the first edition. It was hoped, amongst other things, that publication would call forth criticism of a kind which would help in rendering the work more perfect, but this hope was not realised. Those who read the book were disposed rather to regard it as authoritative, and to say kind things about it. The whole responsibility in the matter thus remained with the author, and he has felt it to be his duty, after the lapse of some years, to reprint it in a revised and extended form. It has been found possible from authorities which were unexpectedly discovered, to make certain chronological

PREFACE TO NEW EDITION

adjustments, and continued inquiry has yielded material for fuller accounts of certain events. The narrative has also been extended to a later date.

It is hoped that the merit of accuracy may be claimed for the book as regards matters of fact; and much of the matter which it contains would not be available now to any more skilful writer who might desire to write on the subject.

As regards the subject, it is felt that it cannot fail to interest a certain number for some time. Amongst the influences which induced and directed the expansion of European occupation, of which the establishment of the *Union of South Africa* is the late culminating event, a prominent place must be given to the doings of the Zulus under their short line of kings. It is believed that the book will indicate in a considerable measure how that influence operated, and also that the deep and wide impression which was created by those people themselves during the nineteenth century has not yet been entirely effaced from the minds of general readers. Whilst hoping, however, with a certain degree of confidence, that the book may prove of some general utility, the author's chief gratification would be derived from the knowledge that it had commended itself to the attention of his fellow-colonists of a younger generation.

Of those for whose kindly help the author is indebted, he would specially mention Mr. H. V. Ellis, late master of Hilton College in Natal, whose continued interest in all that relates to the Colony he served so long and so well, coupled with his sympathetic disposition towards a visitor to this great city from the scene of his labours, has induced him to examine the proofs, and afford advice, the value of which will be fully appreciated by his many friends.

LONDON, *August* 1911.

LIST OF ILLUSTRATIONS

CETSHWAYO KA MPANDE	*Frontispiece*	
MATIWANE AND SOME OF HIS DESCENDANTS .	*Facing p.*	5
ZULU SMITH FORGING AN ASSEGAI . . .	,,	6
TSHAKA	,,	22
From Nathaniel Isaacs' "Travels and Adventures in Eastern Africa," 1836.		
INGXOTA, OR ARMLET	,,	51
ISANDHLWANA	,,	174
ZULU WAR MONUMENT	,,	214
SIR MELMOTH OSBORN	,,	222
CETSHWAYO ON BOARD SHIP	,,	234
USIBEBU	,,	255
ITSHANA, OR ETSHANENI BATTLEFIELD . .	,,	272

	PAGE
ZULU GENEALOGICAL TABLE	317

THE STORY OF THE ZULUS

CHAPTER I

It is said that those tribes who have become known generally as Abantu—a name which might, perhaps, be more correctly written Aba'Ntu—came to South Africa from the north of the continent, "under three thousand years ago."[1] No doubt so long a period might be sufficient, in itself, to account for the entire absence of tradition amongst the people themselves of this migration.

The question is one, however, which lies outside the scope of the present little volume. I desire only to furnish an account of the events, as far as they are ascertainable, of a remarkable evolution of one of these tribes, which commenced in the eighteenth, and was the subject of wide attention during the greater part of the nineteenth century.

But a few words descriptive of the condition which obtained before it was disturbed in the manner to be narrated may not be uninteresting in this first chapter. When Europeans first set foot upon the land which Vasco Da Gama had named Natal, the people who occupied it were of as settled habits as at any time since. This was in 1687, when certain shipwrecked Dutch and English mariners were forced to make a sojourn in the land. They explored it to a distance of

[1] Sir H. H. Johnston's *Colonization of Africa*.

some 1·50 miles inland. They described it as populous. The natives were "friendly, compassionate, strong, ingenious; armed with only an assegai; obedient and submissive to their chief; lived in communities, in huts made of branches, wrought through with rushes and long grass, and roofed like hay-stacks in Holland. The women attended to cultivation and the men herded and milked the cows." They planted corn from which they made "very well-tasting and nourishing bread and brewed beer." They were extremely hospitable: "the men and women vied with each other in offering food and drink, and their habitations for lodgings."

Written records are meagre; but there are remains to be found on the old dwelling-places of these Abantu from which something can still be learned of their habits of life. Where wood was scarce they were compelled to use stones for the construction of their cattle pens, and many of these are still to be found, varying greatly in age, but affording no certain data for fixing the period of their construction. Wherever they occur they are the same in shape, and of nearly the same dimensions. They are all circular, and few of them are more than about fifteen yards in diameter. This circumstance indicates that the people were not in the habit of keeping large herds at their own homes; that the rich saved themselves the labour which would have been involved in increasing the size of their pens to accommodate their increasing herds, and some of the risks of loss from plunder, by apportioning their superfluous beasts amongst the poor. Large families did not live together. They formed separate homesteads amongst the fruitful spots. The habitations were placed around the pens so that the inmates might be in a position to guard them, and the space to be guarded had to be proportionate to the number guarding it. Around these cattle pens, some of them so old that they have become completely covered over with mould, their presence being indicated only by circular elevations, may still be found such relics as pot-sherds, or the stones upon which the cooking pots were supported over the fire, or, more rarely, those upon which grain or snuff was ground.

A monument of the past which is more general, as its coming into existence did not depend upon the presence or otherwise of wood, is the Isivivane—stone cairn. It is unimposing in appearance, and may be passed without notice by the unobservant, but some information may be gained from it as to whether the locality in which it is found has been long or thickly populated. It was the custom of wayfarers to place a stone, and a handful of grass, upon these cairns as an act of propitiation to the guardian spirit of the tribe amongst the members of which they were to seek hospitality; and so, stone by stone, slowly or rapidly according to the number of passers-by, they grew in height and breadth, whilst the tribe remained in the locality to whose guardian spirit they belonged.

The dwellings of the people were so simple, and so temporary in their character, as to suggest the possibility that their design had been derived from nomadic habits. Long wattles or saplings were inserted in the ground, in a circle, and tied together, diagonally, with fibrous grass, the upper ends being gradually drawn together in a dome shape, and the centre supported by one or more posts set in the floor. Over this wattle-work a thick coat of grass was laid, and fastened with plaited grass. The work of constructing the framework was performed by the men; that of thatching by the women.

These huts leaked less as the thatch became more encrusted and solidified by the soot from the fire in the centre of the floor, at which the inmates warmed themselves and upon which their meals were cooked. They were about fifteen feet in diameter, without partition, and each generally served to accommodate a number of persons of both sexes, who slept upon the floor, on straw mats, covered with such skins of animals as they had been able to procure.

The furniture consisted of such articles only as were necessary to the rudest form of comfort. There was little besides the simple bedding and rough earthen pots. An important provision was the Uzwati, or stick for producing fire by friction. This was kept for emergencies. It was a dried stalk of a weed, or shrub, about $\tfrac{3}{8}$ths of an inch in diameter and 18 inches long. In use, the end of this was placed in a hollow near the edge of a flat piece of wood, which was held on the ground by the operator with his feet, and it was made to rotate by rubbing it between the palms, the powder produced by the friction finding its way through a notch, cut for the purpose, to, and forming a pile upon, some powdered grass or other easily ignitible material arranged to receive it. To produce a spark by this means required certain skill which could only be acquired by practice. It was laborious, too, often producing some blisters, and there was a great risk of failure to kindle a flame from the small quantity of glowing powder which resulted. Means were therefore adopted for the preservation of fire, such as burying glowing embers in ashes. If this failed, and it became necessary to fetch it from the kraal of a neighbour, it was done by means of a plant called Inkondhlwana,[1] which, if twisted into a rope and ignited at the end, will glow till the whole is consumed. It was thus used either for conveying fire from a distance or, by placing it, lighted, in a sheltered spot, for preserving it through the night.

The land was tilled by means of a hoe, the production

---

[1] Helichrysum aureo-nitens (Sch. Bip.).

MATIWANE AND SOME OF HIS DESCENDANTS

of which formed the chief industry of the workers in iron. Though rude in its design it was an expensive article, owing to the large amount of labour it cost in producing. It was a rough oval-shaped blade, with a long shank, which was inserted in a hole that had been burnt through the wooden handle.

The art of working in iron was handed down from father to son, and continued as the heritage of families for many generations. There is nothing to show that time effected any change or improvement in their methods, or that a higher degree of skill was attained in one locality than in another. There is no difference in the remains of their forges and furnaces in different localities.

Few smiths now remain, and the operations of these are confined to the making of assegais. They no longer smelt their own iron, but use such scraps of the European article as they can find. Their habitations are usually remote from the haunts of Europeans; their forges are so unimposing that one might pass close to where they are without becoming aware of their existence. It is therefore natural that few are seen at work by those who might be interested in witnessing how implements were made in the olden days, and the weapons with which Tshaka's army carried out its work of destruction in the nineteenth century. For the purpose of the description here given, a visit was paid, at the cost of a twenty-mile ride across hilly and almost pathless country in a remote part of Zululand, to the residence of a man named Matiwane. He was of great age, and the trade at which he had worked while he had strength was now carried on by his son, who, by pre-arrangement, had his appliances in readiness and quickly rewarded curiosity by forging an assegai. His methods, so far as they were exhibited, were identical with those by which his father, and father's fathers, had worked. The hammers and tongs which he used had been made by the elder man from iron of his own smelting.

Their production had cost him much labour, and they had been carefully preserved. The punching of the eyes of the hammers had been an especially difficult task, as was evident, in one case, by the angle at which it had gone through. The heads were square in shape, the largest being about an inch and a half thick and two inches and a half long. They were only used for light work and finishing; heavy stones were employed to reduce large pieces of iron to a manageable size. Stones, partially embedded in the ground, were used as anvils, the operator sitting down to his work. We saw only one pair of tongs, which were used principally for the purpose of taking the iron out of the fire. For that of holding it in position on the anvil, hollowed sticks of wood were employed, into which the colder end was inserted. The bellows, though primitive, were ingenious. They consisted of a bag made of softened ox-hide, about the size and shape of a pillow-case. In one corner of this was inserted a wooden pipe about three feet long, the corner being tightly bound over it with a string to prevent the escape of air. The other end of the bag was open and hemmed over two straight bits of wood, which closed it tightly when pressed together. Loops were fastened on the outside, into which the fingers and thumb of the blower were inserted, so that the bag opened and shut with the movements of the hand. The pipe, with the end of the bag, was held down by a heavy stone laid upon it, and the process of blowing consisted of raising the other end with the mouth held open to admit the air, and then closing and pressing it down again. Two of these were used, the blower sitting on the ground between, and raising and depressing them alternately, with his right and left hand, so as to secure a continuous blast. The ends of the wooden pipes met at the mouth of a funnel- or trumpet-shaped one of clay, the thin end of which was inserted in a charcoal fire, for which a small hollow had been made in the ground. These clay pipes

Zulu Smith forging an Assegai
From a photograph

were not burnt before use; and this accounts for the fact that only the hardened nozzles are to be found in old abandoned forges: the rest, the unburnt part, having perished.

For smelting iron a large number of bellows were used. The blowers sat round the rude furnace, in which the broken-up ore was held in position by clay receptacles, and blew until it was melted, the iron obtained being afterwards rendered malleable by a process which the writer has been unable to ascertain. Steel was not produced, although, probably from the use of charcoal, a metal of a superior quality was obtained, and blades made from it were used for shaving.

The wants of the people were thus simple, and simply supplied.

They were ambitious of authority and praise, and those who were able to acquire a larger number of cattle than their neighbours were in a position to gratify these desires by lending to the needy. They could gather families of such round them, to whom they came to stand in the relation of chiefs, who appealed to them for settlement of their disputes, and amongst whom they maintained social order. They were in a position to command the help of these dependants when their own rights were assailed or their claims disputed. New tribes were thus continually created, to be subdivided, later, by family disputes, producing the condition of things well described by Sir Theophilus Shepstone in a paper read before the Society of Arts in Natal on the 22nd of January 1875.

His information had been supplied by persons who had personally experienced the condition, and he says that "up to about the year 1812, and for how many years before we cannot tell, the country was thickly populated by numerous tribes under independent chiefs. These tribes lived so close together that tribal change of residence was difficult, if not impossible. They intermarried with each other, possessed flocks and herds, lived at ease themselves and at peace with their neighbours; until this luxury occasionally culminated in a quarrel (as is the natural tendency, the natives say, in all that grow fat), and these quarrels were settled by a fight; but these fights were by no means the serious matters they afterwards became. The day was fixed beforehand; the men of the rival tribes met in battle on that day; and the result of a single encounter settled the difference."[1] He estimated that the people living in this condition in the land, which afterwards formed the Colony of Natal, numbered about a million souls. The old man, Matiwane, was able to remember the time when that condition of things had not been entirely terminated, and he described the domains of some then prominent chiefs. The areas which he indicated were so small that it was difficult to realise that they afforded dwelling-place for such considerable tribes as these appear, from tradition, to have been. There were no defined boundaries, even, to divide their several territories.

The people were not troubled with thoughts of national advancement. The condition in which they lived was sufficient for them. They had no conception of a purpose in life beyond mere enjoyment. There was that in Nature which sufficiently gladdened the hearts of all, and they made little modification of Nature's provisions. The interests of a man centred chiefly in his cattle. He would rise early and regard them with placid satisfaction as they filed out of the narrow gate for their morning browse. Their home-coming to be milked at about eleven o'clock, lowing for their calves, while the herd-boys responded by shrilly whistling and reciting their praises, was the gladdest occasion of the day. The men milked them with great leisure, the milk being poured into gourds, to be formed into curds and cream, a prized

[1] Bird's *Annals of Natal*, i. 156.

article of diet. Beyond this the men had little duty to perform. Their days were spent in making milk-pails, spoons or sticks, as their mood dictated, or reposing in their huts. Game was very plentiful, but could only be secured by parties large enough to surround it. The only weapon was the assegai, and this could not be successfully thrown at any great distance. The habit of hunting in large parties necessitated a well-defined Law of Chase, and this has been handed down and continues to be rigidly observed. To the person who first strikes a quarry it belongs when secured, but prescribed portions are due, and readily yielded, to each who contributes to its capture. This law secures a wide distribution of the proceeds of a day's hunting.

Hunting parties were called out by the chief of a tribe, or, on a smaller scale, by subordinate head-men. The men and boys assembled in little companies, into which they had been formed by relationship or proximity of dwellings, and each, following some recognised head, or captain, saluted the master of the hunt on arrival by dancing before him. When all had thus sufficiently shown their respect, and indulged themselves in merriment, they were made to seat themselves on the ground, each company in its place, and were instructed by the appointed director of the hunt as to the position they were to take up in the encircling movement. Each company had some name by which they were called upon successively, and the lines of men streamed out to the right and left, the leaders meeting at a given point, thus surrounding and gradually closing in upon the cover. The startled bucks, after running to and fro, were compelled eventually to seek escape by breaking through the line, and so to afford an opportunity to some of throwing their assegais. Much merriment was displayed at these hunts, and the great activity they entailed contributed largely, no doubt, to the agility by which the race continues to be characterised. The military organisation and tactics of the Zulus owed their system largely to those of the hunting methods of the olden days.

The young boys who herded the cattle met on the grazing ground those from neighbouring kraals. They had boyish fights, which turned their differences into friendship; had their own small hunting parties, sometimes killing birds, rabbits or small bucks; and, when not thus employed, they played together, making little circles on flat stones, with mud, to represent cattle kraals, with dots around for huts. Inside the circles they placed pebbles, or rude models in clay, representing cattle, each of which they would associate with some individual animal in their fathers' herds. They grew up and acquired real kraals and real herds, and pursued the same indolent life as their fathers; and, when they died, neither work nor tradition remained to speak of them to later generations. "He has eaten" came to be a consolatory remark on the death of a very old man. The cause for gratitude, in their minds, was that he had been long spared to enjoy the pleasures of life, not in anything that he had accomplished.

Tradition tells of no events, and there were probably none so important as to make a wide impression. The Abantu, up to the period to be referred to at the commencement of the next chapter, may be regarded as having been a "happy people whose annals were vacant."

CHAPTER II

EVENTFUL history, so far as is known, or can now be known, had its beginning in the last twenty years of the eighteenth century. It began with a man named Godongwana, who in later life assumed the name by which he has become known, Dingiswayo—The Troubled One. He chose this name in reference to circumstances which had set him wandering in his youth. Much more has followed in direct sequence from those circumstances than the wanderings of Godongwana.

It was found, or considered, necessary by all who held authority amongst these Abantu tribes to repress with most rigid measures anything in the nature of pretensions to the positions they occupied. Death was immediately inflicted on any person, whatever his family relationship, who by any act appeared to have assumed the functions of the ruling chief. Jobe, the chief of the Umtetwa tribe, which occupied the coast-land between the rivers Umfolozi and Umhlatuzi, in the country which afterwards became known as Zululand, was led to apprehend danger from a desire his son Mawewe appears to have evinced to succeed him. He followed the usual course by ordering that Mawewe and his brother Godongwana should be put to death. Execution followed in the case of the first, but the second escaped wounded, to return, after wide travels, and gain the chieftainship after his father's death. Romantic tales were told of the dangers he had passed through, and of the prowess and strength he had displayed; but what is of more importance here is the fact that a new idea appears to have been infused into his mind by what he saw in strange lands. He reached Cape Colony, and there came into contact with white men. He witnessed the drilling of European soldiers; and he thought of how his own Umtetwa people might be improved in their fighting powers by subjecting them to a somewhat similar discipline. His home-coming was marked by romantic incidents, but no details can now be gathered from which it would be possible to furnish a complete account of these. He was accompanied by a white man, whose identity has been lost; he rode on a horse, and carried a gun, neither of which had ever been seen in his own country before. The wonder of these accompaniments preceded him through the tribes on his way, and inspired feelings of awe amongst his people, which led to such a force joining him on his arrival as enabled him to overcome the opposition of a brother who had assumed authority in his absence. On establishing himself in the chieftainship, he set about carrying into effect the new ideas which he had imbibed. He called together all the men of the tribe and formed them into regiments, each regiment being composed of men of nearly equal age, and distinguished by a regimental name, by which the members were thenceforth called. There was thus no limit to the number forming a regiment, but each was divided into companies of about fifty men, headed by an induna, or captain, whose duty it was to lead them to the attack. They were drilled so that each company could be made to take up the position assigned to it by the regimental commander, and a systematic attack could thus be substituted for the disorderly assaults which had hitherto obtained. The system conferred such advantage that the neighbouring tribes found themselves unable to oppose effectually the attacks to which they were in turn subjected. One by one they yielded submission, and, from being the chief of a tribe which could not have been very large, and which has never since his day been counted specially warlike, Dingiswayo attained the position of paramount ruler over a wide extent of country. The conquests were generally easy, and the position he assumed was no doubt one which conferred a boon on many who could claim his aid against power which had till then been unrestrained. The royal salute, Bayete, may be conceived, at least in its present form, to have originated then and in these circumstances. There have been differences of ópinion amongst linguists as to the idea it expresses, but it is admittedly an abbreviation of three words, "Ma ba lete," signifying "let them bring." There is this peculiarity in the Umtetwa speech, that the "y" sound is employed where "l" is used in Zulu. Thus their pronunciation of "Ma ba lete" would be "Ma ba yete." It would take the character of a proclamation by the praisers of the king to this effect:—The all-powerful reigns, if there be that which oppresses, or troubles, the people, let them bring it—" and he will give them rest."

The extent to which Dingiswayo carried his conquests is not definitely known, but he appears to have acquired dominion over most of the tribes between the Tugela and Pongolo rivers, and his warlike operations created consternation amongst people at even a greater distance. Tribal migration began, with fighting between those who desired to escape him and those through whose land they had to pass in order to do so. His reign extended over a considerable period, his death occurring, as well as can be ascertained, about the year 1818. The deeds of his life were so much eclipsed by those of a succeeding reign that Zulu tradition furnishes few details concerning them. Many items of interest were gathered by Europeans, who were amongst the first to settle in Natal, from natives who had personal recollections of him. From the account of one of these,[1] based on information so gathered, Dingiswayo

[1] Henry Francis Fynn.

would appear to have been imbued with laudable aims for the advancement and welfare of the people over whom he ruled.

"In the first year of his Chieftainship he opened a trade with Delagoa Bay by sending 100 oxen and a quantity of elephants' tusks in exchange for beads and blankets," and "the trade thus opened was afterwards continued on an extensive scale." "The encouragement held out to ingenuity brought numbers round him, liberal rewards being given to any followers who devised things new or ornamental. Milk dishes, pillows, ladles (of cane or wood), and snuff-boxes were produced. A karosse manufactory was established, a hundred men being generally employed in the work. From the presents he received from Delagoa Bay he selected some for imitation, and a handsome reward was offered for the production of a chair or table. The former article of furniture was actually made. It was cut out of a solid block of wood, and was by no means disgraced even in the presence of its model of European workmanship."

Some few specimens of the kind of chair thus produced are still extant. With the appliances available the work of shaping them must have been very great, and the result, though interesting, could scarcely be considered useful. Probably none but the one artificer ever attempted to make one. It may, indeed, be considered as certain that no permanent fruit resulted from any efforts of Dingiswayo to infuse thoughts of advancement into the minds of the people. Their habits had become too fixed for this to be possible, except by a very slow process.

Such as these were the attributes he is reputed to have possessed, and displayed, in times of peace; but we are told, on the other hand, by an equally good authority,[1] that "Let the weak sow and the strong reap" was his motto, and that "he always halted his army till his

[1] Sir T. Shepstone.

THE STORY OF THE ZULUS

enemy's corn was exhausted." Those described as "enemies" may, perhaps, be more correctly regarded as having been inoffensive tribes against whom he wantonly made war, or whose cattle he desired to possess. His facetious war-song would point to the latter as having been his chief motive:

> "Lezo 'Nkomo, zi 'mbala muni na?
> Zi no 'mland' omkulo,"

which may be thus freely translated:

> "What mean the varied hues of yonder kine?
> Their owners' sins have thereby mark'd them mine!"

The imputation of sin, or wrong-doing, to those whom he sought to despoil is some evidence, however, that he recognised the principle so deeply rooted in the race of which he was a member, that punishment should be justified by some kind of guilt on the part of the recipient.

Most of the tribes readily yielded submission, in order to be allowed to live in peace, but there were some whose submission was very partial, and one at least which he never succeeded in overcoming. This was the Ndwandwe tribe, which occupied the highlands north of the Black Umfolozi River, under a chief named Zwidi. He was married to a sister of Dingiswayo, named Gidjimi, and a high degree of personal friendship subsisted between them, which did not, however, prevent them from frequently going to war with each other. On these occasions Zwidi was generally worsted; he is said to have been sometimes even taken prisoner, but always released again on account of his relationship to his captor. But eventually Dingiswayo's own turn came to be captured, and then he did not meet with the same consideration. The story of his last military expedition is still told by the older Zulus, and their version agrees exactly with that which was obtained and recorded by the early settlers. Malusi, the chief of the Nxumalo section of the Ndwandwe tribe, had appealed to Dingiswayo with respect to some attack or ill-treatment he had suffered at the hands of Zwidi. Dingiswayo sent a remonstrance, but to this an insolent challenge was returned by Zwidi. And, knowing what the result of this would be, the latter anticipated matters, and proceeded with his force in the direction from which he expected the enemy would advance. The meeting took place at Hlabisa, and Dingiswayo, being in advance of the main body of his force, was overcome and taken prisoner. He was brought to the kraal of Zwidi, the site of which is at the north end of the Sigwekwe Hill and near to where the Nongoma Magistracy now stands. The site is marked by a large fig tree, which was planted there in Zwidi's time. There Dingiswayo was put to death: some say by his own desire, as he felt unable to brook the indignity he had suffered in being taken; others that his execution was insisted upon by Zwidi's chief wife.

When Dingiswayo was dead his example was pursued by the chief of the house of Zulu, by name Tshaka. He counted an ancestry of nine chiefs, whose names and order of succession are given as Malandela, Ntombela, Zulu, Nkosinkulu, Punga, Mageba, Ndaba, Jama, and Senzangakona. These lived and ruled successively over their little tribe on the Umkumbane and Unzololo Streams, on the south of the White Umfolozi River, extending their occupation to an unascertained limit towards the Ibabanango hills. The graves of all are still pointed out there, and the district is called Makosini, the place of kings, or chiefs. Nothing is definitely known concerning any of them individually, except the last; but that the tribe should have been called the Children of Zulu, the third in succession, is evidence that he was distinguished by some personal attributes. It was probably he who first acquired authority over other people than the members of his own family.

The last of these nine chiefs, Senzangakona, had attained a position of some importance, but he was included amongst those who became subject to the authority of Dingiswayo. He was, however, but little interfered with in the rule of his own tribe, and, in a small measure, followed the example of that chief by forming the men of his tribe into a little army of his own.

His son, Tshaka, manifested what he regarded as a dangerous disposition, and the course usual in such cases was decided upon. Tshaka escaped, however, and, with his mother, Nandi, went to her father's home in the Langa tribe, then occupying lands in the part of the country which has become known as the Nkandhla District of Zululand. From thence he went to the Umtetwa country, and resided with, and served in warlike operations under, Dingiswayo. He so distinguished himself in valour that he was given the title of Sigidi, Thousand, in reference to the number of the enemy whom he had slain. On Senzangakona's death Tshaka succeeded him as chief over the People of Zulu, being assisted in the attainment of that position by Dingiswayo. He added the strength of his own little army to that of his patron, and together they continued to harass the numerous tribes. He was thus able to establish a reputation as a commander and ruler before the commencement of his independent career.

Dingiswayo had not greatly altered the tribal condition. Submission had been yielded, and tribute paid to him during his lifetime; but the chiefs had been allowed to remain in authority over their several tribes, and, when his personality was removed, they were little disposed to continue their allegiance to his successor in the Umtetwa chieftainship. Tshaka seized upon the opportunity which the circumstances presented to reconquer and establish his own rule over them. To this end he subjected the army under his command to more rigid discipline than had been previously enforced. An

B

experiment taught him that by carrying only one assegai, and engaging the enemy hand-to-hand, his men could fight more effectively than they had been able to do when armed with several, including a certain number for throwing. He therefore deprived them of all but one spear, and this he required that they should bring back with them out of the conflict, if they returned alive. He enlarged his army by adding to its strength the men who remained of the tribes he conquered, and of those who voluntarily submitted to him in order to avoid destruction. He impressed upon his warriors that they had to conquer or die. At the conclusion of each battle the "cowards" were "picked out," under his personal supervision, if he were present, or, in his absence, under the supervision of the man in chief command. They were reported by the sectional leaders, and met with sudden and violent death. Until their doom was pronounced men so selected felt, probably, that they had performed deeds worthy of a different reward. There can be no doubt that much injustice was done in this respect, as in the case of the execution of Zulus which took place at other times and for other causes. But it was a kind of injustice which never strongly impressed itself upon the minds of the nation. It was generally supposed that the victims had committed the offences for which they suffered. In the case of the selection of cowards, the leaders whose duty it was to do so may conceivably have been guided by considerations of personal safety, and have chosen at random for the mere purpose of proving that they had given close attention to the conduct of the men under their command; or availed themselves of the opportunity the situation afforded of securing the removal of persons against whom they entertained a personal grudge. But the effect was that which was desired. The conflicts were close and violent, and the participants were prevented by the necessities of self-protection from observing the con-

THE STORY OF THE ZULUS 19

duct of their comrades with much precision. Cases of injustice would thus escape notice; and this must have been so, for tradition does not say that other than cowards suffered. The practice was certainly a strong stimulus to valour.

Of the several exploits by which Tshaka established and extended his dominion few details can be gathered from the Zulus. There is an exception in the case of his wars with the tribe by which Dingiswayo was tąken and slain. Zwidi, the chief of this tribe, was his most formidable opponent. His lands were not extensive. They lay north from the Black Umfolozi River, and south and east from the Ingome forest, but it is impossible to form a correct idea of their limits, other tribes being also mentioned as having dwelt in the locality. For two years after Tshaka had begun his career of conquest this tribe continued to be superior to his in strength. Zwidi held him in contempt, and failed to appreciate his increasing power. It was impossible that the two could remain long so close together as they were without measuring their strength against each other. About the year 1820 the offensive was assumed by Zwidi. He despatched his army to attack Tshaka in his own country south of the White Umfolozi. Tshaka did not remain there to meet him, but assembled his army and people and retreated south, crossing the Tugela River near its mouth. Zwidi's forces pursued him; but as Tshaka either carried away, or destroyed, all food supplies along the route, their provisions were exhausted by the time they reached the Tugela. Then they began to retrace their steps, but by the time they reached the Umhlatuzi River they were reduced to a famished condition. This was what Tshaka had anticipated, and his warriors overtaking them there, the greater part of the manhood of the Ndwandwe tribe were destroyed. Zwidi had no force left sufficient to battle with that of Tshaka, the advent of which might be immediately expected, and such men as remained were completely unnerved by the slaughter which had taken place of their tribesmen. So there was no course left him but to gather his people and flocks and herds and what else of their effects they might be able to carry, and betake himself to a new land. He was pursued as far as the Pongolo River, but escaped to the Drakensberg, north of where the town of Utrecht stands, and there established a settlement and died.

By the expulsion of this tribe, Tshaka was relieved from the presence of any enemy capable of causing him apprehension. Such tribes as remained in a semi-independent state were necessitated to concern themselves rather with the question how to escape destruction at his hands than with any scheme of making an attack upon him. He had become the ruler of a nation, but a new element soon appeared which was to have an important influence on the nation's destiny. Since the discovery of the Bay of Natal by Vasco Da Gama in 1497, ships had visited it only at long intervals, and merely for the purpose of obtaining supplies. Amongst the people who were united under Tshaka, there were none who had held communication with men who fared by sea. There was some tradition and rumour only concerning them, the latter having reference to the killing by neighbouring tribes of sailors who had escaped from wrecks. Thus when he looked out upon the world, it was upon a world peopled by members of his own race, with little or no variation in their habits or pursuits. He had no example to guide him in the choice of any new aim which he might desire to inculcate; his inherited idea and the circumstances in which he had grown up suggested the formation of the people into an effective fighting force, with his own greatness as the object of their wars. Now during the lull in martial activity which succeeded the completion of his conquests, there came intelligence that white men had been seeking a landing with the object of opening up a trade with his country. In 1823, Lieutenant

Farewell from Port Elizabeth visited his shore with that aim, and on his landing at St. Lucia, he lost through desertion a Cape frontier native named Jacob Msimbiti, whom he had taken with him as an interpreter. This man found his way to Tshaka at the Nobamba kraal in the White Umfolozi valley, which had been the principal residence of his father. Jacob related to Tshaka his experiences, and what his master had sought to effect. He excited much interest, and was given the name of Hlambamanzi, signifying, "Swim-the-water," and accorded a place of distinction in the king's establishment. Although Farewell did not succeed on this occasion, he did not abandon his scheme. In the following year he chartered two other vessels, and, having landed at the Natal Bay, he and his companion Henry Francis Fynn were accorded a hearty welcome at the Bulawayo kraal in July 1824. This was the first meeting of Tshaka with white men, and they were largely indebted for their favourable reception to what had been related concerning them by Jacob, while the records they made are the chief resource of those who would acquaint themselves with any degree of definiteness with the position Tshaka had gained by this time, and with the methods by which he ruled. During this first visit they witnessed two occurrences of considerable interest, confirming the impression of Tshaka which has continued to be held by later generations of his race, that he was a man who ordered his subjects to execution without preferring a charge or admitting of any defence, and showing that he had incurred a high degree of resentment. The first was a summary order that a man who was standing near should be put to death—"for what crime," says Fynn, "we could not learn; but we soon found it," he adds, "to be one of the common occurrences in the course of the day"; the other was an attempt upon Tshaka's own life, to which further reference will be made.

The time at which the visit took place was exceedingly

fortunate. It was during a peaceful interval, and the visitors were thus placed in a position to note Tshaka's habits of home life, concerning which there is little to be gathered from tradition. It is, perhaps, easier to secure increased means than a corresponding increase of capacity for enjoying them. Thus the great wealth which the spoils of fallen tribes supplied made but little change in Tshaka's personal wants. His fare differed but little from that of a native of ordinary means. He knew of no choicer food than boiled beef, and the beer which was the beverage of any man successful in raising a crop of grain. His eyes were reddened by the smoke which filled the ventless hut in which he lived. He slept on a straw mat, with a wooden pillow to support his head, and a mantle made of the skins of animals to cover his body. His apparel was neither so rare nor so costly as to be beyond the means of a common man. The dress in which he appeared on great occasions is thus described by Fynn, who stood by while Tshaka bedecked himself, preparatory to appearing before a multitude of his warriors and people who had assembled at his residence to " make him mirth ": " Round his forehead he wore a turban of otter-skin, with a feather of a crane erect in front, fully two feet long. Earrings of dried sugar-cane, carved round the edges, with white ends, and an inch in diameter, were let into the lobes of his ears, which had been cut to admit them. From shoulder to shoulder he wore bunches, three inches in length, of the skins of monkeys and genets, twisted like the tails of these animals, and hanging half-way down his body. Round the ring on the head were a dozen bunches of the red feathers of the lory bird, tastefully tied to thorns, which were stuck into the hair. Round the arms were white ox-tails, cut down the middle so as to allow the hair to hang about the arm, to the number of four to each. Round the waist a petticoat, resembling the Highland kilt, made of the skins of genets and twisted

TSHAKA

(*From Nathaniel Isaac's "Travels and Adventures in Eastern Africa," 1836.*)

as before described, having small tassels round the top, the petticoat reaching the knees, below which were white ox-tails to fit round the knees so as to hang to the ankles."

His extravagance lay in acts making for the manifestation and recognition of his power. Some 12,000 fighting men were assembled, and were dancing and singing in symphony a song which it pleased him to hear; perhaps one of his own composing, something in the nature of a motto only about eight or ten words in length, perhaps his great war-song—

> "The nations he hath scatter'd far,
> Whither shall he now wage war?"

or words commemorative of some battle in which he felt an especial pride, stress being laid on the enemy's discomfiture on that occasion. While this dance was proceeding (and it was kept up all day, and for several succeeding days), immense droves of cattle were brought near and exhibited by those in charge of them; he derived a great satisfaction from regarding those herds, a satisfaction arising from a simple sense of possession. Many hundreds of women, many of them girls of whom he was as completely the owner as of the cattle, also took part in the singing, and none was more active in the dancing than Tshaka himself.

These proceedings were terminated by the attempt to assassinate him already mentioned. The assegai had pierced his arm, and passed through between the ribs below the left breast, but had not penetrated sufficiently to cause fatal injury. Fynn was called in to attend to the wound, and applied simple remedies. He recorded that the king cried all night from fear, thinking that the wound might prove fatal. But it may reasonably be doubted whether the tears he shed were induced by a fear of this nature. Under the circumstances, a wound of a much less serious nature would probably have caused the same display of emotion. On another occasion (to be mentioned later), he is said to have shed copious tears, although it was considered that their cause was neither fear nor excess of sorrow. This was at the death of his mother Nandi.

Zwidi's people had prospered in their new distant mountain-land, and had become so strong again that Tshaka felt that it would be necessary to proceed against them. They were being represented as a menace; it was believed, or affected to be believed, that the assassin who had failed in his attempt was an emissary of that tribe.

Tshaka's recovery was not long delayed, and he attributed it in some measure to the skill of Fynn and Farewell. His attitude towards them was all that they could desire. He gave them free permission to trade, made them generous gifts of cattle, and Farewell returned to his place at the Bay armed with a signed cession of a large tract of territory, extending one hundred miles inland, and including the Harbour. This cession was dated the 8th of August 1824.

CHAPTER III

LIEUTENANT FAREWELL was considerably astonished by the state of things which his visit to Tshaka disclosed. He had started on his journey with little information as to the condition of the people with whom it was his object to open a trade. He appears to have assumed that there would be no difficulty in the way; he brought with him a considerable number of persons, including Cape Dutch, as if bent on forming a settlement. It was probably with that end still in view that he induced the king to sign a cession of land in his favour. The grant was indeed of little value, the question whether its terms should be held binding being one dependent upon the caprice of Tshaka, in whose power he was. From the subsequent proceedings of the former it is clear that he never intended to concede any other position to the Europeans than one subject to his own authority. The intention of those who had come to settle was soon changed, for reasons which it would perhaps be difficult now to ascertain. Most of them returned by the ship that had brought them; the remainder sailed later, and were lost, and with them the vessel upon which Farewell himself had depended for effecting his departure in the event of any circumstances arising which should necessitate his retirement. The precise number of those who remained with him seems to be nowhere stated, but Fynn, John Cane, and Thomas Halstead are names conspicuously mentioned by those who made note of what transpired, and their names are conspicuous in the subsequent course of events. All four were destined to end their days in the country on the shores of which they had landed; all, but one, to suffer violent death.

During the following year their relations with Tshaka continued to be of the most cordial character. Farewell carried on his trade with the people immediately under that king, while Fynn extended his operations towards Pondoland, Cain and Halstead assisting as occasion required. Then, on the 30th of September 1825, there came another ship, the master being Lieutenant King, an old friend of Farewell, who had accompanied him during the more northerly expedition two years earlier; with him, as a companion, came Nathaniel Isaacs, whose book (where preserved in libraries) will remain a lasting record of their experiences in the course of some succeeding years. The vessel was wrecked at the entrance of the Bay, and both officers and crew were compelled to make a lengthened sojourn.

King and Isaacs entered upon the same pursuits as those who had preceded them. They also visited and were cordially received by the king, and they engaged in trading, while the crew were set to build a craft in which they hoped eventually to be enabled to quit the shore upon which they had been cast. The proceedings of these traders, however, scarcely come within the scope of this history. Their records, which it would not be possible to learn from tradition, show that Tshaka did not proceed upon any important warlike enterprise between the date of their arrival and August 1826. Zwidi was then dead, and his sons, Sikunyana and Somapunga, had disputed the right to succeed him in the rule of the tribe. The former was victorious; the latter barely escaped with his life, and found it needful to devise a way of preserving it. To this latter end, and perhaps with the view of avenging what he conceived to be an injury, Somapunga had made his way to

THE STORY OF THE ZULUS

Tshaka, and preparations were set on foot for a campaign against Sikunyana—Somapunga to go as guide, and Tshaka to command in person.

The whites at the Bay were notified that they would be required to accompany this expedition, and they urged in vain that they might thereby incur the displeasure of their own Government. The matter was, however, compromised; Farewell and Fynn, and some of their Hottentot servants, were compelled to go, the sailors and Isaacs being permitted to remain. King was at this time temporarily absent, having gone to the Cape in a ship which had chanced to call at the Bay.

The army assembled at the Nobamba kraal, and Fynn thus describes it as it left that place on its northward march. "In the rear of the regiments were the baggage-boys, few above the age of twelve years, some not more than six. These boys were attached to the chiefs or principal men, carrying their mats, pillows, tobacco, &c., and driving the cattle of the army. Some of the chiefs were also accompanied by girls carrying beer, corn, and milk; and when this supply had been exhausted these carriers returned home. The whole number of men, boys, and women amounted, as nearly as I could reckon, to 50,000. All proceeded in a close body, and at a distance nothing could be seen but a cloud of dust."

The march seems to have occupied about ten days, including halts for resting, and then the enemy was descried near to a mountain named Ihlongamvula. The battle which ensued is thus described by Fynn:—

"The hill from which we had first seen the enemy presented to our view an extensive valley, to the left of which was a hill separated by another valley from an immense mountain. On the upper part of this was a rocky eminence, near the summit of which the enemy had collected all his forces, surrounding his cattle; and above them were the women and children of the nation in a body. They were sitting down awaiting the attack.

"Tshaka's forces marched slowly and with great caution, in regiments, divided into companies, till within twenty yards of the enemy; and then they made a halt. Although Tshaka's troops had taken up a position so close, the enemy seemed disinclined to move, till Jacob (Hlambamanzi) had fired at them three times. The first and second shots seemed to make no impression on them, for they only hissed and cried in reply, "Inja leyo!" (That is a dog!). At the third shot both parties, with a tremendous yell, clashed together, and continued stabbing each other for about three minutes, when both fell back a few paces. Seeing their losses about equal, both armies raised a cry, and this was followed by another rush, and they continued closely engaged for about twice as long as on the first onset. Then both parties drew off. But the enemy's loss had now been more severe, and this encouraged the Zulus to a final charge. The shrieks now became terrific. The remnant of the enemy's army sought shelter in the adjoining wood, but were soon driven out. Then began the slaughter of the women and children. They were all put to death."

This was perhaps the most important of Tshaka's battles. Fynn estimated that the spoil he secured numbered about 60,000 head of cattle. Sikunyana's tribe, numbering according to the same authority about 40,000, was all but annihilated. He personally escaped, but with what remnant of his people history does not say. He is supposed to have found his way to the north of Delagoa Bay, and relationship is still acknowledged between some of those people who were at war with the Portuguese in 1896 under Ungungunyana,

THE STORY OF THE ZULUS

and the family of Somapunga, who resumed the old Ndwandwe sites in Zululand under Tshaka.

Resistance was not yet entirely overcome, however, although what remained was only of the kind which desperately attempts to ward off destruction. Upon the way back from the desolating operations just described, two sections of the army were detached to deal with two minor tribes who had, at one time, been tributary to the old chief Zwidi. They both resisted with considerable success. Umlotsha at the Mapondwana mountains, some way north of the Ingome forest, held his own for some time, and is recorded to have submitted on terms. The other, Beje, "succeeded in cutting to pieces one of Tshaka's regiments numbering two thousand men. . . . A few escaped and came to the army . . . but orders were given to put them to death at once as men who had dared to fly."

This was no doubt the same Beje against whom Tshaka found it necessary later on to impress the aid of the Europeans with their firearms.

No doubt the Sikunyana war added to Tshaka's fame, but his name already inspired terror from the Limpopo to St. John's River. Immense territories had been depopulated, including that which afterwards became the Colony of Natal. A few stragglers remained, amongst whom cannibalism was afterwards found to prevail. The straits to which they were reduced by his devastations are said to have caused them to adopt this habit, which is abhorrent generally to South African natives, and which did not long continue to be practised. Of the tribes which were dispersed from the land of Natal a list was prepared by order of Governor Scott in 1864. Their names, to the number of ninety-four, show them all to have spoken the language of the Zulu. What became of them can only be traced in the case of a few, notably the Fingoes of the Cape Colony. Of those who left the territory which afterwards became known as Zululand that which took the most conspicuous place in later history was the Kumalo tribe under Umzilikazi (whose name is generally written Moselekatse by historians). Two names will serve to commemorate his association with the Zulu country in the days of Tshaka—Bulawayo and Nombengula (commonly written Lobengula). The first signifies "one being killed," and was given by Tshaka to his principal kraal in reference to the circumstances which drove him from his father's home in his youth; the second, signifying "with-a-fire-brand," was probably chosen by Umzilikazi as a name for his son in reference to those events in which he set out on his own career. He was a son of Matshobana by Nompetu, a daughter of the Ndwandwe chief Zwidi. He occupied the northern slopes of the mountain range on which grows the beautiful Ingome forest. His tribe was not powerful, nor does he appear at that time to have been held in much distinction. He yielded submission to Tshaka, as well as can be ascertained, about the time when the latter obtained his first victory over Zwidi. He and his tribesmen were incorporated in the Zulu army and associated with the Bulawayo as their headquarters. At a later time he became a freebooter and broke entirely away, establishing himself eventually in what became known as Matabeleland, with a great place of his own named after that from which he had set out.

The expansion of Tshaka's dominion was sudden, and left him master of vast territories, very sparsely peopled, which he was not able to place in official occupation. He was only able to establish effective authority over a small portion of the land he had conquered. He extended his personal occupation as far as practicable. The Bulawayo was far from his ancestral domains, between the Umlalazi and Umhlatuzi rivers in what has become the Eshowe Division of Zululand. He built an important residence

THE STORY OF THE ZULUS

on the Natal coast, on the site of which now stands the village of Stanger, giving it the name of Dukuza. He also established other minor kraals farther south, the name Congella (or Kangela, a well-known place at the head of the Durban Bay), being derived, according to tradition, from that of a kraal, afterwards conspicuously mentioned in Zululand, which he temporarily erected there. Towards the north he planted several personal kraals, notably one in the Black Umfolozi in charge of Ngqengelele, whose son Umnyanana was destined to become celebrated as Prime Induna under Cetshwayo. The territory lying to the north-east of the Nongoma range he assigned to Mapita, a son of his father's brother Sonjiyiza, who had greatly distinguished himself in martial operations, and who established a power there, of the doings of which under his son Usibebu it will be necessary to make especial mention in this narrative.

Tshaka returned from his campaign against Sikunyana towards the end of October 1826, and Isaacs has described a scene he witnessed at the Bulawayo kraal on the 11th of the following month. The writer has never heard this incident mentioned by Zulus, and the statement has thus to rest upon Isaacs's sole testimony. On the other hand, it may be argued that it was not so conspicuous amongst Tshaka's acts as to be specially remembered. Under the rule of the Zulus, conjugal infidelity was a capital offence; both the erring woman and her paramour were put to death on proof of their guilt. But this law was probably never so rigorously carried out as in the case of those women who were either the wives of the king or attached to his household, and in respect to anything in the nature of an advance towards them by men. Tshaka was not married, but he adopted and carried out, to an extent probably unprecedented, a custom which had prevailed in past generations amongst chiefs generally. Men in want of cattle, or perhaps of agricultural implements (which in those days were valued as highly), were in the habit of transferring, as a consideration to those in a position to supply their wants, their paternal power over daughters. In cases where tribute was required by the chiefs, its payment was sometimes made in this form; and daughters were sometimes translated into families of chiefs as voluntary acts by men seeking favour. These girls resided in the kraals into which they had been translated, and were obliged to comply with the wish of him to whom they had been given, either by becoming his wives or marrying any other men of his choice. The number of such girls at Tshaka's kraals was very great. They were called the women of the Great House. Their position required that their conduct should be as precise as if they were married. Tshaka appears to have discovered that this character had not been duly maintained during his absence at the Front. It was Isaacs's opinion that he merely affected to have satisfied himself on the point in order to be in a position to give licence to his inhuman disposition. He rose early and proceeded to a place some distance off, pretending to be in search of a suitable site for a new kraal. Instead of this, however, when he had attained a sufficient distance to avoid being heard, he announced to those who accompanied him the conclusion at which he had arrived. He asked what should be done in the circumstances, and the expected answer was returned, "Kill them, Father." Then he ordered his men to surround the kraal before suspicion of his design could be aroused. "Their number amounted to a hundred and seventy boys and girls." Tshaka advanced and personally superintended their slaughter. So far as was known, they had not so much as been told the cause.

The Bulawayo kraal was sometimes called Gibigxeku, a name which signifies literally, "Take-out-the-old-man." This was in reference to the killing of certain men too old to go out to war, and whom Tshaka therefore regarded

THE STORY OF THE ZULUS

as an incumbrance. The mention of the name to a Zulu may still evoke a smile.

Towards the end of the year Tshaka removed to the Dukuza kraal, and from such records as exist, he would appear to have generally resided there during the remainder of his life.

Operations for the subjection of Beje were in progress at the beginning of 1827. This object was effected with the aid of certain of the Europeans, which Tshaka exacted as a penalty for certain offences committed by Hottentots in their service.

Gradual progress was being made with the building of the ship at the Port, and by the middle of this year there was reason to hope that a voyage in her might be practicable within a reasonable time. And Tshaka conceived the idea of sending a friendly mission by her to the English king, of whom he had heard much from his white visitors. There was some importunity displayed by the latter in respect to ivory, of which they felt that they had not received a quantity commensurate to the articles which they had presented to the king, and on the 24th of July Tshaka told Lieutenant King that he was going to hunt elephants, and that whatever ivory he procured would be sent to King George. He seems to have set out upon this expedition soon after that date. He had gone a considerable distance (Fynn says he was eighty miles from home), when intelligence reached him that his mother was seriously ill. He hurried back, Fynn preceding him, in time to find the sufferer still alive, but on the point of death. Her end came about the 9th or 10th of August, and, according to what appears to be good evidence, at her kraal named Nyakamubi just outside Dukuza, and near where Tshaka himself lies buried. The event was to prove an important one as a turning-point in South African history.

There was reason for the people to apprehend that

some important result might follow from it of such a kind as to seriously affect themselves. Tshaka's mother is the first woman to whom Zulu history or tradition assigns greatness, but it would perhaps not be safe to say that he was the first of the kings or chiefs to give to his mother an exalted position. He probably exaggerated a custom which had prevailed in previous generations. Although there appears to be little known of the mother of his immediate successor, Dingana, those of Umpande and Cetshwayo long continued to be named in asseverations. The greatness of Nandi was second only to that of Tshaka himself; the respect he required the people to accord her impressed them with a sense of her importance in his eyes. It behoved them to assure him that they were grieved by her death. From far and near they made haste to the scene with that object; those who arrived early found the king in an attitude which boded some grievous issue.

It is said by those who have hunted lions, that there is a certain tone in the growl of those beasts, when wounded, which serves to warn their assailants of danger. In certain circumstances a Zulu's tears serve the same purpose. They flow most freely when induced by a desire for vengeance. When Tshaka found that his mother was dead, he appeared outside the hut and stood there, his head bent forward and the tears rolling down his cheeks. He stood so in silence for some twenty minutes, and the people knew what was in his mind. His attitude and emotions told them plainly that he attributed his loss to the secret craft of some evil-disposed persons, and that his dignity had been hurt by their audacity. Each member of the assembled throng perceived the importance of establishing his own innocence of so terrible an offence, and of manifesting a readiness to destroy the guilty. They therefore exerted themselves in the display of grief and in the killing of such as seemed to be lacking in that direction. The dreadful scene continued all night and all next day, by which time thousands were dead. Some had died from exhaustion, but most from violence, having been beaten to death on the pretext that their grief had fallen short of that which was to be expected from the innocent. Then the massacre was extended to distant residents who had failed to present themselves, and carnage and desolation were spread far and wide. It is even said that the young calves were killed in order that the lowing of their bereaved mothers might make it appear that the cattle joined in the mourning.

In six months the ship was completed, and the terrible expressions of grief consequent on the death of Nandi appeared to have subsided. The project of sending a mission was now matured. The ship was Lieutenant King's; he had quarrelled with Farewell, and had largely supplanted him in Tshaka's affections.

In the arrangement under which he was to conduct the mission, he was to act independently. The document appointing him to the duty embodied a cession of territory, which included an important portion of that land which had been ceded to Farewell four years earlier. It was dated February 1828. It directed King to take under his charge and protection Sotobe and others, including Jacob, or Hlambamanzi, and, having reached their destination, to "represent that they were sent by Tshaka on a friendly mission to His Majesty King George's dominions; and after offering him assurances of friendship and esteem, to negotiate with His Majesty a friendly alliance between the two nations."

Fynn appears to have now associated himself with King; he himself voluntarily remained as hostage. The party sailed on the 30th of April, and reached Algoa Bay on the 4th of May, where they remained until the 2nd of August. Sotobe was severely questioned as to the object of his visit, and was not shown the courtesy which he had expected. He was told that he might proceed to Cape Town to see the governor, but, as King was not permitted to accompany him in the capacity in which he had been appointed, he declined. Therefore he and King were sent back to Natal in His Majesty's ship *Helicon*, the Natal schooner being taken back by Isaacs, both reaching the Bay on the 17th August.

In the meantime Tshaka had complicated matters. He had sent a large expedition along the south coast, which seemed to threaten the Cape frontier natives, whom it was the duty of the English Government to protect. Its object was, according to Fynn, to attack those tribes whose cattle were to be considered as tears shed for Nandi. It was held out as a continuation of the cleansing rite in respect to her death. It placed Sotobe in a position of anxiety. He heard of the complications likely to arise with the English Government, and expressed a desire to be permitted to return to his master to warn him of the error into which his ignorance appeared likely to lead him. But the expedition did not proceed a great distance. It captured a great number of cattle from the Pondos, but its success was not otherwise considered to be great. It is said to have been recalled on the advice of Fynn, who perceived the trouble it was likely to create. But before it had been long back it was ordered to set out again along the north coast, and attack Sotshangana beyond Delagoa Bay, and had left before Sotobe's return.

The result of the mission did not satisfy Tshaka, as he considered that he had been slighted. But neither did he give practical effect to his resentment, nor, apparently, let it be known to the Zulus generally that his object had not been gained. It remained a tradition with the latter, during their continuance as a nation, that Sotobe had crossed the water and entered into a treaty of friendship with the English king.

The character of Tshaka, as it is known to the descendants of the people over whom he ruled, was largely made up of the two qualities of generosity and wanton cruelty. He is reputed to have been liberal in his gifts to those who had been so fortunate as to earn his favour, whilst acting towards the generality of the people in a manner to make it appear that he derived a kind of amusement from seeing them killed or placed in situations of such danger as to preclude almost all hope of escape. His object in practising the first of these attributes might have been that of securing support, but his aim in indulging the second is not so easily to be perceived. Tradition is vague in regard to it. It merely refers generally to the nature of the things he was in the habit of doing, without specifying any act in a manner which might afford a possibility of authenticating it, or assigning a cause. As Fynn's account of his proceedings during the absence of his army is in agreement with the general impression of his conduct, it may be taken as a fair example.

He affected, as is not uncommon amongst savage chiefs, to be possessed of some form of supernatural power. He proceeded to practise the divining art, taking the wives of his absent warriors as his subjects. "He collected the people of the kraals, and subjected them in rotation to some operation, selecting some who were to be put to death. Though he went through the ordinary custom of dream-doctors, yet those who were not selected for death did not on that account escape their fate. He inquired of them if they were possessed of cats, and whether the answer was in the affirmative or negative, the result was the same. During three days the bodies of women numbering not less than three or four hundred were seen carried away to the rivers, or left to the wolves."

The northern campaign was not successful. The army marched, it is said, as far as Inhambane, but it met with difficulties with which it could not successfully contend. The enemy against which it had been sent employed baffling strategy. Food supplies ran short, and fever attacked the men. In September they began to straggle back into their own country, greatly reduced in number and greatly disheartened. The expedition became known as " Impi yo Balule," or the *Balule* campaign, that being the native name for the Limpopo River. A reference to it fixes the date of other occurrences of about the year 1828.

What the reception of the defeated army might have been under the circumstances in which it returned, can only be a subject for speculation. Intelligence met the home-coming men that Tshaka was no more. A new prospect had opened.

CHAPTER IV

It is recorded of Tshaka that he gained the chieftainship of the Zulu tribe by causing the assassination of a brother who had assumed that position. Of this event no definite information can be gained; nor as to whether any of the other sons of Senzangakona fell victims to his ambition. It is clear, however, that at the period to which reference is now being made, when Tshaka had enjoyed an independent career for about twelve years, there were still a considerable number of his brothers living. They joined in his wars, and it may be assumed that some of them fell in battle. One named Unzibe succumbed to fever after his return with the expedition to the Limpopo. To him it will be necessary to refer again. Another brother named Umpande was married, but his descendants assert that his first sons, born in Tshaka's time, were killed, as were any that chanced to be born to Tshaka himself.

Tshaka owed the position to which he had attained so entirely to his own personality that he might, with apparent safety, have regarded himself as free from the possibility of intrigue on the part of his brothers. The example of Dingiswayo was before them, and they might well have been supposed to doubt their ability to maintain authority over the nation, even if placed in a position by its creator's removal to assume the kingship over it. There were no open signs of intrigue. There is, perhaps, no race in which greater circumspection is exercised by those in authority than is the case amongst the Zulus. The habit of watching for any sign of evil design on the part of a neighbour is, indeed, not confined to the chiefs. Even young children at the present day seem to be affected, by some process of inheritance, with the necessity which was felt in days past of guarding against surprise. They scarcely ever answer to the first call. It seems to have become an instinctive habit of mind not to let it be known where they are until they have satisfied themselves, by hearing the voice a second time, as to the identity of the person calling. The disposition of chiefs is to believe the most incredible tales as to designs against themselves, and there are those amongst the people who are ever ready to report any semblance of suspicion. The circumstances of Tshaka's death are therefore remarkable. Until he was pierced by the spears of his murderers, he appears to have been entirely unconscious that a plot was in existence against him.

The plot was carried into effect on the 24th of September 1828, the participators being his brothers Mahlangana and Dingana, and his confidential servant Umbopa; and the description of how it was done is best given in the words of Fynn, who acquainted himself with the circumstances shortly after the event: "Some Kafirs had arrived from a remote part of the country with crane's feathers, which the king had sent them to procure, and the king was dissatisfied at their having been so long absent. He came out of his hut and went to a small kraal fifty yards distant. There these people sat before him. Unguazonco, brother of Nandi, an old man much in favour with the king, was also there. Tshaka asking in a severe tone what had detained them so long with the feathers, Umbopa ran up to them with a stick and called upon them to state why they had been so long in fulfilling the king's orders, and struck at them. Being aware that their lives were in danger, and supposing that Umbopa had, as was usual when some one was ordered to be put to death, received the private signal, they ran away. Tshaka, seeing them run, asked Umbopa what they had done to deserve being driven off in this way. Mahlangana and Dingana had hidden themselves behind a small fence near which Tshaka was standing, and each had an assegai concealed in his kaross. The former, seeing the people run off, and the king by himself, stabbed him through the back on the left shoulder. Dingana also closed upon him and stabbed him. Tshaka had only time to ask: 'What is the matter, children of my father?' But the three repeated their stabs in such rapid succession that he died after running a few yards beyond the gate of the kraal. The body remained out all night. In the morning people were selected to bury him; and his body was then placed in an empty corncellar," that is, in a pit in the cattle-kraal which had been excavated for the storage of grain. Not so much trouble was taken, apparently, as to dig a grave for him.

The circumstances of Tshaka's death, in all their details, form one of the few incidents of Zulu history that have been, thus far, carefully preserved by the Zulus themselves.

Tshaka being dead, the question at once arose between his two brothers who had slain him, as to which of them should reign in his stead. Mahlangana appears to have had reason for believing that he possessed a preferent right to the succession, but he soon perceived that Dingana was also an aspirant. It was apparent to both that the question could only be solved by the death of one of them. Mahlangana was seen suspiciously sharpening an assegai, and disclosed his design to Umbopa, who was in the confidence of both, but who secretly favoured Dingana. He at once warned the latter, and placed him in a position to strike the first blow. Mahlangana was quickly despatched; then it was found necessary to forcibly overcome and remove Ungowadi, a son of Nandi by a second husband, who was discovered to have pretensions to the kingship supported by a considerable force.

The way being thus cleared, there was little difficulty in conciliating the people. They were thankful for the removal of Tshaka, and their affections were easily won by the announcement of a more pacific policy. Dingana declared himself to be a man of peace. He maintained this pretence to his people, and perhaps to himself, during the greater part of his reign. But other measures were necessary to repair the ruin into which the nation had been brought. The bloodshed that had followed the death of Nandi had made the scenes of its occurrence repellent to the people. The Natal coast-lands were almost immediately abandoned. A traveller to the Zulu country, in passing the Dukuza some three years later, found some ruins only of that great place. The kraal had been, or was later, re-established in the valley of the White Umfolozi River, accompanied by a translation thither of the spirit of Tshaka, his body only remaining at, and thus lending little sentimental interest to, his burial place. The old inhabitants had been driven out and the new population withdrawn; the country south of the Tugela was almost unoccupied.

The satisfaction with the accession of a new ruler with peaceful professions was shared by the white residents. They both felt and expressed their confidence in the good intentions which he evinced. The friendship which they had established with Tshaka seemed to be placed on a still better footing with the new king.

Dingana established his principal seat, the Umgungundhlovu, in the fork of the Umkumbane and Unzololo streams, in the tribal lands of his ancestors, a place which was destined to be the scene of tragic occurrences. He soon determined to follow the example of his predecessor in sending a friendly mission to the British authorities at the Cape. Lieutenant King had died almost immediately on his return with Sotobe, and Farewell was absent. It therefore devolved upon Cane to take charge of the new mission. Overland traffic had been opened in 1828, and there was no longer occasion to travel by sea. Proceeding along the coast, the mission reached Grahamstown on the 21st of November 1830, and the Civil Commissioner there reported its arrival, and the nature of the message it had to convey, in a letter to the Secretary to the Government, dated the 26th of that month. By this time Cane had resolved on disposing of the ivory, which had been entrusted to him as a present to the authorities, and on purchasing with the proceeds a suitable present for Dingana. He represented that, by delaying, he would incur the risk of being stopped by swollen rivers on his return journey. The rivers did detain him, and he did not reach Natal till the 10th of March 1831. He had been accompanied, amongst others, by Jacob, or Hlambamanzi, who proceeded on the journey much against his will and with feelings of resentment against Cane, whom he suspected of having induced Dingana to send him. Cane, on arrival, did not go to Dingana personally, contenting himself with sending the articles which he had brought as presents. Hlambamanzi proceeded to Umgungundhlovu and made reports to Dingana which alarmed and incensed him. His relation appears to have been coloured by the ill-feeling which he had contracted towards Cane, and it found more ready credence in consequence of the latter's apparent want of respect. There had been little in the nature of reciprocation of Dingana's message, and Hlambamanzi told him nothing but what was calculated to disturb his confidence in the friendly intentions of the British authorities, and of the British residents in his own country. He spoke of the white people's methods of expansion. They came first and took part of the land. Then they increased and drove the natives back, and had repeatedly taken more land as well as cattle. They had built houses amongst the frontier people, for the purpose of subduing them by witchcraft; there was a mission-house in every tribe; no less than four kings had died, and their deaths were attributed to the witchcraft of the whites. During his stay at Grahamstown, the soldiers had frequently inquired what sort of a country the Zulus inhabited, if the roads were good for horses, if the people had plenty of cattle: and they had remarked, "we shall soon be after you." He had heard that a few people intended to come first to get a part of the land, as Fynn and others had done; that they would build a fort and then more would come and demand land and build houses, and subdue the Zulus and keep driving them back, as they had done in the case of the Cape frontier tribes. He reported (which was a fact) that one Cullis was on his way to Natal with a number of white men, bent on forming a settlement, and said that the British troops, which had been dealing with the frontier tribes, would advance to see Dingana. Dingana expressed alarm at the latter part of the story, and his suspicion that Cane had remained behind for the purpose of guiding the troops. He sent a force to seize Cane's cattle, which object was carried out, Cane and other Europeans vacating their settlements, and thus probably averting more serious misfortune. Friendly relations were, however, soon again restored. Dingana was induced to believe that the representations of Hlambamanzi were entirely false, and then the tables were turned upon him. Cane was authorised to kill him and take his cattle.

The withdrawal of Dingana from the south of the Tugela, and the deserted condition in which it left that part of the country, gradually induced the European residents to consider that it was theirs. Tshaka had permitted them to shelter certain tribal remnants, and a continuous accession to their adherents and dependents now took place. The peaceful professions of Dingana conduced to the return of scattered members of tribes, and fugitives from the decrees of Dingana made frequent additions from the north of the Tugela. A feeling that they were becoming independent steadily gained ground, but they were conscious of Dingana's superior strength, and of the expediency of avoiding a conflict with him.

There is no doubt that a period of national prosperity succeeded the death of Tshaka. Dingana scarcely relaxed the military discipline, but his warlike expeditions were few and unimportant. According to the account of Captain Allan Gardiner, who visited him at Umgungundhlovu in 1835, his state and military strength would appear to have been not inferior then to that which Tshaka had held and displayed. The Umgungundhlovu was counted a great place. It contained about 1000 huts, surrounding spacious enclosures in which cattle were penned and military exercises performed. At the head of the circle, a certain number of huts were screened off, one of which was of larger dimensions and of neater workmanship than the rest. This was the dwelling of the king himself, the remainder being occupied by the "Girls of the Great House." The manner in which he lived and derived gratification from the things within his power is well described by Captain Gardiner. If solicitude for the peace and happiness of the people formed an element in the motive which led Dingana to adopt those measures by which he gained the kingship, that element had then been largely supplanted by growing selfishness.

It is indeed difficult to discover anything in that or any other accounts, whether by Europeans or natives who were acquainted with him, which disclosed any loftier aspiration in Dingana than the gratification of his personal desires. His private apartments were called "Isigodhlo," signifying that by which anything is held to one's self. As in the case of his predecessor, numerous women occupied these apartments with him; the name implied their being kept away from the rest of mankind and belonging to himself alone. Their number appears to have been a hundred or more at this place; but each separate kraal contained a somewhat similar number. These women were a source of danger to the public, for any man who by ill chance was caught in conversation with any one of them was liable to be instantly put to death, and they were avoided by men for this reason. Men pledged themselves by way of asseveration to enter the Isigodhlo, should their words prove untrue—'ꝑngi ngene (esigodhlweni)."

Under these circumstances, notwithstanding that they enjoyed in a large measure the two conditions so agreeable to the nature of the Zulu—idleness and plenty—their lot must be held to have lacked many of the conditions necessary to happiness. Yet it was part of their duty to amuse the king by a continuous display of merriment. "A messenger," says Captain Gardiner, "running and breathless, came to inform me that Dingana was waiting to see me. I found the king seated near the fence of some detached houses at the back of the Isigodhlo, where I was joined by my interpreter, who informed me that several messengers had already been despatched for me in several directions. Dingana appeared in high good humour, but with a degree of mystery which rather prepared me for some strange antics. He began some trifling conversation to eke out the time, when, suddenly, the head of a column of the most grotesque-looking figures debouched from their ambush on the right and marched past, four deep, raising and lowering their bent arms, as though in the act of tugging at steeple-bell ropes, and repeating two lines of a song as they passed, which may be thus translated:

"'Arise, Eagle,
Thou art the bird that eateth other birds.'

"When they had passed and repassed in this order

they appeared again, broken into irregular companies, according to their dresses; and, seeing that I admired the arrangement of their beads, with which they were literally covered, they were ordered to advance in file and approach nearer so that their dresses might be inspected. They proved to be no other than the king's women, about ninety in number."

In such, and other ways, according to his capricious wishes did these women contribute to the king's diversion. The dancing and military display of his men occupied, also, much of his interest, while to an extraordinary degree did he revel in that form of praise which is elicited by giving. Amid thunderous adulations he daily issued in person the rations of all the occupants of his kraal.

He was of an inquisitive disposition, and in the gratification of his curiosity he had no regard for the feelings and sufferings of those upon whom he might find it convenient to conduct an experiment. He took much interest in the products of civilisation which he received as presents from Europeans. Some person had presented him with a burning-glass, with the harmless intention, no doubt, of merely exciting his wonder. He examined Captain Gardiner's eye-glass, and inquired whether it would burn. He then sent for his own glass, and proceeded to give an exhibition of its powers. "His first essay was to ignite the dry grass on either side of his chair; but this was too tame an occupation, and, beckoning one of his servants near, he desired him to extend his arm, when he firmly seized his hand and deliberately held it until a hole was actually burnt in the skin a few inches above the wrist." During this operation, which was afterwards repeated on another, the victim, while obviously "writhing in pain, dared not utter a groan."

The Zulu ideal of the refinement of cruelty is derived from the wanton operations he is said to have been in the habit of performing on women.

He has been remembered as well by less harmful indulgences. A favourite at his kraal was a man named Manyosi, who possessed an insatiable appetite, and he was wont to amuse his mind with watching this glutton's consumption of the great quantities of food he caused to be placed before him. It became a proverb that "Even Manyosi died," signifying that much indulgence in good things could not alter the general fate of mortal man.

As time advanced, and his position became more secure, Dingana came to value the lives of his subjects as lightly as Tshaka had done. Tradition tells of how he caused the destruction of large numbers apparently from sheer wantonness, and he is credited with having always accomplished his design in that respect by means of treachery. It is related how he was wont to cause large numbers to be seated in order to partake of food which he had provided, and then, by a prearranged signal, to call upon a force to massacre them. Places are pointed out, where it is said that so many bodies of persons killed in this wise were cast that several days were required for their removal thither. It may be that these stories have been multiplied and varied from one incident which formed a dark day in the annals of his reign. Of its authenticity there is no doubt, but at the time of writing this account it is necessary to depend for particulars upon men who heard of it from their fathers. What definite cause may have led to it must remain a matter of conjecture. It is probable that some difficulty was felt in exercising sufficient control over the different sections of the people and the chiefs who immediately ruled them. The method resolved upon for dealing with the situation, whatever it may have been, was the removal of the chiefs. To this end a great feast was appointed, and a general invitation extended to these. There was a great assemblage at Umgungundhlovu, and

THE STORY OF THE ZULUS

a vast concourse of people. Many cattle were slaughtered, and other provisions supplied, and the numerous groups which dotted the precincts of the kraal gave themselves over unsuspectingly to enjoyment. In the meantime, certain regiments had been disposed so as to surround the kraal and this assembly, and emissaries were appointed, furnished with a list of the doomed. These then traversed the grounds, accompanied by bands of executioners to whom they pointed out the victims as they were found. Chief after chief fell under their clubs. No one knew who might be pointed out next, and great was the consternation amongst the living as the day advanced. Many men of high distinction died that day, and those who found themselves alive at its close were filled with thankfulness.

Senzangakona is reputed to have had many sons, but only two of them are known to have survived Dingana. Some died in war; but the execution of one, which was witnessed by Captain Gardiner, may serve to indicate how others were removed from the scene. There was some report that this brother was intriguing. Whether any trial was held or not is not recorded. He was seen to be suddenly hurried out of a gate and across the Umkumbane stream to the top of a low stony ridge beyond, and there put to death. At his own desire he was strangled, this form of death being more in keeping with his rank than clubbing. This ridge was called, and has retained the name, "Kwa Matiwane," signifying the place of Matiwane, from the circumstance that a chief of that name, prominently mentioned in other histories, and whose descendants and their Amangwane tribe now occupy a slope of the Drakensberg, in the Upper Tugela Division, was sent to it on a like errand. After this man's many vicissitudes he determined to trust himself to Dingana's mercy, and repaired to Umgungundhlovu almost unattended, and tendered his submission in abject tones, saying that he had no cloak to shelter him but the king. Dingana, having heard him, ordered his death. Kwa Matiwane came to signify proverbially a place at which a man arrived for the last time. It was still to receive the bones of many, and to be made memorable by yet more important events.

When this brother of Dingana's, Gowujana by name, had been slain, a party was despatched to kill all those of whom he was chief, and seize their cattle; from the induna who went in charge of that party Captain Gardiner obtained the following account of what happened: "The principal property belonging to Gowujana was in the neighbourhood of the Tugela, and thither this officer was sent with a party of men, not exceeding thirty, to destroy the entire population of the villages. On reaching the first of these devoted places, he entered with one man only to avoid suspicion. In the course of the evening one or two more dropped in, and so on until the whole number had arrived. He then informed the principal men that he had a message from the king, and, as it was addressed to all, it would be better for the men to assemble in a place together where all could hear. This being arranged, he so contrived it that his men, with whom a previous signal had been concerted, should intermingle with the party and endeavour to divert their attention by offering them snuff. While thus apparently upon the most friendly terms the fatal blow was given, each of the induna's party at once rising and stabbing his fellow with an assegai. The houses were instantly fired, and the women and children butchered. The same horrors were perpetrated at each of the remaining villages, and it is said that very few escaped by flight out of the whole number."

There is no mention in anything that has been written, nor have the Zulus preserved any account of any important military enterprise in which Dingana had

Ingxota, or Armlet

engaged up to this time. The name of Umzilikazi was referred to in the boasting of warriors; but it does not appear that any successful attack had yet been made upon him. There were no tribes near from whom he had reason to apprehend attack, and there was no reason why he and his people should not spend their lives in peace.

Dingana is described as having been "tall, corpulent and fleshy, with a short neck and heavy foot," but, withal, active and agile in dancing. His colour was somewhat darker than usual, but his countenance was not unpleasant. "There was nothing sanguinary in his appearance," said the Reverend F. Owen, on visiting him two years later, "and I could hardly believe that those hands had been so often imbrued in blood."

Being fond of ornaments, a smith was employed in the manufacture of brass "throat-rings and armlets, and of knobs or studs" for the ornamentation of women's girdles. The man who acquired the requisite skill in the moulding of brass was held in high distinction.

His son, Mahloko, and grandson, Zuya, followed him in the craft. The last-named now occupies the position of a chief. He lost his occupation when Cetshwayo fell, his wares being no longer required. Neck-rings were probably not worn after Dingana's time; there are none extant among the Zulus. But the brass armlet continued to be a badge of distinction for men till the end of Cetshwayo's reign. It formed part of the court dress. It was called "Ingxota." It weighed from two to three pounds. The privilege of wearing it was accorded by the king, and the individual upon whom it was graciously conferred presented him with an ox in acknowledgment. The decoration was then purchased from the maker with another ox. The Zulus claim that, when worn on important occasions at court, its effect was most striking. The wearing of it occasioned much pain, as did the operation of removing it from the arm, which was performed by prising it open with the shank of a Kafir pick. The brass was imported. So far as is known, the Zulus never mined any other metal than iron. This man, who had to some extent acquired the art of founding brass, was of the Ndwandwe, not of the Zulu tribe. But where he learned the craft can not now be ascertained. He had probably been taught it in some other country, as no improvement in its practice in Zululand was effected during the three generations. There was nothing in the habits, in the wearing apparel or implements, or in the weapons or utensils of this time differing in any important respect from those followed or employed by the Zulu of the present day.

Dingana was disposed by reasons of policy to respect the protection which was afforded to his fugitive subjects by the few Englishmen at Natal. Amongst those reasons was the fact that Sotobe was supposed to have established certain relations with their nation. But he was gradually led by frequent desertions to manifest a degree of irritation which alarmed them; and, in the year 1835 on the 6th of May, a treaty was concluded in the following terms:—

"Dingana from this period consents to waive all claim to the persons and property of every individual now residing at Port Natal in consequence of their having deserted from him, and accords them his full pardon. He still, however, regards them as his subjects, liable to be sent for whenever he may think proper.

"The British residents at Port Natal, on their part, engage for the future never to receive or harbour any deserter from the Zulu country or any of its dependencies, and to use every endeavour to secure the return to the king of every individual endeavouring to find an asylum amongst them."

The want of an "asylum" was before long to produce an important revolution in the affairs of the country.

CHAPTER V

THE English residents at the Bay seem to have regarded the fact that Dingana signed the Treaty as implying that he recognised their title to the land on the south of the Tugela. On the 23rd of the month succeeding that in which it was signed they laid off a township, naming it D'Urban, after the then Governor of Cape Colony, and framed a petition to the English king, praying "that it would please his Majesty to recognise the country intervening between the Umzimvubu and Tugela rivers," to which they gave the name of Victoria, in honour of the princess who was to become queen two years later, "as a Colony of the British Empire." This petition was entrusted to Captain Gardiner for conveyance through the British authorities at the Cape, but his attempts to reach that Colony were to be frustrated by various causes, and his object long delayed.

In the meantime another movement was in active progress. There were amongst the British subjects at the Cape those who desired as strongly to free themselves from the rule to which they had been subjected as did certain Zulus to get away from that of Dingana. The Dutch, so far as their occupation extended, had constituted themselves masters of the native inhabitants. Their industries depended upon the labour they exacted from them. They had learnt by time and experience by what methods labour could best be exacted, and had cultivated a habit of mind which perceived nothing either harsh or unjust in those methods. A new idea was introduced, however, with British rule. What had come to be regarded as legitimate persuasion was now held to be criminal, and white men were punished on the complaint of their black servants. It is not my purpose to trace here the causes of the "great trek," to which ample attention has already been given by historians, but its main motive lay in the altered relations between white and black which followed the cession of the Cape to England in 1806. The discontent of the Boers with the new order of things, after manifesting itself in various forms and passing through various phases, ended by their casting about for some new land where they might be free from the restraints under which they felt that prosperity was impossible.

In 1833, Carl Johannes Trichard and Hans van Rensburg at the head of a party numbering thirty-one families, actually left the Colony. A writer,[1] to whose work the Boers are mainly indebted for what knowledge they possess of their history, describes their object to have been to "go as far afield as possible, wholly beyond the reach of the British flag, where neither English missionaries nor Anglicised Hottentots could aggrieve them, where the Kafirs were tame, where good pasturage for flocks and herds was to be found, and also large game, such as elephants, buffaloes and giraffes, and where men could live in freedom. Such a land was, according to report, to be found in the vicinity of Delagoa Bay, a thousand miles distant, but not beyond reach."

A remnant of this party reached Delagoa Bay in a lamentable condition in December 1836.

Those who formed the trek which concerns this story were less precipitate. They sent out "Commissions," parties of men commissioned to explore and report. One of these reached the Bay of Natal in 1834. It included a man who, of all the Voor-trekkers, has been best remembered by the Zulus, Johannes de Lange. He was destined to take a prominent part in the subsequent proceedings of the trekkers, to acquire great fame amongst the Zulus

[1] F. Lion Cachet.

THE STORY OF THE ZULUS

as a warrior and a hunter, and finally to die on the scaffold in 1861 for taking the life of a native.

The report of this party confirmed the impression that had already been formed as to the suitability of the land of Natal for the purposes of the contemplated new settlement. It was practically uninhabited; had a seaport, and was well adapted to agricultural and pastoral pursuits. To Natal, therefore, would they go. In 1835 a beginning was made in that direction. Families moved to the north of the Orange River, with all their possessions, and waited there for others not yet ready to start. After some time had elapsed a body of these moved forward, being impatient of delay, and were attacked and reduced to sore straits by Umzilikazi, who had by this time gathered much strength and was at the head of a formidable army. He had dispersed and despoiled many tribes, and was rich in herds.

In October 1837 Pieter Retief, the Governor of the Emigrants, was at the Bay of Natal, and on the 5th of the following month he arrived at Umgungundhlovu, applying to Dingana for permission to occupy the land lying on the south of the Tugela River, and, while negotiations were still in progress, a large body of the people for whom the land was required descended the Drakensberg and occupied it. Captain Gardiner had returned from his mission. The British Government had declined to entertain the request contained in the petition he had borne, but had appointed him under a statute then recently enacted (6 and 7 William IV. chapter 57) to be a Justice of the Peace, the object being to arm him with authority to send back to the Cape for trial such British subjects as might commit irregularities. This arrangement was not at all satisfactory to those whom he had represented. They declined to recognise his authority, and welcomed the arrival of the Boers, which they viewed as establishing a condition of things in which the menaces of Dingana might be ignored, and his authority over them disowned.

It is a matter for regret that fuller accounts of the journeyings of these people have not come down to us. Not even their number is known. By the time Retief returned "at least a thousand wagons" had descended the mountains, and many families followed at a later date and spread themselves in groups over a large extent of country. They entertained no fear of attack from the Zulus, although in the course of their journey they had been compelled to defend themselves on more than one occasion from the unprovoked attacks of the people of Umzilikazi, whom they knew to have formerly dwelt in Zululand and to be of the same race, and possessed of the same characteristics, as the Zulus. With their victories over those people Dingana had become fully acquainted. In September of this year his army returned from the great campaign of his reign. This formed the only one of his warlike expeditions that has been specially remembered by the Zulus. The year 1837 is known to them as the year of the expedition against Umzilikazi. If, in after years, a very large number of cattle were brought together the old men would compare their multitude in their minds with that of those which were brought back as spoil on that occasion.

Amongst the cattle the army had captured were some of those that Umzilikazi had taken from the Dutch emigrants, besides many of their sheep. There were also brought back some captured women, and these were able to describe to Dingana how the Boers fought, and how difficult it was for men armed only with assegais to hold their own against them. Indeed, there was much in the advent of the Boers to give rise in the mind of the Zulu king to misgivings as to how their presence might affect his own security. The action he took against Cane, on the report of Hlambamanzi, should have served as a warning, but it is not known whether the Boers were made aware of this.

For long these Boer families had journeyed and sojourned in trackless and cheerless wastes. For the sick and the aged, and for the young children, they had no other shelter than that which their covered wagons afforded. The hardships that were endured by mothers of families it is not easy to fully realise. Ill-provided with servants, with little other food than the flesh of antelopes, remote from any place at which their stock of clothing might be replenished or medical comforts procured, they journeyed through a country that was destitute of fuel, and in which the winter season was extremely cold. It was desirable that they should soon take possession of the land for which they had gone out from their old homes, in order that they might make themselves new ones there. And they now saw that land spread out beneath their feet, and it seemed good. In these circumstances they were lightly impressed with possible danger. They had not heard anything of Dingana to inspire them with confidence as to his peaceful intentions; and there was no reason to believe that their coming was an event that he would be inclined to welcome. By taking up their abode in the country they manifested an intention to remain there, whatever answer they received to their request for permission. The reputation which had preceded them was calculated to make Dingana doubtful as to his ability to enforce a refusal. He was placed in the position of having to grant the permission sought or to refuse it, and then eject them. Their necessities were pressing, and account largely for their apparent indiscretion in not awaiting the outcome of Retief's negotiations. But, on the other hand, the situation was capable of being viewed by Dingana as one calling for special measures.

CHAPTER VI

DINGANA had reigned nine years. Relations between him and the English settlers had occasionally been somewhat strained, but none of these had suffered actual violence at his hands. The friendly feeling which they had established with Tshaka had been generally maintained. Missionaries had also been permitted to commence work, although, for the time, with but a poor prospect of success. The country of the Zulus had presented attractive features as a field for missionary enterprise. To the mind of the Christian the people were without religion, and their social and moral condition was lamentable. The conviction was a terrible one that all these people were doomed, by reason of not having been taught the Gospel of Christ, to eternal torment in the life beyond the grave. Referring to a conversation he had with a Zulu boy on the subject, one of these pious men recorded this: "He asked me whether those who were already dead were happy. I gave him to understand that only those who had learned God's Word would rise in happiness; that the rest would be cast into fire which would never be extinguished." The white men with whom the people had for some thirteen years been in a sense associated were only traders, and did not make the elevation of those with whom they abode and traded one of their objects. Their tendency was rather to descend to the adoption of the habits of those people. The governing power was subject to no moral restraint; its acts were dictated largely by caprice. Conspicuous amongst those acts were such as presented themselves to the mind of an

English Christian as "cold-blooded murders," and the king was regarded as the chief murderer. The system of government precluded higher aims than the aggrandisement of the king. His ambition necessitated much killing and misery. The hope of modifying this condition of things by the introduction of Christianity was an inspiring one, and the difficulties in the way of its acceptance by the king and people did not take away from the attractiveness of the undertaking to men who had consecrated their lives to the good of mankind.

The first to be stimulated to definite action by the hope of bringing the Saving Faith to this people was Captain Allan Gardiner. As has already been noted, he was, in March 1835, at Umgungundhlovu, petitioning the king for permission to bring the teaching of the words that were in the "Book" to his people. He urged that it was very far from his thoughts to interfere in any way with the laws or customs by which the people were ruled; that respect for kings, and all in authority, was a prominent feature in the religion which the "Book" taught. What he desired was only the spiritual instruction of the people. He "enlarged upon the blessings attending Christianity, both individually and nationally." But, for answer, he was told that the kind of teaching Dingana desired for his people was in the use of guns; and his mission was, for the time, fruitless. To the "laws and customs" with which he expressed himself as having no intention to interfere he referred in his narrative with extreme horror. Doubtless Dingana perceived something in his teaching which seemed to "say there was another King," and, having betaken himself to Natal, and been well received, Captain Gardiner established a mission house on the high land overlooking the Bay, and called the place "Berea," because his circumstances reminded him of the experience of St. Paul when he found the people "more noble there than those in Thessalonica."

The permission thus withheld was provisionally granted about the beginning of the following year on the application of members of the American Mission, and two of these, and the Reverend F. Owen of the Church Missionary Society, were established in the country at the time of Retief's visit. Mr. Owen had his residence at Umgungundhlovu. The admission of these missionaries was capable of being regarded as additional evidence of friendly disposition on the part of Dingana towards Europeans, but vanity was no doubt the real motive which actuated him in the matter. It was gratifying to his sense of dignity to have about him men of a distant race who could talk strange things, and their numbers were so few that no harm could result to his position from their presence. In the object for which they had gone into the country they made no progress. Dingana was, perhaps, their chief hindrance. He was unable to perceive that any good could be derived from what they taught. Their preachings amused rather than enlightened both him and his people. At times he was displeased with what they told the people. The attributes of God, which they described and extolled, were the opposite to his own, and God's powers were represented as infinitely greater than those of any man. He naturally suspected that the tendency of such preaching might be to lower the people's estimate of himself; and so his feelings were occasionally manifested by the entire absence of those who had habitually attended the services. When events had occurred which induced Mr. Owen to resolve on departure, Dingana gave expression in a definite form to his feelings on the subject.

"He referred," wrote the missionary in his journal, "to our native servants, who, he said, reported that I spoke evil of him; that we praised God, but when we did so we always had him in our hearts. We praised God but reviled him."

Even had this form of opposition been absent the implanting of the Christian Faith would have been extremely slow. The minds of the people were not in a condition to realise readily the possibility of an after life depending for its felicity on good conduct in this. In their own belief as to spiritual life there was no trace of this idea. Their propitiation of ancestral spirits was only to secure their good offices in the ordering of earthly affairs. Moreover, Christian ethics involved the sacrifice of many of those things upon which the happiness of their lives depended. Whatever these missionaries did in the way of building has been effaced by time, and that they ever were in the country has been forgotten by those for the good of whose souls they for a brief space laboured.

The precise thing which operated on Dingana's mind so as to induce the resolution he had adopted respecting the Boers cannot now be ascertained. It was probably known to few besides himself. If there was anything more definite than may be inferred from the circumstances which have been indicated, it would appear never to have become known to more than those who were his counsellors at the time. The actual execution of that resolution was witnessed, and described, by Mr. Owen, and little more can be gathered from the Zulus than what is stated in his account.

The substance of Dingana's reply to Retief's application for the land of Natal is contained in a letter he caused Mr. Owen to write, dated the 8th day of November, on which date the Boer deputation had returned to the south of the Tugela; but it had, according to the narrative of Wynand Bezuidenhout who was present at the interview, been stated verbally at Umgungundhlovu. From the latter account it appears that Retief offered to purchase the land he sought to acquire.

In the letter referred to, Dingana said: "As regards the request you have made to me as to the territory, I am almost inclined to cede it to you; but, in the first place, I desire to say that a great number of cattle have been stolen from my country by people having clothing, horses and guns. The Zulus assure me that these people were Boers; that the party had gone towards Port Natal; the Zulus now wish to know what to expect.

"My great wish, therefore, is that you should show that you are not guilty of the matters alleged against you; for at present I believe you are. My request is that you recover my cattle and restore them to me; and, if possible, hand over the thief to me. That proceeding will remove my suspicion, and will give you reason to know that I am your friend; then I shall accede to your request."

The cattle here referred to had been raided by a chief named Sigonyela, who dwelt with his tribe on the west of the Drakensberg. Retief had become acquainted with him, and negotiations had taken place in reference to the passing of the Boers through his country on their way to Natal. They had, moreover, promised him some payment for the right of way. Having observed that some of the members of this tribe had horses and guns, and wore clothes, Retief at once concluded that they were the raiders, and undertook the task of recovering the cattle.

He proceeded at the head of a sufficient force to a mission house near to Sigonyela's residence, and invited him to an interview there on the subject of the payment he had promised him. Sigonyela, not suspecting any other object, came to see him, and sat down to discuss the matter which he understood was to be considered. He was then suddenly seized and handcuffed by one of Retief's followers, and held prisoner until he had delivered up Dingana's cattle and paid a fine in guns and cattle to Retief. The latter thus accomplished his mission without bloodshed, although by a method not unlike those sometimes employed by Dingana in the carrying out of his designs.

THE STORY OF THE ZULUS 63

With these cattle, numbering some 300, he arrived at Umgungundhlovu on the 3rd of February 1838. He was accompanied by his son and sixty-eight other Boers, and by Thomas Halstead as interpreter. When Dingana heard of his approach he sent him an invitation to bring all his people with him, promising them a hospitable reception. He desired, he said, that they should dance upon their horses, and that there should be a dancing competition between them and the Zulu warriors. This was probably with the view to the more effectively carrying out the dark design he had formed. Retief had been disposed to take a force of 200 men with him; but, the opinion of his advisers being averse to this, those whose number has been given accompanied him as volunteers. They had with them some 30 native servants; their horses numbered about 200. They entered the kraal, and proceeded to show how they "danced on their horses" by exhibiting a sham fight and firing volleys. The Zulu regiments also danced after their fashion, and general cordiality seemed to prevail. Dingana appeared highly pleased to have recovered the cattle. Matters proceeded, to all appearances, most favourably to the desires of the Boers. No objection was made to the cession of the land; and, in fact, it was ceded by a document signed by Dingana next day. The restored cattle were taken as full consideration. No question of further payment appears to have been raised.

"Whereas," this document declares, "Pieter Retief, Governor of the Dutch Emigrant South Africans, has retaken my cattle which Sigonyela had stolen; which cattle he, the said Retief, now delivers unto me: I, Dingana, King of the Zulus, do hereby certify and declare that I thought fit to resign unto him, Retief, and his countrymen (on reward of the case hereabove mentioned) the place called Port Natal, together with all lands annexed, that is to say from Tugela to the Umzimvubu River westward, and from the sea to the north, as far as the land may be useful, and in my possession." This document was signed by Dingana and three men who were designated "Great Councillors," but whose names are not elsewhere to be met with amongst those of the prominent men of the time. It has been found on inquiry that two of them, Umnwana Ka Celo and Magonondo Ka Kondhlo, were respectively a private servant of and a medicine man in attendance upon Dingana.

The negotiations Retief had opened with the view of the purchase of this land, which, to some extent, was in occupation by Dingana's subjects, were interrupted by the professed suspicion of the latter that the Boers had raided his cattle. The cattle had been recovered with the object of removing that suspicion. Now their return was accepted as the price in full of a vast territory.

The readiness shown in ceding the land, and the easiness of the terms, might have struck one acquainted with the Zulu character as strange; but it could scarcely have suggested the existence of so terrible a design as that which Dingana had formed, and was soon to carry out. There had been no occurrence to suggest to the Boers the possibility of their being subjected to violence, and they accepted Dingana's professions of friendship as sincere. They believed that by signing the document with which they had presented him, he had intended to cede to them the extensive territory it described as a reward for the services they had rendered. They entered the cattle-pen on the morning of the 6th of February, entirely unarmed and free from apprehension of injury, to partake of some refreshment prior to taking their departure to their newly acquired land. They had piled their arms beneath two euphorbia trees that stood near the gate, one of which still stands, after more than sixty years, and is reputed to mark the burial place of Nkosinkulu, one of Dingana's ancestors. Their hearts were gladdened by the feeling

THE STORY OF THE ZULUS

that their wanderings were over; that the land, to possess which they had journeyed so far and suffered so much, was now theirs; that in a few days they would arrive amongst their families with the good tidings. They sat down in friendly conversation and to drink some milk which the king caused to be placed before them. They had been accustomed to see large bodies of armed men continually near the king, and counted it nothing strange that the walls of the enclosure were lined by a large force, who were presently ordered to dance for their entertainment. But Dingana's friendly tones suddenly gave place to one of stern command: "Seize them!" he cried; and, in the words of one who participated in the execution of the order, "the dust rose!" There was no escape; but the one short journey remained for them—across the Umkumbane to Matiwane's. According to the testimony of several Zulus who took part in the massacre, one white man broke away and ran for his life, and was not overtaken and killed till he had reached the Itala, some fifteen miles distant in the direction of the Boer camp; and more than sixty years after the event, it is claimed by a man named Roman, that he got away on horseback and conveyed intelligence and warning to those who had remained with the wagons. Thomas Halstead was amongst the slain. As has been seen, he was amongst the firstcomers of 1824; he was the first Englishman who is known to have met his death at the hands of a Zulu.

The next day large forces were sent off to destroy the remainder of the Boers in their camps in Natal. These unsuspecting people were in a very defenceless state. They were living in small groups long distances apart, and many of the men were absent hunting large game. Women and children were thus in many instances unprotected; and the progress made towards their annihilation by the Zulus was, at first, subject to little check. The news of their onslaught, however, gradually spread; and the deadly fire of the Boers, when they had to some extent got together and taken up a position of defence, was ill to face. Heavy loss was, in their turn, inflicted upon the attacking forces, and they were eventually forced to retire across the Tugela. They had killed some 280 of the Boers, chiefly women and children, and about 250 of their black servants. They carried off large numbers of cattle, and thus reduced many families to poverty.

Except by a few of the older Zulus this event has been forgotten. There was no special feature in it that they would remember; but to the Boers it was a memorable event. It is commemorated in Natal, too, by the names it gave to streams and places. Moord Spruit, "Stream of Murder," and Weenen, "Weeping," are two that were suggested by the attack and its consequences.

The occasion also called forth deeds of heroism by which some Dutch names have been, and will long be, remembered, especially those of Wynand Bezuidenhout, Martenus Ossthuisen and Sarel Celliers.

The missionaries left Zululand shortly after the death of Retief and his companions; and for some time subsequently there were no Europeans north of the Tugela.

CHAPTER VII

ALL attempts to form separate homes had, therefore, for the time, to be abandoned by the Dutch. The necessities of mutual defence required that they should draw together with what speed they could. Life in a large camp, in their peculiar circumstances, was fraught with hardships that were ill to bear. It was the rainy season, and a very wet one. The incessant downpour, the large number of people living close together, the immense flocks and herds necessarily kept close to the camp, resulted very soon in such a muddy state of the ground within it that boots could not be worn. Women had to go about their duties with kilted skirts and bare feet. Bedraggled by day, and with only such scant comfort as is afforded by canvas covering at night, even the robust constitutions their habits of life had given them began to be impaired. It was urgently necessary that preparations should be made for planting. The land, being scarcely inhabited by natives, was practically destitute of grain. For food there was little else than flesh and milk to be obtained. Those whose cattle had been carried off by the Zulus had to depend almost entirely on game, which was happily in great plenty and easily procured.

It was urgently desirable, on the part of the Dutch, that no time should be unnecessarily lost in attempting to end this unhappy state of things; and, being strengthened by a small body of men under Piet Uys, who had remained on the west of the Drakensberg with a portion of the emigrants, an expeditionary force was got ready on the 5th of April. They had also entered into an alliance with the English at the Bay. These desired to avenge the death of Halstead, whom they highly esteemed. They also felt it to be desirable that Dingana's power should be broken. With a native force, partly armed with muskets, they arranged to advance upon the Zulus along the coast, crossing the Tugela near its mouth. On the 8th of the month was fought what became known to the Zulus as the battle of the Itala.[1] The exact locality of the battlefield it would be very difficult to ascertain; but the Itala Hill, near the source of the Umhlatuzi River, is that which gave it its name. The Boers had taken only such stores as could be carried by horses, and had thus been able to traverse the rugged and precipitous valley of the Tugela by way of a crossing to the north of the Isipezi Mountain.

In this battle the Zulus were entirely victorious. They killed Uys and his son and nine of his companions, captured most of the baggage horses with their burdens, and pursued the Boers a considerable distance. They were recorded by the Boers to have sustained heavy losses; and this would naturally have been the case in the circumstances in which they fought. They had no guns, and had to charge their enemy in the face of most deadly fire in order to get sufficiently near to use their assegais. The result of the battle greatly discouraged the Boers. News of it, much exaggerated, reached the camp the same evening by one De Jager, who, in a great fright, seized a black charger named "Tromp," which was already famed as the swiftest in the trek, and fully maintained its reputation by the immense distance it carried its fugitive rider in the course of the day. Great was the wailing that was produced by the intelligence he brought. One of the

[1] A kind of fatality would appear to attach to this place and name as regards Boer enterprise. It was destined to be the scene of a serious defeat to a commando under Louis Botha in September 1901; while Talana, or the little Itala, was that of the first reverse the Boer arms sustained in the great war on the 20th of October 1889.

THE STORY OF THE ZULUS 69

commanders of the expedition was Hendrik Potgieter, the subsequent founder of the Transvaal Republic. He had claimed, and been allowed, equal rank with Piet Uys; and when the time came for attacking had failed to join with the men he commanded in carrying out the plan of battle on which the latter had decided. He has been chiefly blamed for the adverse termination of the enterprise. So impressed did he become with the strength of the Zulus that he and his followers decided to abandon all further attempt to cope with them. They betook themselves across the Drakensberg, leaving those who still hoped to overcome their foes much weakened in numbers. The English with their native forces set out three days after the defeat of Uys. The difficulty of communication prevented them from becoming aware of what had transpired. They occupied four days in marching along the coast and crossing the Tugela. Then, on the 15th of the month, they were confronted with a greatly superior force, flushed with the victory which had been attained over the Boers seven days earlier. Seventeen Englishmen were with the expedition, of whom Cane seems to receive the most conspicuous mention. Of the battle no reliable account can be obtained. It appears to have been of short duration, the natives who had no firearms running to take shelter behind those who had, and thus causing a panic. Cane and other twelve whites remained dead on the field. The other four eventually reached their homes, but the story of how they eluded their pursuers over the intervening sixty miles of wilderness has not been told. Dingana's army pursued them to the Bay, but it chanced by good fortune that a ship lay at anchor there.

Four months later Dingana made another attempt to destroy the Boers. On the 10th of August his army made a determined attack on one of the Boer camps, some five miles west of the site of the present town of Estcourt. They continued the siege for three days, but were unsuccessful. They had, on this occasion, brought with them the guns they had captured in previous engagements; but they so lacked skill in their use that they failed to hit one man, though "continually firing." Only one Boer, who had gone out of the camp and was cut off, was killed during the siege.

From that time for four months there was nothing done on either side. Of how the Zulus employed themselves during that time there is no history. It may be assumed that Dingana, while keeping his men in a state of readiness to resist attack, had abandoned for the time the idea of acting on the offensive. The Dutch were soliciting aid from the Cape Colony; and this came in time to enable them to get ready another commando in December. On the 16th of that month 600 of them were at Ingcome Stream; which from that date has been known to Europeans as the Blood River, because of the colour given to its water by the mingling with it of the blood of slain Zulus.

That 16th of December became memorable to both Zulus and the Dutch South Africans; to the latter, perhaps, the more so. While the expedition was still on the south of the Buffalo River, its members had assembled and made a solemn vow "to the Lord their God, that if He were with them and gave the enemy into their hands they would consecrate to the Lord the day in each year and keep it holy as a Sabbath day." It has been so kept, and is, till now, annually observed and called Dingana's Day. It was a Sunday. The Boer army had camped near to the river on the one side and to a deep watercourse, or sluit, on the other. The river at the place chosen had formed a long and deep reach which could not easily be crossed; the watercourse had banks some 14 feet high, and prevented approach from its side. Thus the Zulus could attack the camp from two sides only of the quadrangle in which it was formed. The wagons were drawn together as a fortification. At daybreak the Zulu army had surrounded the camp. They determinedly charged it several times; but the losses they sustained through the accurate fire of the Dutch forced them to retire. Then they were charged by horsemen and completely routed. Many sought refuge in the water, but were shot there, their blood tingeing it with red. They had only wounded two Boers, including the Commandant-General. The loss on their side was estimated by the Boers to have been not less than 3000. The event is remembered by the Zulus as one in which they suffered a defeat of great severity. Its story is told by father to son, and there are few even amongst the younger generation who are not acquainted with it. Amongst the killed were two brothers of Dingana, sons of Senzangakona's wife Langazana, who lived, thus bereaved, to an extreme old age, dying in 1882, having exercised power in the land, during successive reigns, second only to that of the kings. Tradition says of these princes that they had escaped out of the battle, but, knowing the fate that would meet their return at the hands of Dingana, they preferred to await death at those of the pursuing Boers.

The effect of this defeat it was not easy for the Zulus to overcome. They offered no resistance to the forced march of the Boers, by which they reached Umgungundhlovu on the 20th of the month, in four days. The condition of things they found there was calculated to impress the Boers with the belief that their victory had been complete. There was no force to oppose them; the king's residence and neighbouring family kraals had been burnt on their approach by a man whom he had left for the purpose. He had betaken himself across the White Umfolozi River. There was, indeed, no living person to be seen. They found the bones of their late governor, Retief, and his companions, on the ridge upon which they had been bleaching since their massacre ten months earlier. These were identified by means of fragments of clothing still adhering to them. In a satchel amongst those of Retief was found the document which, on the 4th of the previous February, had been signed by Dingana as a cession of the land of Natal.

All the bones which could be found were collected and buried in a grave, still to be seen, after sixty years, at the base of a small conical hillock, on the ridge-slope facing the site of Umgungundhlovu and about 100 yards from the spot on which their bodies had been cast to the wild beasts—a spot marked by numerous small cairns of stones erected at the time wherever identifiable bones were discovered. The grave is about eight feet long, and, although the name of Retief has been a household word throughout South Africa, the spot where his bones mingle with those of so many of his countrymen has remained unmarked up to the present time (1911) except by the few stones placed upon it by those by whom they were buried.

It appeared as if there was nothing more to be done. One of the objects of the expedition had been to recover the cattle of which the Boers had been deprived by Dingana's forces; but in that respect it appeared likely to prove fruitless.

Soon, however, a man was seen hurriedly seeking hiding in a clump of trees. He was promptly seized, and, with exhibitions of tremor, had much to disclose. He had been sent as a decoy, and played his part well. His name was Bongoza. No common man of the Zulu race ever attained such fame as he. His name and what he did is known to every Zulu of an intelligent age. If a man be employed as a guide he will answer to the name as his own.

Dingana's army, he said, had dispersed after the battle of Ingcome. Left undefended, he had burnt his kraal and fled. He had left his cattle behind in the hope that the Boers, when they found these, might refrain from further pursuing him. These cattle were in the valley of the White Umfolozi; they were very numerous; Bongoza was in a position to guide those to the place who might go to fetch them. By some this story was disbelieved; but by most it was given credence. Therefore, on the 26th, the day after the man's capture, the camp was moved some eight miles in a south-eastern direction to the top of the Mtonjaneni Heights; and on the 27th Bongoza was leading 300 Boers towards the east along the ridge. He was mounted on a horse and being made much of. As the eastern brow was reached a small body of Zulus were seen, but on being fired upon they retired. Bongoza is said to have pointed to this as a proof of the correctness of what he had said: "See," he is reported to have exclaimed, "I told you that there were no men left who would fight." That brow has since been known by the name of Sanqonqo, a name made up of an imitation of the sound of gun-shots. From this point the party descended by a steep path, still in use, along the narrow back of a spur which projects itself into a sharp and deep curve of the White Umfolozi River. The path reaches the bottom of the valley near to where the Upate stream joins that river, the final descent being a broad hill-face strewn with rocks and studded with stunted mimosa trees and aloes, the stalks of which it is sometimes difficult to distinguish at a distance from the bodies of men who may be standing near to them. When they had entered the gorge and nearly reached the river, they were made suddenly to realise the peril into which they had placed themselves. On a sharp, rocky, and bush-clad peak towards their right front, and on the far side of the river, there sat the sentinel Xwana; and now, in those clear, high-pitched tones by which a Zulu is able to make himself heard so far, he uttered the words, "I si pakati" (with prolonged emphasis on the initial and penultimate syllables), meaning that the enemy was enclosed. From all sides the impis rose and advanced. In the confusion which ensued Bongoza made good his escape, but of his later life, or how it was ended, nothing can be learned with certainty.

The Boer detachment was under the command of Carl Landman, but the man who saved it was Johannes De Lange. He held little rank, but the perilous life he had been accustomed to lead had fitted him to assume the guidance in a crisis such as that which presented itself. There was some consultation, the Commandant being for standing back to back and fighting; but De Lange saw what the situation demanded, took the lead, and was followed by the whole force. To return by the way by which they had come was scarcely possible; they had not sufficient ammunition for a prolonged action such as threatened; the difficulties that lay ahead were unknown to them; but, as he rightly perceived, the greater hope lay in going forward.

It has to be concluded, after a careful inquiry and an examination of the ground, that there was some considerable distance between them and the several posts occupied by the surrounding Zulus admitting of less precipitate movement than has generally been ascribed by historians. It is not easy to credit that a body of 300 horse could gallop over the ground which it was necessary to immediately traverse. It is closely bestrewn with jagged rocks, overgrown by various thorny trees and aloes, and intersected by numerous steep-sided ravines. They had no acquaintance with the ground and no guide. It appears most probable that the greater part of the rougher ground had been passed before the Zulus were able to close with them. At any rate, they succeeded in crossing the river and attaining the open ground without having suffered any loss whatever, and thereafter in keeping their assegai-armed foe at a safe distance by occasionally turning and firing. They thus traversed the

Ulundi plains, bearing gradually to the west, and re-arriving at the river where it is joined from the south by the Umkumbane stream. In the meantime the young Udhlambedhlu regiment, viewing their movements from that direction, had ascended the river and were awaiting them at the crossing. Here five Boers were killed, and also Alexander Biggar, who had accompanied the expedition with a number of natives from Natal, of whom none are supposed to have escaped. The pursuit continued for some distance beyond this place, and there was still some fifteen miles of difficult ground to cover. But eventually, though late and in a state of complete exhaustion, the party reached the camp without further loss. Owing to their circuitous retreat they had covered, since setting out, some forty miles of very rough country on a summer's day and in a valley noted for heat. They had been fighting most of the time. They recorded their belief that they had killed 1000 Zulus, but this was necessarily a mere guess.

Thus ended the second Boer invasion of Zululand. Before recrossing into Natal they attacked and shot some cattle herds and captured some 5000 head of cattle; but no more fighting of any importance took place. Concerning the period occupied in the retreat the records left by the Boers differ from the history of the affair as it is known to the Zulus, as does also the impression as to the result of the campaign. The Zulus, both those remaining of the warriors who took part in it and those who know of it from what their fathers have told them, declare that so precipitate was the retreat of the commando that, although the Zulu army marched after them next morning, it was found impossible to overtake them; that they had marched during the night, and made for the border with great rapidity; that, as a result of the experience they had met with, they never again attempted any operations against Dingana, but on the contrary sent frequent overtures of peace, until they had been joined by half the Zulu nation under Umpande. They claim to have repelled the enemy, although the invasion cost them many lives, and they speak warmly of the valour the Boers displayed.

On their side the Boers considered that their campaign was successful; and, with regard to their retreat, they recorded that they continued in occupation of their camp for three days, during which time they sent out patrols in the hope of drawing the Zulus on to an attack upon it, but without success; that their horses being rendered unfit for offensive operations, they retreated very slowly in the hope that pursuit might give them an opportunity of finishing the war; that on arrival at the Buffalo River they encamped again three days for the purpose of sending out a patrol to capture cattle. In support of the Zulu version it has to be observed that the commando had arrived at the Tugela, in Natal, and the spoil was distributed on the 9th of January; and, considering the distance and the roughness of the road by which they travelled, it scarcely appears as if they had time for the deliberateness they professed to have displayed.

Although the Zulus claim that they finally repelled the invasion, there is no doubt that its effect had been to discourage them greatly. Dingana was not to return to Umgungundhlovu and the fair Umkumbane stream, which he appears to have greatly loved. It is said that while he continued at the place to which he retired, some fifteen miles distant, he had his private supply of water carried thence by his serving men. Soon he rebuilt the kraal in the Hluhluwe valley, between Hlabisa and the coast, but the prevalence of malarial fever caused him to abandon that site in favour of one on the south of the Ivuna stream, eight miles from the present magistracy at Nongoma; this also he was permitted to occupy only for a short space. These spots are still pointed out as sites of the Umgungundhlovu kraal. He showed by another act that he felt weakened in fighting force. He directed the members of his youngest regiment, the Udhlambedhlu, lads of about twenty years of age, to assume head-rings, thus according to them the status of men. These lads, as has been seen, were conspicuous in the attempts to carry out the object for which Bongoza had led the commando into the valley of the White Umfolozi River, and Dingana announced as his reason for thus distinguishing them, that the Boers had stipulated it as a condition of peace, describing them as "the boys who had sprung from the bones of the warriors they had slain." His object was doubtless to encourage them to fill the places of these.

In the meantime the emigration from the Cape of the Boers, and their wars with the Zulus and other tribes, had been causing much concern in the minds of the British Government, whose subjects they were, and who felt responsible for their actions. The feeling that their proceedings should be checked had taken practical shape. With this object a small body of troops, under the command of Major Charters, had landed at Port Natal on the 4th of December; and that officer had despatched, on the 6th, a message to the Boer camp at the Tugela, addressed to Chief Commandant Pretorius, and warning him not to proceed with the expedition, the result of which has just been described. But the Boer army had already gone out when the messenger arrived at the camp; nor would the earlier arrival of the message have availed to effect the object for which it had been sent. The rights of the British Government to interfere with their proceedings were not admitted by the Boers, and their Council, by whom Major Charters' warning was received and acknowledged, took no steps to carry out its requirements. The instructions the officer in command of the troops had received included one to seize all arms and ammunition in the possession of the Boers; and this order was carried into effect in regard to a few families who had taken up their abode near the Bay. The act gave rise, some time later, to a protest from the Boer authorities; but, except for this, the most friendly relations subsisted between them and the troops up to the time of the departure of the latter about the end of the following year.

On the 7th of February 1839, Major Charters had left Natal, and Captain Jarvis had succeeded to the command. Upon that date this officer commenced negotiations with the view to bringing about peace between the emigrants and the Zulus. In the sending of the message to Dingana on the subject he was assisted by an English resident named Ogle. The message was this: "Send Sotobe; the representative of the Queen desires to communicate with you through him." Sotobe had acquired a fame, which has made his name familiar to the Zulus down to the present time, by having been deputed by Tshaka to carry the message from him to the English king across the water.

Sotobe was not sent; but Dingana lost no time in responding to the message. His representative arrived at the British camp on the 23rd, sixteen days later. He was named Gambusha. He expressed, on Dingana's behalf, the wish that the Boers might be sent out of the country, but his tone manifested an eager desire for peace, and a willingness to accept it upon any terms that could be arranged. Being instructed as to the message he was to convey to his king, Gambusha left on the 24th. A month later he returned fully empowered to act on the king's behalf. He brought with him about 300 of the horses that the Zulus had captured from the Boers. On the 23rd of March peace was concluded, the terms being "that the

Boers should protect the Zulus in case of their being attacked unjustly; that the Zulus should remain on the other side of the Tugela until everything was settled, nor come on this side without a pass. A place was to be appointed at once where the cattle were to be given up"— the cattle which the Zulus had taken from the Boers since their arrival in Natal, and which Gambusha undertook, on Dingana's behalf, to restore to them. So definite was the agreement that the British Government soon considered the object to have been accomplished for which the troops had been sent to Natal, and made arrangements for their withdrawal.

After this Dingana committed no aggressive act against the Boers, but he fell short of compliance with the conditions of peace in that he did not return the Boers' cattle.

Dingana continued to manifest uneasiness in regard to the future. He sent an expedition to Swaziland with the serious object of seizing and occupying that country. A severe battle was fought, in which, while the Swazis admit that they were beaten, they claim to have inflicted such heavy loss on the invaders that the object of the expedition was wholly abandoned.

Discontent with his system of government had been growing amongst the Zulus for a considerable period. It is remembered as one of unsparing slaughter. The absence of some power which could afford protection to such as might be compelled to flee from its decrees had long been felt. The slender protection which the few Englishmen who resided at the Bay of Natal were able to afford had been sought so frequently, that the force with which these attacked him in April 1838 was largely composed of refugee Zulus. Except in one instance the agreement by which the English had bound themselves to surrender all such to Dingana had neither been observed by them nor enforced by him.

CHAPTER VIII

It was a natural outcome of the methods by which law was administered amongst the tribes of whom the Zulu nation had been formed, that a condition of things should have arisen by which the kingdom was constantly menaced. For most recognised crimes the punishment was death or confiscation of property, or both. The establishment of guilt was usually effected by means of consulting those persons called Izangoma, who have come to be known to the English as "witch-doctors," and sentence in such cases was pronounced in the absence of the supposed culprit.

The belief of the people concerning the functions of these persons was essentially similar to that which led Saul to consult the witch of Endor. They were regarded as, and believed themselves to be, the media of communication between the earthly and spiritual world. The guardian spirits were supposed to make known through them to the authorities the persons by whom wrong was being done to their earthly charges.

What the sentence would be was at once known by the individual declared to have been pointed out as the wrongdoer by the invoked spirit, and he lost no time in effecting his escape to some neighbouring tribe. Escapes of this kind had become so common that places of refuge from the decrees of their chiefs had become generally recognised as imperatively necessary. The conquests of Tshaka gave him dominion over so great an area that to get outside the range of his power was scarcely possible to those who might fall under his displeasure; but even

THE STORY OF THE ZULUS 81

he was in the habit of accepting the intercession of those to whom such might fly. The case of those who were protected by the Europeans at the Bay of Natal is an instance. It became the custom, indeed, to grant the prayer of any one having sufficient influence to get it presented, for leave to "gather the bones" of persons condemned to death. The prayer was accompanied by a present to the king, and it was understood that the man whose bones were asked for was dead only in that he had incurred the king's displeasure, and that the person making the petition would be responsible for his future good conduct. Thus persons holding any sort of authority waxed in power continually by gathering round them, as did David in the cave of Adullam, those who had got themselves into trouble. The growing power of subordinate chiefs was constantly calling for vigilant watchfulness on the part of the king. At the time at which we have now arrived Dingana's position was becoming endangered by the growing power of his brother Umpande, on the one, and of his cousin Mapita on the other, side of the country he ruled.

The life of the former had been spared, and he had been allowed to marry, because he had evinced no dangerous attributes. He had gone out with the Balule expedition in 1828, but since the death of Tshaka had taken no part in warlike operations. He had attained middle age, "the traces of wrinkles were beginning to be perceived" on his countenance. He dwelt peacefully at his kraal, called the Gqikazi, close to the site of the present town of Eshowe, and had gained the affections of a large number of people occupying the land lying towards the Tugela and the sea.

Six months had elapsed since the conclusion of peace with the Boers. There had been no breach of its terms on either side, except by Dingana as regards the restoration of cattle. In his attack upon the Swazis he appears to have been actuated by a hope of escaping the pressure of the Boers by conquering and occupying that country, and apparently he had not altogether abandoned the enterprise.

The lack of activity shown in this campaign by Umpande gave a definite form to a suspicion as to his loyalty; and there is no doubt that at this time his disaffection was well developed. He had ascertained, according to his own statement to the Boers some time later, that he was in agreement with a northern chief, who was, however, unable to get through Zululand to join him. This chief was probably Mapita, who had acquired a considerable following since taking up his abode in the land of the Amandwandwe.

It was in September, in the year 1839. Dingana's dissatisfaction with the manner in which compliance with his orders had been yielded by Umpande had manifested itself, amongst other ways, in a peremptory summons to the latter to attend personally at Umgungundhlovu; and there remained but one course open to the latter if his life were to be saved, namely, to immediately carry out the design he had secretly formed of crossing the Tugela and joining the Boers.

This accordingly he at once did. He first showed his peaceful intention by presenting a number of cattle to Johannes De Lange, whom he found killing hippopotami near the mouth of the river. Then, proceeding along the coast, he encamped near the Tongati River, and opened up communication with the Boer authorities at Boesman's Randt, or Bushman's Ridge, as their capital, now Pietermaritzburg, was then called.

His friendliness was at first doubted, and the question was mooted in the Boer Council of surprising and annihilating the force by which he was accompanied. By entering the territory south of the Tugela he had broken the treaty between the king and the Boers, and justified steps, on the part of the latter, for his forcible expulsion. But perhaps the effect of his arrival on the minds of the Boers is best told in the words of M. Adulphe Delegorgue, a French naturalist, who was present and took part in the discussion of the situation which followed: . . . "Great excitement was caused . . . by the fear of these neighbours: it was difficult to believe that they were refugees. The grave proceeding resolved on by Umpande was," in the eyes of the Boers, "only a great scheme for authorising the entrance into their territory of the army of Dingana, this sworn enemy, who refused the payment of an acknowledged debt, and whose dishonest intentions had been so well unmasked. Umpande was as much distrusted as Dingana himself. Little was needed to give immediate effect to the opinion of the women, for African ladies have a voice in the councils, and to them is due the action of their husbands. An onslaught was to be made on the refugees without any warning, a butchery that would oblige them to return from whence they came."

But wiser and more temperate counsels ultimately prevailed, and an alliance was concluded on the 27th of October, the object of which was a combined attack upon, and the overthrow of, Dingana, and the establishment of Umpande as Zulu king. For their assistance in securing this object Umpande undertook to pay the Boers the cattle that had been stipulated in the treaty with Dingana, and he promised that when secured in the kingdom he would not permit "any woman, or child, or defenceless aged person to be murdered, nor allow any war or hostile action on the part of his people against any neighbouring chief or tribes without the consent of the Assembly of Emigrants."

These terms had been definitely concluded when a scene occurred which has been remembered by the Zulus. The Boers had requested Umpande to nominate three persons of those "particularly attached to his person" to be his "Chief Captains." He did so, and the three he chose included one Umpangazita (whose name, for some reason now inexplicable, was written in the records Umpangazowaga), who had held a prominent position as one of Dingana's indunas at Umgungundhlovu. The men were addressed by the chief of the Boer representatives on the gravity of the responsibility attaching to their office, and general satisfaction seemed to result. But no sooner had they retired than Umpangazita was set upon by a considerable body of men and beaten to death with sticks. There was no apparent reason for this act. It was believed by his sons, who became old and well-known men in the nation, that Umpande did trust this man, and that his execution was the spontaneous act of the people, who felt unable to do so because of the position he had held under Dingana. On the other hand, M. Delegorgue says: "In our eyes Umpande had cleared himself of crime. His eloquence made us believe him innocent. Some days elapsed before we learned that the act had been his first exercise of kingly authority." And what may perhaps be regarded as a second "act of kingly authority" was the almost immediate despatch of an armed force against some petty tribe in the neighbourhood, which the Boers had sanctioned in the course of these negotiations at the Tongati.

Those who had accompanied Umpande in his flight were estimated as numbering some 17,000; and such fighting strength as could be supplied by that large number of people had been added to that of the Boers and taken away from Dingana.

The treaty into which the Boers had entered with the latter was now entirely laid aside; and, as soon as the troops at Port Natal were withdrawn by the British, which took place in December 1839, preparations were begun for an attack upon him by the combined forces of the new alliance. The march was commenced in the following month. The campaign was fruitful of great results; it was the last in which the Boers engaged against the Zulus. It was arranged that the forces of Umpande and the Boer commando should proceed by different routes, the former by way of the Lower Tugela and Eshowe, and the latter by the route of their last campaign. Umpande was personally to accompany the Boers, his men being commanded by his chief induna, Nongalaza.

The ground alleged in the official journal as justifying the breaking of the treaty and the renewal of hostilities against Dingana was the failure on his part to pay the cattle stipulated in it; they claimed that he was in default to the extent of about 40,000 still due. He had sent only "some fifty to a hundred cattle, 2000 lbs. of ivory, and vain promises that the cattle still due by him would be paid." Having, on these grounds, divested themselves of the obligations into which they had entered, they returned to the position of things before the treaty, and resolved, not only that Dingana should be deposed, but that he should expiate the wrongs he had done them with his life, as also his two chief indunas, Unzobo and Undhlela. He and they, the journal states, "were the monsters who stained the earth with the innocent blood of our peaceful whites." They offered a reward of fifty head of cattle to any who would deliver up Dingana, and twenty-five for Undhlela. Unzobo they had with them "in chains."

The development of affairs had seriously alarmed Dingana. He scarcely knew what to do. He perceived that it would not be possible to hold his own against the force combined against him. Flight was not likely to secure his safety, because he had incurred enmity on all sides.

The Swazis on the north were hostile to him, so were the people of Umzilikazi on the north-west. From the south and south-west the impi of Umpande and the Boer commando were threatening to advance against him. What could be done in the circumstances he did. He sent Unzobo (known in histories as Dambuza, his war title) to the Boers at Pietermaritzburg to make what terms he could with them, promising to agree to anything which his ambassador might undertake on his behalf.

Unzobo and Undhlela, as Dingana's chief advisers, were credited with having urged him to commit the wrongs of which he was held guilty. Their names are conspicuously mentioned in connection with all the negotiations that took place between him and the white men who had dealings with him. The feeling they had evoked in the minds of the Boers was expressed in the Journal of the expedition, and was given practical effect to, in Unzobo's case, by his immediate arrest. He was to accompany the commando for a time, as a prisoner, and then suffer the doom which it was desired that there might be opportunity of inflicting on all three.

Dingana did not long feel safe in his new residence at Ivuna. His enemies were advancing upon him. He therefore moved another thirty miles away, himself reaching the Magundu Mountain, which stands conspicuously about eight miles to the south of the Pongolo River; his army remaining at the Maqongqo, a group of round hills a few miles to the south of it, whose name has been well known since.

There the issue of the situation was determined on the 29th of January 1840. The date is a useful one to remember, because the event is referred to by Zulus for the purpose of fixing the dates of other occurrences.

Umpande's men had been somewhat rash to stake everything on their own strength. The battle was fiercely contested, and for a time the issue was doubtful. A survivor of Dingana's men stated, in 1899, that at one time they believed the victory to be theirs, but that they were afterwards overpowered. There were a great number killed on both sides: "for many years the place was white with their bones." But Nongalaza did ultimately gain the fight, and a new course of events began.

Undhlela died on this occasion. He was in command of Dingana's forces, and was wounded. So incensed was his chief at his failure that he immediately ordered his execution.

Unzobo, the other "monster," was to die the next day.

The Boers had "arrived within a day's march of the capital"; they were thus more than sixty miles away from its scene when the battle took place. They were not aware of the success which had been gained by their side. The Commandant-General resolved to "decide the fate" of their prisoner, and of a man named Kambazana who had accompanied him on his mission.

A court-martial was convened, of which the Commandant-General was the President and Umpande a member, although he was also the chief witness against the accused. The charge against Unzobo was, indeed, stated by him, and the essence of it was as follows: (1) that the accused had been a consenting party to the king's (Dingana's) acts of bloodshed; (2) that the destruction of Zulu families by the king's orders had invariably resulted from proposals made by the accused; (3) that it was the accused who prevailed upon Dingana to kill Retief and his companions, and order the subsequent massacre of the Boers in Natal; (4) that the accused had on one occasion induced Dingana to authorise the execution of Umpande himself, which authority was, however, withdrawn.

Unzobo was asked whether he had anything to say with regard to these accusations and replied in the negative; but declared that his companion, Kambazana, was entirely innocent of anything set forth in them. Umpande was thereupon appealed to, and, "declared that he (Kambazana) had always instigated the king against others by false reports in order to remain in favour with the king"; and thereupon, "with the advice and consent of the court-martial," the Chief Commandant proceeded to pass sentence of death upon the prisoners, who were straightway led out and shot by a party of Boers.

The death of Unzobo is a well-remembered incident in Zulu history. Strangely, the Zulus believe that he was tied to the spokes of a wagon-wheel and killed by being carried round with it when the vehicle was in motion.

But nothing connected with this trial and execution has been remembered with resentment. It is believed that the cruelty of Dingana, and the large number of deaths he ordered to be inflicted, were due largely to the advice of Unzobo, and that security for life demanded that he should die. The action of the Boers was agreeable to the feeling of the party who had severed themselves from Dingana and given their adhesion to Umpande. That chief gave expression, at the trial, to what his party felt on the subject; and this, no doubt, largely influenced the Boers in the course they took. But the feeling was only against Unzobo personally, and his family were not made to lose their position of distinction. His son, Umgamule, grew old in honourable employment under the succeeding rulers. The same has to be said of Undhlela. His sons, Godide and Mavumengwana, became prominent amongst the notables of the country.

The news of the defeat of Dingana reached the Boers on the 1st of February. They had then reached the rough country near the Black Umfolozi, and their wagons could not proceed further. A party of 250 horsemen went in pursuit of the defeated enemy, and nearly had an engagement at the source of the Isikwebezi stream. Dingana, having been accustomed to hold Umpande in contempt, was extremely annoyed at the termination of the battle at the Maqongqo. He lost no time in despatching what force he could still muster to renew the conflict. The two impis were about to meet, when that of Dingana beheld the Boer force advancing through the mist which enveloped the hills, and withdrew. The pursuit was continued as far as to the Pongolo River.

The work of the expedition was now accomplished. Mapita had yielded submission to Umpande and to the Boers. He and Umpande were to continue on terms of close friendship as long as they both lived; and during that time he was to gather the strength that was destined, under his son, Usibebu, to produce marked effects in the future—as will be seen.

The Boers had collected 31,000 head of cattle to take back with them, and had done no fighting and lost none of their number. They were in high spirits. On the 10th of February the Commandant-General ceremoniously declared Umpande King of the Zulus, and an alliance was agreed to between them.

But, four days later, he read a proclamation setting forth that whereas the Zulu nation was still indebted to the Boers in the sum of 22,600 rix dollars (£1725) for horse and wagon hire and other war expenses, and as there was no hope of recovering this sum in consequence of the flight of Dingana, therefore the land between the Tugela and the Black Umfolozi, from the mouth of the latter to the mountains near its source, and thence along the high lands to the Drakensberg, was taken in satisfaction of the debt, and would thenceforth be a portion of the South African Company's territory. This done, they returned to Pietermaritzburg and their homes, satisfied with their success, and feeling that an ever-imminent danger had been overcome, and that a peaceful prospect lay before them.

Regarding the proclamation, which if given effect to would have taken away from Umpande the greater portion of the land upon which the people dwelt over whom he had been made king, a Dutch historian has this question and answer: "How is this proclamation reconcilable with the other whereby Umpande was acknowledged King of the Zulus? Very simply. The Boers had made him King of the Zulus but not of Zululand. He might go with his Zulus whither he listed—to England, if necessary." [1]

It will be convenient, now, to follow Dingana to his end. He crossed the Pongolo River and took refuge on the Lembobo Mountain, by Hlatikulu, the great forest. He rested there for some time. He had with him a considerable people; and it was no easy matter to find food for their maintenance. He therefore meditated a descent on, and occupation of, Swaziland, but his hopes of accomplishing this were vague. In the meantime most of his fighting men had to be employed in foraging, and he had little personal protection, while impatience was beginning to be manifested at the non-payment of the cattle he had promised for grain supplied by the inhabitants of the locality. This payment it did not seem that he would ever be able to make, and some individual, more impatient than the rest, conceived the idea of getting rid of both him and his people by means of the Swazis. He offered his services as guide, and an impi was sent by the king (or Queen-Regent, the King Sobuza being said to have been then dead) to attack him. The kraal he occupied was surrounded at night, and, in escaping, he was wounded by an assegai in the side. In three days he died of this wound, and his people buried him. Those who had followed him, Umdidi ka 'Ndhlela, or the tail of Undhlela, as they were thenceforth satirically called, then returned to their own country glad to submit to the new rule.

It may be interesting to give the account of the matter as recorded by a Boer, to whom the story had obviously been furnished by one who desired to tell something pleasing. This story has since been adopted by historians as a true account of Dingana's death. "Sobuza

[1] Cachet.

took Dingana prisoner. On the first day (according to the statement of the Kafirs) Sobuza pricked Dingana with sharp assegais, no more than skin-deep, from the sole of his foot to the top of his head. The second day he had him bitten by dogs. On the third day Sobuza said to Dingana: 'Dingana, are you still the rain-maker? Are you still the greatest of living men? See the sun rising, you shall not see him set!' Saying this, he took an assegai and bored his eyes out. This was related to me by one of Sobuza's Kafirs who were present. When the sun set Dingana was dead, for he had neither tasted food nor water for three days."

CHAPTER IX

THE circumstances in which Umpande had gained the kingship, as has been seen, threatened to dispossess him of the major portion of the land upon which the Zulu people dwelt; that described in the proclamation mentioned at the conclusion of the last chapter included nearly all the king's personal places of residence. The proclamation had been read in his presence and hearing, and there is no reason to suppose otherwise than that it was intended to be effective. Favourable circumstances would probably have resulted in its provisions being carried out.

But circumstances were soon to bring about a change upon which neither party had reckoned. The Boers, being now free from the dangers which had overhung them, soon began to spread themselves freely over the land they had acquired. They built and planted, and soon established themselves in a condition of life very similar to that which they had left in the Cape Colony. Facilities for obtaining such articles as are considered necessary in civilised life were wanting; but the people were not without resource, nor the ability to secure such comforts as health required. They were generally well-to-do. They had regained by recent successes nearly as many cattle as they had lost to the Zulus in previous reverses. Of money they had but little, but many were able to procure from the traders, who soon established themselves amongst them, some few luxuries in exchange, mainly, for hides and ivory. Large game was very plentiful, especially in Zululand, which now became a free hunting field. The hunting exploits of Johannes De Lange have not yet been forgotten. It is still told how he attacked a herd of elephants in the Umbekamuzi Valley, and, having driven them into a corner, slew so many that the valley stank; how the herd included a mighty patriarch which was spoken of in tradition, and had been given a name signifying " taller than the trees." De Lange spent much of his time in Zululand. He adopted many of the habits of the Zulu people, perhaps in a worse form. At festive gatherings he and they were wont to discuss, in loud but friendly tones, the several battles in which they had been opposed, and to dispute as to which side had been victorious.

The produce of the land furnished such food as they had been accustomed to eat. They were, perhaps, falling away somewhat from civilised ways, but they were generally content with their lot. They were scarcely affected by the Government at Pietermaritzburg; they enjoyed almost complete freedom.

They were, however, sometimes subjected to a kind of annoyance which a Boer is least able to bear. In certain parts of the settlement they frequently missed portions of their flocks and herds, and there was evidence that they were stolen and taken in the direction of Pondoland. They persuaded themselves that the thefts had been committed by the Mabaca people, the chief of whom at that time was a man named Ngcapayi; but it has been contended that the real thieves were a race called Bushmen.

Poor Bushmen! It is not easy to see one now, so few have they become. But at the time to which reference is being made they were numerous. They dwelt partly in caves, partly in such rude shelters as they were able to construct. They did not plant, but lived on what game they could kill, or what they could steal from those who owned stock. They were a low type of mankind, very short of stature; of a light, almost yellow, colour; with black, woolly hair, which gathered in tufts, leaving intervals of bare scalp; very high cheek-bones—very ugly generally. But they did not lack intelligence, and were capable of being trained to high usefulness as servants. As such they were very highly valued by the Dutch. Their natural aptitude for horsemanship rendered them especially useful as rough-riders. In their natural state they were regarded rather as wild animals than human beings. If seen in the proximity of a herd of cattle or flock of sheep they met with scant consideration at the hands of the owner. Their minds, perhaps, were scarcely able to appreciate the rights of ownership. They were a continual source of annoyance to cattle owners, and a kind of war of extermination was waged against them. Sir George Napier, the Governor of the Cape Colony, in a despatch dated the 25th July 1842, stated that it was a well-known practice of the Boers to attack them, kill those that were grown up, and bring up the children as servants. In their captivity they became so separated as seldom to meet with members of their own race; so that they soon disappeared off the face of the earth, leaving, as memorial, only the rude paintings which they executed in the caves they inhabited, generally depicting wild animals and man equipped for slaying them.

By the end of 1841 complaints of stock thefts had become numerous and loud, and, whatever may have been the true facts of the case, the Boer authorities felt satisfied that Ngcapayi and his tribe were the thieves. They subsequently found certain of their stolen animals in the possession of these people, which fact they held to have justified their action. Commandant Pretorius, at the head of 200 men, attacked the tribe, and, after a "desperate fight" in which some 150 of the natives were killed, and none of the Boers, "as many cattle were seized as would repay the people what they had been robbed." A number of native children were also brought back by the expedition and "apprenticed" to their captors or other Boers—a form of contract which was in some quarters considered to place the apprentice in a position differing little from slavery. The children so taken and disposed of were termed orphans. It was either believed, or affected to be believed, that they had been rendered destitute by the death in battle of their natural supporters, or by their abandonment through the flight of these. The Boers never failed to find some such orphans in the course of their military expeditions; even in that against Dingana, in the beginning of 1840, in which they did no fighting, being far away from the scene of it, a considerable number of young Zulus were so found and provided for by means of apprenticeship.

Although neither this system of apprenticeship nor the breach of the treaty with Dingana had attracted much notice, these new proceedings gave rise to a very grave concern in the minds of the British authorities at the Cape. The Pondo chief, Faku, while professing friendship with the Boers and affecting to approve of their action against Ngcapayi, sent a message to the Governor asking for protection against them. A report of the raid reached him at Grahamstown on the 5th of January 1841; by the 27th he had confirmatory intelligence, as well as Faku's appeal for protection, and, in response to that appeal, had ordered Captain Smith, with a detachment of the 27th Regiment, to proceed to the Umgazi River, in the territory of that chief, to take up a position there, and afford him the protection for which he asked. In the meantime some correspondence had passed between the Governor and the Council of the Boers at Natal on the relations that should subsist between them and the British Government. When asked for a statement of their views on the subject the Boers asserted that they were a free and independent people; while, on the other hand, they were regarded by the Queen's representative as British subjects, for whose acts of aggression the British Government was responsible. The correspondence promised no satisfactory settlement of the question. The Boers were informed by the Governor, in a letter dated the 27th of September 1840, that the Queen could not acknowledge a portion of her own subjects as an independent republic; but that, on their receiving a force from the Colony, their trade would be placed on the same footing as a trade with a British Colony, a proposal which the Boers rejected in a letter dated the 11th October. They contemplated a step, moreover, which seriously alarmed the Cape Government. Since their occupation of the land of Natal large numbers of natives had come from Zululand and elsewhere and taken up their abode in it, feeling, probably, that they could enjoy greater security there than under their own chiefs. The rapid increase of the native population from such sources soon became a subject of alarm to the Boers, and, with a view to averting the danger they feared, it was resolved by their Council on the 2nd of August that the land lying between the Umtamvuna and Umzimvubu rivers should be set apart for native occupation and that those inhabiting the land they desired should be removed thither. The Commandant-General was instructed to see this measure carried into effect. It was considered that, apart from the severity of the measure itself, the placing of so large a native population on its frontier would be dangerous to the peace of the Cape Colony; the territory to which these people were to be removed was that of the Pondo chief, Faku, and his permission had not been asked.

These were among the reasons which led to the resolution, which was arrived at by the Governor at the end of 1841, to resume military occupation of Port Natal. It was the wet season, and the movement of the troops stationed at the Umgazi, who were designed for that service, had to be delayed till the following March. In that month

THE STORY OF THE ZULUS

Captain Smith began his march; he reached his destination early in May 1842, and established a camp near the Port.

The Boer authorities, having sent him formal protests, which he declined to receive, began to collect at Congela, where they were soon in considerable force. On the 23rd of the month Commandant-General Pretorius demanded that Captain Smith should instantly break up his camp and withdraw across the borders of the territory which the Boers claimed, besides paying the expenses incurred, threatening war unless these demands were complied with. Captain Smith determined to attack the Boer camp, which he accordingly did, with disastrous results to himself, the same evening. The Boers were prepared for his advance, and suddenly rained a deadly shower of bullets upon him from behind trees, killing seventeen and wounding thirty-one of his men, and forcing him to retire to his camp. There he withstood a vigorous siege till relieved, about a month later, by reinforcements from Cape Colony, whither news of his position had been carried on horseback by one Richard King. The Boers opposed but feeble resistance to the landing of these forces, being unable to stand against the fire from the ship's guns, under cover of which the landing was effected. While manifesting great unwillingness to submit to British authority, they did not oppose any further active resistance to it; and, military occupation having been continued till the end of 1842, the English Government reluctantly determined to take possession of, and establish an administration in, the territory of which the Boers had acquired possession, and which later became known as the Colony of Natal. That decision having been received by the Governor at the Cape in April of the following year, steps were soon taken to give effect to it, the Honourable Henry Cloete being appointed Her Majesty's Commissioner for the purpose in the following month, and arriving in Natal on the 5th June 1843.

Favourable conditions were offered to the Boers, who, after considerable opposition and threatened resistance, submitted, a document embodying their submission being signed by the members of their Council at Pietermaritzburg on the 8th of August 1843.

Umpande had maintained friendly relations with the Boers, but matters had remained in a somewhat unsettled state. No definite line of division between his and their territory had been agreed upon. Claims by Boers to farms on the north of the Tugela had been registered, while the Zulu king had kraals on the south of the Umzinyati, or Buffalo River, which subsequently formed the boundary. A settlement of this matter was of urgent importance, and two months after Natal had become British territory Commissioner Cloete proceeded to the kraal of Umpande with the object of effecting it. The king readily extended to the British the friendship which he had established with the Boers. He was very desirous also that a frontier should be agreed upon, and readily fell in with the proposal that his territory should be limited on the south by the Tugela and Umzinyati rivers. A treaty to that effect was signed on the 5th of October. On the same day Umpande granted to Her Majesty the Queen a cession of St. Lucia Bay, which was to prove of political utility forty years later.

The condition of the Zulu people at this time was in no important respect different from that of previous reigns. Shortly before Mr. Cloete's visit Umpande had removed the only possible cause of political disturbance which then existed. Of his father's numerous sons he and one other only remained alive when he became king. Two had successively reigned over the Zulu nation, and in turn had been destroyed by brothers who desired to reign in their stead. Some had perished in war, but most had probably been killed because of suspected aspirations to the kingship. About the middle of 1843 Umpande's only brother,

Gququ, was thus suspected. He was married, and had established himself on the Sigubutu Hills on the north of the Black Umfolozi River. The impression has remained with the Zulus that he was beginning to feel his strength; that the suspicion was justified. Captain Smith, who inquired into the matter at the time, declared that their had been no ground for it; that action was taken against him merely on the word of a man named Tengwana, a resident in Natal, who stated that he had heard of the conspiracy on the part of Gququ against the king.[1] But, upon whatever evidence, the king's order went forth; the kraal on the Sigubutu was surrounded suddenly, to Gququ's surprise, and he and his family were entirely destroyed. That a large portion of the people were attached to him is evident from what immediately followed. His aunt, Mawa, who resided near the Tugela, fled into Natal, and was followed by nearly the whole of the people in that part of the country. Commissioner Cloete found nearly all the kraals, which had been numerous, as far north as the Inseleni stream deserted and in ruins; their inmates had been added to the rapidly increasing native population of Natal.

The "Crossing of Mawa" is one of the events in Zulu history which mark periods in time.

There was no one left to dispute the right of Umpande to reign, and tranquillity thus prevailed within the borders of his country. There could be no further cause of civil war until his own sons should grow up and dispute the succession with each other.

Umpande was residing at the Sixebeni kraal, near the abandoned site of the Umgungundhlovu, long after the chief residence of Langazana. He was indulging in the same forms of amusement as his predecessors had done. Bands of fighting men performed war-dances before him.; large numbers of women sang to him in his private apart-

[1] *Annals of Natal*, ii. 316.

ments. He had done nothing in the direction of adopting such civilised habits as he had seen during his association with the Boers. Mahloko was engaged in the manufacture of the clumsy brass armlets already described, and he evinced a deep interest in the work, asking, as Dingana was wont to ask, to be presented with files for the purpose.

Missionaries had endeavoured to establish themselves in the country after his accession, but had lately become alarmed and left. Umpande refused them permission to return. But he allowed traders free access to his country, and any of his subjects who stole or injured their property, or that of any white man, was liable to be put to death. The property of white men was thenceforth to be most rigidly protected in the Zulu country; perhaps in no country in the world did greater security prevail. The French naturalist already mentioned went, shortly after Umpande's accession, into the valley of the White Umfolozi River to collect specimens. He pitched a tent there and left it for a time without any one in charge. Upon his return he found that it had been entered and certain articles or specimens removed or injured. There was evidence that this had been done by a human being, and he reported the matter to the king. The result was interesting, as showing the degree of reprobation in which such acts were held by the king, and how justice was, and continued to be, administered. Certain men of position were sent to investigate the matter in the locality of its occurrence. They called the people of the neighbourhood together and subjected them one by one to searching examination. At last one showed some hesitation in answering the questions addressed to him, from which it was at once perceived that he had some knowledge of the subject; and, when closely questioned, he admitted that he had seen a certain person leave a hunting party and go in the direction in which the tent stood, and mentioned other circumstances which he thought might cast suspicion upon this man. Thereupon the person referred to, who was also present, was interrogated, and being unable to evade the searching questions addressed to him, eventually made a full confession. His guilt being thus established, he was removed a short distance and put to death.

CHAPTER X

UMPANDE had always been regarded as the fool of the family. He scarcely took any part in politics. He took to himself wives, chiefly of the daughters of commoners, and was permitted, by reason of his supposed harmlessness of disposition, and his lack of ability to do any important thing, even had the disposition been present, to live and bring up a family. That his position was not always free from danger may be inferred, however, from the name which he gave to his eldest son. Cetshwayo signifies "The Slandered One." It most probably had reference to some accusation brought against Umpande, from which he had exculpated himself to Dingana's satisfaction at the time of the boy's birth. His sudden rising had been a surprise to his reigning brother, and now that he had established himself in the position of king the lack of ability by which he had been characterised soon began to mark his reign. His weakness was so much felt by the people that their hopes early turned to his sons. The eldest of these were in this year, 1843, about fourteen years of age. They were named Cetshwayo and Umbulazi, and the chief event of the remaining years of their father's reign was to arise from their rival claims to succeed him.

Cetshwayo's mother was singular, amongst the wives of Umpande at this time, in being the daughter of a chief. The name of her father was Manzini—In-the-Water—and it afterwards became necessary for the women of the nation, from respect for him through his queen-daughter, to call water by another name, which they still do. Her name was Ngqumbazi, and was, and continues to be, held in high veneration.

The mother of Umbulazi was named Monase. She was the mother of three sons besides him, all born to sorrowful purpose, and three daughters.

The section of Umpande's family presided over by Ngqumbazi continued to reside on the south of the Umhlatuzi River, while the residence of Monase was established at the Umfaba Hills on the south bank of the Black Umfolozi River. The two sections were thus about eighty miles apart, the chief residence of the king being between them, at the White Umfolozi. Parties began gradually to associate themselves with these two centres, and gave to themselves the names respectively of Izigqoza and Usutu, the latter being the party of Cetshwayo and the former that of Umbulazi. By the time Umpande had reigned sixteen years the nation was thus divided against itself, and he had no power to control the two parties into which it was formed. Matters reached a crisis in 1856.

Umbulazi conceived the idea of applying for help to the Natal Government in the conflict which became inevitable, and, following the example of his father, he gathered his people together, and proceeded with them in the direction of that Colony. He arrived at the Tugela River in November, at a place near its mouth known to the natives by the name of 'Ndondakusuka. To reach this place he had traversed the district occupied by Cetshwayo with his Usutu section, which was gathered to attack him. He crossed the river personally to solicit aid in his cause from the British Border Agent, but, this being declined, he returned to his people, and abode with them the attack. His force was much weaker than that against which he was to be opposed, and he was at the further disadvantage of having the aged and the women and children of his people with him.

John Dunn, of subsequent notoriety, was at that time

a young man employed as a clerk in the Border Agent's office, and volunteered, with a small force of natives, in Umbulazi's service. He has stated the number of the opposing armies respectively as 7,000 and 20,000. The fight, which took place on the 2nd of December, was short and decisive. As is usual in native battles, the Izigqoza, when once put to flight, never rallied. They made what speed they could to the river, which was swollen. There a terrible scene followed.

Umbulazi's non-combatants were placed between his fighting men and the river. Their whole dependence for safety was upon the arms of their warriors. With the failure of these they were placed in a pitiable position indeed. The whole people became a confused crowd, resistless as sheep. On the one side advanced the relentless enemy, while on the other rolled the broad and treacherous Tugela. On the far side of the river their lives would be safe, but there only, and the desperate choice had to be made quickly, whether to cast themselves into the flood and try to gain that haven, or trust to the mercy of the advancing host. It is hard to say to which alternative the preference was given. The sea shore, as far south as to Durban, bore evidence on succeeding days, in the dead bodies which the sea cast up, to the fact that those who had trusted themselves to the mercy of the flood rather than to that of their angry countrymen had been many. The northern bank of the Tugela long testified by bleaching bones to the fate of those who hesitated.

Sharp were the moments of terror and anguish of many a mother that day. For themselves they did not much fear death. But oh! if their little ones might be permitted to live! These many offered as free gifts to such as they thought might be able to save them; but it is doubtful whether acceptance was in any case met with.

In this battle six of Umpande's sons were killed or drowned, including Umbulazi, the claimant, Mantantashiya

THE STORY OF THE ZULUS

and Madumba, both sons of his mother, Monase. The names of the others are well remembered by the Zulus, but nothing more is known of them than their names.

Monase's other son, Umkungo, Umpande surreptitiously sent into Natal, where he was to spend an uneventful life, returning to Zululand in his old age, when it had become British territory.

The effect of this battle was to place Cetshwayo virtually in possession of the kingdom. His father retained the position in name only and on sufferance. It is said that the suggestion was made that he might be removed, but that Cetshwayo declined to entertain it on the same grounds as those on which Dingana had spared Umpande —that he was harmless. But an incident which occurred some time later indicated that he was not disposed to allow filial respect to stand in the way of his own aspirations. Umpande showed some disposition to prefer a wife whom he had married after he had gained the kingship above those who had become his wives while he was still a subject, and she obviously hoped that the succession might pass to her sons. Her name was Nomantshali. Her kraal was called the Umdumezulu, and was within a short distance of the Nodwengu, Umpande's chief residence north of the White Umfolozi River, whither he had now removed. Cetshwayo resolved upon the extirpation of this family, and despatched an impi under the command of Umbomvana, the induna of the Ubazini kraal, to carry that resolution into effect. Nomantshali had three sons, Umtonga, Umgidhlana and Umpoiyana. The two former were absent; their mother was with Langazana at the Sixebeni, Umpoiyana alone being at home when the impi arrived. He left, accompanied by several young men, intending to join his mother, but without a definite plan of escape. He was captured in the part of the White Umfolozi valley into which Bongoza betrayed the Boers, and brought back to Nodwengu. What then took place shows how completely Umpande's authority had passed away by this time (1860). He was sitting outside the kraal. When he saw his boy arrive he uttered a cry, and advanced as if to take hold of him. Before he could do so, however, a body of men seized the lad, and threw him violently against a hut, from whence he arose bleeding from the ear. He was also crying, and inquiring how one so young could dispute the succession. He was immediately hurried through an opening in the kraal-stockade, across the cattle-pen and out by the gate which faced the Umdumezulu kraal, from which point it has been found impracticable to trace him further. Umpande could but weep and address unavailing prayers to his ancestral spirits. Intelligence was sent by Langazana of Nomantshali's presence, and a body of men were sent to kill her. Umtonga and Umgidhlana escaped to the Boers who occupied the land between the Buffalo River and the Drakensberg, with results to be recorded later.

Another cause of trouble in respect to the kingship was growing, but it was not suspected then to have that tendency. A full brother of Umpande, named Unzibe, had died shortly after his return with the Balule expedition in 1828. He resided on the ridge which has now taken the name of Usibebu's kraal, Xedeni, on the road from Nongoma to Hlabisa, where the Xulu family reside, of which the head was then Unzibe's henchman, Umfinyeli. His grave may be seen there. So strong is the belief in some form of spiritual life that Umpande actually took wives for the spirit of this man, and there was born, and considered to be born to him, a son, to whom the name was given of Uhamu. This family of Unzibe's spirit was located on the hills sloping from the Ingome forest to the Umkuzi stream, and a strong section with independent tendencies began to be formed there, of which notice will have to be taken.

Beyond domestic disturbances there was no important

event to mark the reign of Umpande. There was one campaign undertaken, of necessity against the Swazis, there being no other accessible foe, but the date of it cannot be ascertained. It was regarded more as a military exercise than a serious warfare. It was not due to any quarrel, but had for its object merely to enable the regiment to which Cetshwayo belonged, the Tulwana, to see active service. It has been remembered as the "Fund' u Tulwana,"—Teach the Tulwana—campaign. Its success was not great. The Swazis betook themselves to the Umdimba Mountains, and waited in security there till the invaders retired; then, with a view to appeasing so formidable an enemy, they sent a present of cattle to the king. This incident is remembered by the Swazis as one which involved them in obligations to the Transvaal Boers. On hearing of the Zulu advance they sent a large number of cattle into the Transvaal for safety, and for the protection which they received they acknowledged that they owed a debt. This debt, in subsequent negotiations, they claimed to have discharged by capturing a number of Tonga children on the east of the Lebombo Mountain and handing them over to the Boers.

The disturbance caused by the rivalry of Cetshwayo and Umbulazi resulted in a great exodus of people. It was the greatest influx into Natal since the crossing of Mawa. The Natal Government considered it to be necessary to issue what became known as the Refugee Regulations. These were issued on the 23rd of the month in which the battle of 'Ndondakusuka was fought, and remained in force until Zululand became a British possession. They provided that each Zulu capable of work and coming into Natal should be placed in the service of a white master for a period of three years.

These were the most important interruptions that occurred in Umpande's reign of the tranquillity of the people. His long rule was otherwise characterised by general quietness. While for various reasons some of the people found it necessary to seek refuge in Natal, it has to be noted that in the year 1858 a chief named Matshana, son of Mondise, sought the protection of the Zulu king to escape action that was being taken against him by the Natal Government. He and his tribe fled across the border and were assigned land on the Malagata Hills near to it, where they were destined, twenty years later, to contribute indirectly to a sorrowful mishap to a portion of the British Army.

Of notable events there were few others. In 1863 the country was sorely stricken with small-pox: many still bear the marks which the disease left on their faces. The scourge was stamped out by means of vaccination, which was introduced by Europeans and carried out by the people themselves.

In 1861 the Secretary for Native Affairs in Natal, Mr. Theophilus Shepstone, visited the king and obtained the formal recognition of Cetshwayo's title to succeed on his death.

The laws governing the conduct of the people were perhaps scarcely different in principle from those that had been in operation before a central government had been substituted for the independent rule of numerous chiefs. There were then neighbouring tribes to whose protection men might fly when the death sentence had been pronounced against them; this condition had now been restored by the governments that had been established in Natal and in the Transvaal. When the guilt of an accused person had been established with such certainty as to be considered seriously to demand his execution, great secrecy was observed; when there was any doubt, or when the execution of a condemned man was not held to be urgently expedient, rumour was permitted to reach him as to what was intended, and he escaped, leaving his property to be collected on behalf of the king.

THE STORY OF THE ZULUS 109

Two authenticated cases which occurred about this time may be given by way of illustration. In the one the accused man resided in the north of the country. He had given it as his opinion that a relative of his who had died had been the victim of some practiser of witchcraft, and indicated in what direction his suspicions lay. The matter was referred to Cetshwayo, then residing at his Landandhlovu kraal, in what is now the Eshowe District, and exercising the authority of king, and he ordered a consultation of witch-doctors. These pointed to the complainant as the man who had done the evil deed, and this being reported, Cetshwayo ordered that he should be killed. The man from whom these particulars were obtained was the one to whom instructions were given to carry this order into effect. He had to travel a journey occupying four days, and was alone, supported only with verbal authority to call upon Umnyamana for assistance in the execution of his orders. Umnyamana was a man scarcely likely to yield ready compliance with such a request if the condemned man, as was the case in this instance, happened to be in any sense an adherent of his own. He was already waxing strong, and his strength was in an especial measure made up of those whom he had sheltered. He professed inability to act without direct instruction, for which he promised to apply, telling the messenger that if, in the meantime, he were satisfied with his orders, he might of course carry them into effect. The necessity for further reference to the king afforded the man ample time to remove out of danger, which he did by proceeding into the Transvaal.

The other case was that of a man who, having become separated from, and lost sight of, his own family, had attached himself to that of a man of such position that he had been entrusted with the charge of some of King Umpande's cattle. A disease broke out amongst these animals, and it was necessary to give some account of this in reporting the deaths that resulted to the king. A witch-doctor was consulted, and, having no doubt had his mind in some way influenced in the matter, he pointed to the resident stranger as the man who, by some occult art, had induced the disease. This evidence satisfied Umpande, and he ordered the man's execution, and granted the petition of him in whose kraal he had dwelt to be permitted to take, and adopt for his own benefit, the children he left.

The regimental system was actively pursued during Umpande's reign. He reigned thirty-two years, and the regiments given by the Zulus as having been enrolled during that time number thirteen, a list of which, with the approximate year of the birth of their members, is given at the foot of this page.

Of the first on the list there remain few alive at the time of writing this, but of the yet older, the Udhlambedhlu regiment, one may still at times be met with.

There being no restriction in regard to trading, various articles of commerce were brought within the reach of most, and imported articles of European manufacture substituted largely for those that had been produced by native industry.

Great licence was allowed to sportsmen and hunters, and while it may be lamented that many valuable wild animals were thus lost to those who came into life at a later period, there are many lovers of the chase who look back, in their declining days, with great pleasure to what they term the "good old days of Zululand."

LIST OF ZULU REGIMENTS

1. Indaba-ka-Ombe . . 1820
2. Ingwegwe . . . 1823
3. Izingulube . . . 1825
4. Isangqu 1828
5. Tulwana, Inkonkoni or Umboza . . . 1830
6. Indhlondhlo . . . 1833
7. Dhlokwe 1835
8. Dududu 1837
9. Umxapo 1840
10. Umbonambi . . . 1842
11. Nokenke . . . 1845
12. Kandempemvu or Umcitshu . . . 1847
13. Ingobomakosi . . 1850

Umpande died in 1872. No portrait of him remained. In his later days he became so fat that he was unable to walk. In the prime of his manhood he would appear, judging from a description by M. Delegorgue, to have conveyed a different impression from that which led to his being characterised by his family and nation as a "fool": "A brilliant black eye, deep set, well-guarded by an advancing frontal angle; a high forehead, straight at the sides, on which the traces of wrinkles were beginning to be perceived; a nose of usual mould, with gristles boldly shown; a large mouth often smiling with the smile which means 'I understand'; a square chin, indicative of resolution; in fact, a large head, well formed, borne on a superb body shining with plumpness, but of which the carriage was so noble, the members so well under control of his will, the gestures so precise, that a Parisian might well have believed that Umpande, in his youth, had frequented the palaces of kings."

CHAPTER XI

THE death of Umpande for the first time rendered the Zulu throne vacant by the process of nature. It was shortly to be formally assumed by his son, Cetshwayo; but before describing that event it is necessary to take a brief note of a long train of other issues from which a condition of things had resulted involving it in difficulties.

It has been seen how strongly Hendrik Potgieter was impressed at the battle fought at the Itala on the 8th of April 1838 with the strength of Dingana's army. He lost no time after that event in placing himself beyond the reach of so formidable an antagonist. On the west of the Drakensberg there were no warlike tribes. Umzilikazi had, since his attack on the Boer immigrants and defeat by them and the Zulus, betaken himself farther north, leaving only scattered and impoverished remnants of the tribes through whose lands he had travelled. From those Potgieter experienced no important opposition. He travelled far, and found a country which at first appeared sufficiently remote from British influence and otherwise suitable, in what afterwards became known as the Rustenburg District of the Transvaal. He formed a settlement there and established a capital town, to which he gave the name of Potchefstroom—Pot-Chef-Stroom or Chief-Potgieter-Stream. In this country fighting took place, but it was attended, if the accounts that have been given of it be true, with little danger to the Boers.

The manner in which they prosecuted their wars and

the treatment to which they subjected the natives are described by Dr. Livingstone, who was personally acquainted with Potgieter, and had opportunity of noting the proceedings of the people of whom he was the chief. The licence they had allowed themselves might be regarded as largely explaining that objection to British rule which had impelled them to seek remoteness and freedom.

"It is difficult," says Dr. Livingstone, "to conceive that men possessing the common attributes of humanity (and the Boers are by no means destitute of the better feelings of our nature) should set out after caressing their wives and children and proceed to shoot down men and women whose affections are as warm as their own. It was long before I would give credit to the tales of bloodshed told me by native eye-witnesses, but when I heard the Boers either bewailing or boasting the bloody scene in which they had themselves been actors I was compelled to admit the validity of the testimony."

These further remarks may be quoted: "In their own estimation they are the chosen people of God, and all coloured races are black property or creatures given them for inheritance. However bloody the massacre no qualms of conscience ensue. Indeed, the leader, the late Hendrik Potgieter, believed himself to be the peacemaker of the country," while, on the other hand, the natives who had lately experienced the passage through their country of the Matabele chief whose attributes have been described as so terrible, declared, according to the author quoted, "that Umzilikazi was cruel to his enemies and kind to those he conquered, but that the Boers destroyed their enemies and made slaves of their friends."

Their methods of warfare Dr. Livingstone thus describes: "One or two friendly tribes are forced to accompany a party of mounted Boers, and are ranged in front to form a shield; the Boers then coolly fire over

H

their heads till the devoted people flee and leave their wives and children to the captors. This was done in nine cases during my residence in the interior, and on no occasion was a drop of Boer blood shed."

Potgieter is described as having possessed an especially strong antipathy to the British. He vehemently opposed any attempt to open diplomatic communication with them; he desired only to be so far away as to be free from the possibility of their interference.

He and his people occupied the country he had chosen till 1845, but it was found to possess disadvantages. It was far inland. The only port through which merchandise could be introduced was British. It was south of the degree of south latitude up to which British subjects—and he was still a lawful British subject—were liable to be tried for their acts on return to the jurisdiction of British Courts of Justice. Hopes arose of escaping these disadvantages by opening up a trade with Delagoa Bay. His mind was attracted thither by another cause. A Dutch ship, named the *Brazilian*, had been sent by merchants in Holland to trade with the emigrant Boers in Natal. The Boers had been anxious to establish political relations with Holland, and the super-cargo of this ship, one Smellekamp, had been tempted into making promises on behalf of the king of that country. Believing that he had acted by authority, the Boers were encouraged by the protection they were led to hope for in resisting the British Government.

It was, therefore, considered necessary to prevent their further intercourse with Smellekamp, and being forbidden to land in Natal, on his return trip from the Netherlands, he had steered for Delagoa Bay. Potgieter hoped that if that port could be reached it might yet be possible to accomplish the object which it had been attempted to effect through this man, and to secure the merchandise the *Brazilian* had brought to, but been prevented from landing at, Natal. With this view he set out, accompanied by a number of his countrymen, in 1843. He did not reach the Bay on this occasion, but a second expedition in the following year was more successful. He arrived at his destination without loss of man or beast. The Portuguese authorities were friendly to his proposal to open up a trade through their port; Smellekamp was there, and encouraged a hope that a regular trade would soon be established with Holland. But the settlement Potgieter had formed was too far inland, and for this, and the other reasons given, he determined to move to a tract some 200 miles from the coast, whose features had tempted him in the course of his journey and whose locality would be more favourable to his scheme.

Accordingly he organised a new trek in 1845, when, with most of those who formed the Rustenburg Settlement, he proceeded to, and established himself in, that part of the Transvaal territory which has become known as the Lydenburg District. The country was occupied by weak tribes, the principal one of which was the Bapeda, under Sikwata, whose son, Sinkukuni, in after years became of some importance. They did not oppose the Boer advent, and the settlement was quietly effected. No arrangement was come to with those inhabitants, and, some time later, when a Volk's Raad, or People's Council, was appointed, one of the first questions they took into consideration was whether they were lawfully possessed of the land. The Council determined that such possession had still to be acquired, that it was necessary to purchase the land from the Swazis by whom the local tribes had been conquered. Accordingly a "commission" was despatched to the Swazi king, a step which was so contrary to the wishes of Potgieter, and so drew forth his resentment, as nearly to involve the young settlement in civil war. The commission, however, carried its object, with results that were to be of importance to the subject of this story. Its members brought with them a document, remarkable alike as regards its spelling and composition and its substance. It purported to be signed by Umswazi as king and Somcuba as regent, and declared that for and in consideration of the payment to him of one hundred breeding cattle, fifty of which were to be delivered within one month, and the remainder within two years, he had ceded to the Dutch South African Nation the territory lying between the Portuguese possession of Delagoa Bay on the east, the 26th degree of south latitude on the south, the Olifants River on the north, and extending to Eland's River on the west. Upon this territory and under these circumstances was formed the Lydenburg Republic, which was to have an independent existence as such till 1859.

In Natal good relations were not successfully established between the British Government and those Boers who had remained there. The Government failed to satisfy the claims which the Boers set up in respect to land or their desires in other respects. When six years had passed they had come to regard themselves as so sorely aggrieved that steps had become necessary to obtain redress. They despatched their late Commandant-General, Andries Pretorius, to the Cape, with instructions to lay their grievances before the Governor there. He returned both dissatisfied and angry. His representations had not received the consideration to which he considered they were entitled; he had been denied the interview he sought with the Governor. Meetings were thereupon held; he was re-elected to his old position of Commandant-General, and under his leadership a new "trek" was begun; people gathered together and betook themselves across the Drakensberg, in search again of a "free" country. When they reached the Tugela they met Sir Harry Smith, who had in the meantime succeeded to the Governorship of the Cape Colony, and was on his way to Natal. He manifested great concern at what he saw, and expressed himself as

THE STORY OF THE ZULUS

most anxious to remove the cause of discontent. He promised at once to appoint a Lands' Commission, with Pretorius as one of its members, and to do everything he could to further the interests of the people. But they were not to be turned back. They crossed the mountain forming the border of the British Colony of Natal only to find themselves, to their intense chagrin, still within British territory; on the 3rd of February 1848, all the country as far north as the Vaal River had been proclaimed a British possession, and British authority established at Bloemfontein. Pretorius was not in a mood to submit to this condition of things. He called his countrymen together, to the number of some 400, and marched on Bloemfontein, where he gave the Administrator one hour to consider whether he would remove to the south of the Orange River or abide attack. The first alternative was chosen, and British authority was not restored till August, when Sir Harry Smith engaged and defeated the Boer force at a place named Boom-plaats, between the Orange River and Bloemfontein.

Pretorius and his followers were proclaimed rebels, and had to go for safety across the Vaal River—to the country lately occupied by the followers of Potgieter. Negotiations which followed resulted in the signing four years later, on the 17th of January 1852, by British Commissioners, of the Sand River Convention, by which the "Emigrant Farmers beyond the Vaal River" were granted "the right to manage their own affairs and to govern themselves according to their own laws, without any interference on the part of the British Government."

The object for which the Boers had so long striven had thus at last been gained. They had a vast country where entire freedom from British interference could be enjoyed. But happiness and peace did not immediately follow. Parties had been formed amongst the emigrants themselves, and some years of dissension and strife had to be passed through, sometimes nearly culminating in civil war, before the several republics that had been formed were finally merged into one—the South African Republic.

The portion of the land composing that Republic, the acquisition of which was of most importance to the subject of this story, was that known as the Utrecht District. By the Sand River Convention the Boers had been granted independence " beyond " or to the north of the Vaal River, and by the treaty entered into by Commissioner Cloete with Umpande in 1843 the British territory of Natal was limited on the north-east by the Tugela and Umzinyati or Buffalo rivers. The Vaal River, flowing west, takes its rise in the Drakensberg; in the same range is the source of the Umzinyati, which flows to the opposite coast. The territory of Natal ended at the source of the latter river; that to the north-east of it was regarded as belonging to the Zulus. As no limit was set to the extent to which the Boers might expand their possessions towards the north, so was the northern limit of the Zulu territory undetermined. No effect was ever given to the proclamation of Pretorius at the coronation of Umpande; no Boer occupation followed of the land it described. Those people of the Zulu race who dwelt along the Umzinyati up to its source were subjects of the Zulu king, but near the Drakensberg they were few in number. There was a large tract of country but barely inhabited, and its verdant slopes and fertile valleys presented temptations to the eyes of those Boers who resided near to its border in Natal.

One of these, a man who had become well known, and who long continued to be held in high distinction by the Zulus—Cornelius Van Rooyen—obtained permission, about the year 1847, for himself and a few other Boers to reside and graze their stock in it. They acquired no rights, but continued for seven years to occupy the land on the same

THE STORY OF THE ZULUS

terms as Zulu subjects. In 1855, however, they professed to have acquired the land by purchase; to have bought it from Umpande for 100 head of cattle. Their title consisted of a written cession purporting to have been signed by the king. After it was considered to have been thus acquired it was united to Potgieter's Lydenburg Republic. Its boundaries, where it joined Zululand, were but vaguely described by the deed of cession, and at subsequent times this was interpreted in different ways, being construed, on each occasion, as including more land on the Boer side. The boundary which the Boers ultimately claimed was the Ingcome or Blood River, from its junction with the Umzinyati up to where it was crossed by the "old hunting road, and thence along that road to the Pongolo River," the road-boundary passing near to where the town of Vryheid now stands.

It was to this district that Umtonga and Umgidhlana fled to escape the fate which their mother and brother Umpoiyana had suffered at the hands of Cetshwayo's executioners; and in 1861 Cetshwayo, fearing a possible alliance such as that which had secured the kingdom for his father, opened communication through Cornelius Van Rooyen with the view of securing their surrender. The negotiations which followed resulted in this, and the possession by the Boers of a document signed by Cetshwayo and his brothers Usiwedu and Usiteku, ceding to the Dutch additional land, subsequently beaconed off, the boundary running from Rorke's Drift to the Pongolo River, and including many Zulu subjects. In addition to the surrender of the young princes, Cetshwayo was given twenty-five head of cattle.

The territory professed to have been thus acquired was afterwards known as the "Disputed Territory," about which more will be seen.

CHAPTER XII

NEVER had the Zulu nation been more powerful than it was at the time of Cetshwayo's formal accession. For some thirty-two years there had been a condition of peace that was interrupted only on occasions when the aggressive was assumed by the Zulus against tribes from whom they met with but feeble resistance. There had been regular enrolment of the men into regiments, so that all those between the ages of twenty and fifty had been made soldiers. Those forming older regiments were still numerous and capable of active service. The whole strength of the able-bodied male population was organised and ready to be launched, with short notice, against any possible foe. The fame of the nation had spread far and wide over South Africa. Its greatness formed the favourite topic of conversation amongst all tribes. Wild conceptions were formed everywhere of the king's court and character, but above all of the number of Zulus. Comparisons were formed with the idea of impressing the minds of listeners with a sense of how incomputable they were. A story was widely told, and as widely believed, which may have had an imaginative origin, that Cetshwayo on one occasion, after he had become king, sent to the Secretary for Native Affairs in Natal a sack-full of the grain called Upoko (millet) with the message, "if you can count the grains of it then you may also be able to count the Zulu people"; but it was admitted that as difficult a task was set by the return of an ox-hide, the hairs of which were stated to represent the number of English. The habit grew of discussing the Zulu strength in comparison with that of England; and there was danger of that being counted the greater which was present and could be seen. What they could see of England's greatness was in the Colony of Natal, and there but little fighting force was visible. And the Zulu nation was well united. Strong sections had been formed under various chiefs. In the northern part of the country there were three whose personal following gave them great power, who were in a position to command certain respect and consideration at the hands of the king. These were Usibebu, Uhamu and Umnyamana. In the south also there were strong chiefs. But amongst them all there was none who evinced, or felt, a disposition to oppose the accession of Cetshwayo. They had no other design at this time to exercise their influence otherwise than in tempering his rule, or maintaining their rights as against other subjects.

Some time elapsed after Umpande's death before formal steps were taken by Cetshwayo to assume the kingship. He designed first to send an expedition against a tribe which dwelt on the north of the Pongolo River, but was dissuaded by John Dunn, who had ingratiated himself since fighting against him in 1856 at 'Ndondakusuka, and now held a high place among his counsellors. The reason Dunn urged against the step was that the tribe against which he desired to wage war was armed with guns, while the Zulus were still without those weapons. He promised to seek permission from the Government of Natal for their purchase and introduction through the Colony; in the fulfilment of which promise he so far succeeded as to be able to procure for Cetshwayo 250 firearms. Thus, and at this time, was the beginning made of a general arming of the Zulus with guns. Many continued to be brought through Natal by a system which was called "gun-running," but most were introduced through Delagoa Bay.

About the middle of the year following that of Umpande's death preparations were begun for the king's progress to Mahlabatini, where the royal seats were. There was probably some feeling of uncertainty as to the unanimity of sentiment amongst the various sections of the people. Whether on that account and with a view to making his position the more certain of general recognition, or as a mark of respect to the British Government and without any definite purpose, it is somewhat uncertain, but a message was despatched as from the nation requesting that a representative of that government might be present at the ceremony of the assumption by the new king of his office. The message was that "the nation found itself wandering because of the death of the king." There was no king, and the ambassadors brought from the nation four oxen, representing the "head of the king,"[1] to the Natal Government. They also asked that Mr. Shepstone, who had been present at the nomination of Cetshwayo, might go and establish what was wanted, and, at the same time, "breathe the spirit by which the nation should be governed"—a request to which the Natal Government acceded.

In his progress Cetshwayo was accompanied by a very large number of people from the southern part of the country, where, till this time, he had dwelt.

As they proceeded, the men branched out of the track and indulged in hunting,—there was such hunting and killing of game as would long be remembered. Wild animals that were then plentiful in the Umhlatuzi Valley have since been comparatively scarce.

Thus pleasurably did the journey proceed, without consciousness of danger ahead. And yet there was a real,

[1] NOTE.—The message was probably not quite correctly understood in this respect. The term "Kanda," or "Head," was applied to certain chief kraals which formed the Army Divisional Headquarters, or centres of government, and it was from the cattle belonging to these that the oxen were probably represented as having been taken.

smouldering danger there. Mapita's strength had grown great. He had held the first place among the counsellors of the late king. His people had done signal service in the interests of him now about to assume the kingship and had turned the tide when his other forces were wavering at 'Ndondakusuka, thereby securing that victory to which he owed his title to assume it. Mapita had died soon after Umpande, and those people, proud of the strength they felt and had manifested, proud of the obligation they felt that the king owed them, were now governed by Usibebu, whose courage, resolution and daring stood above those of any living Zulu. Uhamu had also waxed strong. It was thought that he aspired to the succession, but there were most probably no grounds for this idea. As has been seen, the circumstances of his birth placed him in the position of a nephew rather than that of a son of the late king; and the Zulus did not consider that he had a legitimate claim. But he possessed a formidable following which would obey his command, and he was in a position to demand consideration. He and Umnyamana, no less powerful, dwelt with their people on the land extending northward from the Inkonjeni range.

Neither of those three were represented in the royal retinue. They were apprised of the king's progress towards the place of his ancestors, and there were mutterings of "Who are these people that are bringing home the king?" Usibebu especially manifested a resentful disposition.

The procession had reached a place called Emakeni, the site of one of the king's ancestral kraals, some four miles to the south-east of the Umgungundhlovu site, and not far from the base of the Mtonjaneni heights. The king had walked most of the way. He possessed a carriage drawn by four horses, with John Dunn as a willing driver; but policy had forbidden the devotion of so much of his society to that chief as riding in it would have involved. He did not realise that the northern chiefs had been given the same cause for jealousy.

After he had waited three days at Emakeni these appeared with their followings. There were two bodies, Usibebu's contingent forming the one and the combined adherents of Uhamu and Umnyamana the other. They were advancing from different directions. Presently Usibebu's force was observed to make a rapid forward movement. It was an anxious moment. But a timely message to him caused his force to be halted; explanations followed, and a collision was averted which might have had important results.

On the day following Cetshwayo was formally proclaimed King of the Zulus by Masipula, the prime minister of his father, after which the progress was continued to the north-east of the White Umfolozi River, where, at the kraal called Umlambongwenya, that of Umpande's mother Songiya (by whose name Zulus may still be heard to swear), Mr. Theophilus Shepstone repeated the ceremony in August 1873, placing a crown upon Cetshwayo's head and proclaiming certain laws or principles by which he had promised to be guided in his government.

In this way it was sought, on behalf of the Natal Government, to establish a condition of greater security than had existed hitherto against the execution of Zulu subjects whose guilt had not been formally established, or for offences of a minor character: the punishment of death being considered to be too generally applied under the existing Zulu law. The proclamation set forth that there should be no more indiscriminate shedding of blood in the land; that no Zulu should be condemned to death without open trial and the public examination of witnesses, for and against, and that he should have the right of appeal to the king; that no Zulu's life should be taken without the previous knowledge and consent of the king, after such trial had taken place and the right of appeal had been allowed to be exercised; that for minor crimes the loss of property, all or a portion, should be substituted for the punishment of death.

The terms of these laws, or principles, could have been but vaguely understood. The first aimed at restraining the king personally in the exercise of his power. It required that he should not wantonly order the death of subjects who had done no wrong. It does not appear whether Cetshwayo explicitly admitted that a condition had existed in which indiscriminate shedding of blood had prevailed; but an admission was apparently implied in its being proclaimed, with his approval, that that condition should cease. Nor does it appear whether the person accounted responsible for such a state of things in the past was the late king or Cetshwayo himself. It may, however, safely be asserted, that at no time would Cetshwayo have acknowledged that he had wantonly and without cause taken the life of a subject.

The next three clauses of the proclamation affected those charged with the administration of justice rather than the king personally, although there may have been an implied undertaking on his part to restrain them.

There were chiefs who had the power to award death as a punishment for offences committed by certain of their adherents; but the right excluded any member of the king's army. No man who "bore a shield" could be put to death without the king's authority. These bore the proud designation of "Umpakati." But there were, no doubt, many, especially women and resident strangers, who might have benefited by the enforcement of the provisions of the proclamation.

It may be assumed to have been designed that the king should elaborate these regulations; that he should lay down detailed orders of procedure for the apprehension and keeping in custody of accused persons; for the nature of the evidence to be admitted and the manner in which it should be taken; for the report to the king of the evidence taken at trials; for the conveyance to his presence of the person condemned, if required. Not only was the system entirely new, but the circumstances of the country would have rendered exceedingly difficult the carrying out of the details it would have involved.

The requirements as to the examination of witnesses naturally precluded the evidence of witch-doctors, for one of these could not have been called to disprove the evidence of another. It was upon such evidence that the discovery of Abatakati entirely depended. Their supposed methods of working evil were obscure to the ordinary mind; only those in communion with the spirit-world were believed to be capable of detecting their deeds of darkness. And nearly all the ills to which the people were subject were attributed to practisers of a kind of art called Ukutakata.

The conception which had been formed by the native races of the powers and methods of these evil-disposed persons, called Abatakati, was as vague as the ideas which prevailed in olden times in Britain concerning those of witches. The main difference was perhaps this, that whereas the latter were supposed to be in league with an evil spirit, the natives ascribed to the potency of medicines the powers supposed to be possessed by their evil-doers. By means of unknown and unnameable concoctions they were believed to be able to accomplish strange things. As their deeds were dark, so they favoured the night for their performance; and, as their medicine-pots were supplied mainly from the bodies of the most repellent of animals, so were these employed in various ways, in their living state, in the execution of their nefarious purposes. A favourite caprice was to ride upon a baboon, and the footprints of one of these animals seen near to a homestead, if it happened to be at a distance from their usual haunts, gave rise to grave fears as to the consequences that would follow to the family from something that its supposed nocturnal rider might have deposited near to the kraal. So fixed was the belief, that there were individuals who actually believed themselves capable of exercising supernatural powers by means of mixtures.

It is plain, when the circumstances are considered, that either Cetshwayo did not fully realise the significance of the "laws" he was required to adopt, or that he promised to adopt them without serious intention to give effect to that promise. It is certain that they were never put into practice.

While awaiting the arrival of Mr. Theophilus Shepstone, Cetshwayo organised and attended a large hunting party, from which he returned to find that a grass-fire had destroyed one of his kraals. It was afterwards discovered that, in the confusion attending the conflagration, some of his property had been stolen. A tin box containing two dozen bottles of chlorodyne was missing. It was afterwards reported that a similar box had been seen in the possession of one of the king's attendants who had returned to his home on the coast, and Cetshwayo sent a detective to investigate the matter. The poor delinquent supposed that he had come into possession of some kind of rare drink. He had not a clear idea as to its nature, but, during his entertainment of the man sent to discover his guilt, took occasion to try it. He produced the bottles and emptied the contents of some of them into pots of beer, which he thereupon gave to the women to drink in order to observe the effect. Hilarity gave way to overpowering sleepiness, and this was succeeded by somewhat serious illness. Having by this means become assured of the guilt of his host, the detective sent a message to the king, before whom the thief was summoned, shortly after Mr. Shepstone's departure. The fact charged against the accused was so clearly established that no defence could be offered. He may thus be regarded as having had a fair trial. But the case being one of simple theft was, perhaps, of the class which it had been intended to signify by the term "minor crimes." What followed may be best described in the words of John Dunn, who witnessed the scene, and by whom the story is told:

"One morning, about eight o'clock, I was sitting in front of one of my wagons, when I saw a gathering of indunas in front of the king's kraal. After they had been talking for some time I saw, all at once, a scrimmage, and a man knocked down and pounced upon. Seeing me in view the indunas sent to tell me that they had been trying a thief, and that he was to be killed. The poor fellow lay on the ground for a short time, for he had been only stunned. His arms had been twisted round and tied together over his head. As soon as he recovered his senses he prepared to march. Having often witnessed similar scenes he knew their routine. So he got up of his own accord, and, without being told, took the path leading to the place of execution, followed by about a dozen men who had been told off to finish him."

John Dunn remarks concerning this incident: "This was the first man killed after the coronation—almost before Mr. Shepstone could have reached Pietermaritzburg. But it served the fellow right, for he was guilty of a great breach of trust. The Zulu is only to be ruled by the fear of death or the confiscation of his entire property."

It is recorded by the same authority that shortly after this event one of Umpande's old servants was put to death, whether for any offence is not stated; but he observes it "was the opening of the ball of killing without trial which was usual in Cetshwayo's reign."

Notwithstanding the immense concourse of people by whom the function was attended, the coronation had been accomplished in a remarkably orderly manner, no disturbance of any kind being incidental to it.

Matters of state had still to be discussed. An account had to be given of the acts of the late reign; and the person from whom this was due was Masipula. He had gained the position which he held under Umpande, of first induna, by his own merits, not being an hereditary chief; but so high had he risen in the estimation of the nation that the sons of the king sought their principal wives from amongst his daughters. Like other high officials he had acquired a considerable, though not yet great, following. His lands lay between the Umkuzi Stream and the Pongolo River; he even had adherents on the north of the latter. He is worth remembering for results of which his people were the cause, at a later time, under his son Maboko.

What the "giving of an account" consisted of must remain obscure. Returning from the meeting which had been held for that purpose, Masipula called upon John Dunn and informed him that his work was finished; that he had resigned his position, and was going to lie down and rest. The same night he was taken violently ill, and in the morning he was dead. It was supposed by some that, having given displeasure to the king, poison had been put in his beer. It is curious that Cetshwayo was himself destined to die in circumstances calculated to give rise to a like suspicion.

Whether the Zulus are possessed of deadly poisons has not been ascertained. Death sometimes results from the drugs administered by the medical practitioners, and suicidal attempts are sometimes made by a like means; but whether they have ever been able to make a preparation in so concentrated a form as to be capable of being taken in food without its presence being detected, is doubtful. It is certain that they have never made use of it for the destruction of obnoxious animals.

Of the Zulu ceremony of coronation it is impossible to learn the details. The receiving by the king of his inheritance in cattle formed an important item. These were brought from all parts of his dominions and exhibited to him. So important was this held to be, that although lung-sickness prevailed at the time in some parts of the country, and the danger of spreading infection by bringing cattle together was recognised, the ceremony could not be dispensed with. For days the king sat watching the herds pass before him, no doubt retaining an impression as to their approximate number, appearance and the place from which each had been brought. The number of his cattle was very great. There had been little disease in the country other than that known as Nagana, and this being confined to certain localities could be avoided. John Dunn has stated that about half of them died as the result of this concourse, and that never again did cattle become so numerous in the land as they then were.

The accession of Cetshwayo may be regarded as having been attended with happy circumstances. His father had died at an advanced age, peacefully and happily; the people had received him as their king in a manner which assured him of their loyalty; he was at the head of what he believed to be the strongest nation of South Africa, every member of which would yield ready obedience to his will. Feeling secure in his own strength, he might enjoy his wealth and the adulation of his people without fear of interruption; nothing stood in the way of the gratification of his most extravagant desires. Thousands of ready hands were already employed in the building of the Ulundi kraal, to be constructed after his own taste, providing for his physical comfort according to his highest ideal. There appeared to be but one object which might possibly make it necessary for him to exercise the force at his disposal—the regaining of that portion of his territory upon which the Boers had established themselves and which according to their contention formed part of the South African Republic.

CHAPTER XIII

By the people he ruled Cetshwayo was generally considered to be a good king. There were those who felt aggrieved, in some respects, by the form in which he exercised his power over them. Some felt it to be burdensome that their attendance should be so frequently required at the royal kraals, as was the case for military exercises. So rigidly was this attendance enforced, especially towards the end of the reign, that some who believed themselves excused by age or illness were killed by armed parties for having failed to present themselves at their headquarters. They had to find their own food. For those who resided at great distances the arrival of supplies carried by the female members of the household was uncertain, and generally at long intervals, and there was considerable hardship in the hunger they had to suffer. The constant movement of bodies of armed men, who supplied themselves from the crops which they found in the fields on their way, was felt to be a hardship by the owners. Many who suffered the penalties of the laws under which they lived doubtless felt that they were the victims of injustice. But the general impression created was that the reign was not an oppressive one.

He was proud of his people, and the people were proud of and loyal to him. They recognised in him those qualities that the salute "Bayete" implied. If they were threatened with famine because of a visitation of locusts, or the withholding by the heavens of the customary showers, they appealed to him; and those who were his subjects grew old in the firm belief that, through his means, they were able to secure relief. He did not claim to possess the gift, believed to belong to northern chiefs, of being able to control the harmful insects or to cause rain to fall; but he could propitiate those chiefs in the one case, and the spirits of his fathers in the other. A herd of black oxen was especially maintained for this last purpose. When the drought was so severe and general as to call for a public supplication, these were driven to the localities believed to be inhabited by the several spirits of the past chiefs, and one ox sacrificed to each, while the whole army sang in symphony the songs that were wont to delight their ears during their earthly life. On certain occasions the war-song of Dingiswayo was also sung, showing that his spirit was believed to dwell with those of the Zulu chiefs. How it became to be believed that rain resulted from these rites can only be guessed.

The reverence paid to the king's ancestral spirits was so profound, that a condemned criminal was considered to be entitled to pardon who could so long escape execution as to be able to reach the locality in which they were understood to dwell and claim their protection.

There was general peace amongst the tribes who formed the nation, and little fighting with those outside his dominions. Only two small military expeditions are mentioned, of which, there being no written record, the date is difficult to fix. A shipment of guns had been landed on the north coast, and the king ordered the people of certain tribes occupying the land between the Lebombo Mountain and the sea to carry them to him. They failed to do so, and Usibebu was ordered to punish them with that portion of the army which belonged to his own tribe. The people thus attacked were unwarlike and unable to resist the invasion by force; but the lakes and woods of their country afforded shelter for both themselves and their cattle, and they suffered but little injury. The other expedition, or foray, was directed against Sambane, on the Lebombo Mountain, and designed to punish him and his people for their treachery to Dingana in 1840. It was also fruitless, the extensive forest and the precipitous character of their mountain dwelling-place affording shelter to the people till their assailants had withdrawn. These events are scarcely remembered except by those who took part in them, having produced no result of importance to the nation.

An incident which made a lasting impression, which served to mark a period in time, occurred about three years after Cetshwayo's accession. The women of the nation, like the men, were classified according to age. They were assigned a regiment from amongst the members of which to find husbands when those men should have received the king's permission to marry. They also, like the regiments, were distinguished by a name. Since the battle of 'Ndondakusuka in 1856, the Isangqu regiment had taken wives from amongst the girls called Gudhludonga, the Tulwana from amongst the Isitimane. A considerable time had elapsed since these marriages; the Indhlondhlo and Dhlokwe regiments were unmarried, and aged respectively about forty and thirty-seven years at the time of Umpande's death. Cetshwayo gave the permission to these two regiments simultaneously; they were the only regiments to whom, during his reign, he gave it. The girls from amongst whom they were to find wives were called Ingcugce. They were comparatively young; but what their age was it is not practicable now to ascertain. It was soon found that many of these girls had engaged their affections to men younger than those to whom leave had been given to marry, and various devices were resorted to with the object of evading the regulation which now required that they should separate themselves from the men they loved. Amongst others was that of pretending that they were married to the elder brothers of their real husbands. Complaints to the king by those who, for this reason, found it difficult to avail themselves of the privilege which he had accorded were numerous. He was determined that the regulation should have proper observance; and, other means having failed to secure that end, he gave the order in 1876 which caused consternation throughout the land. Armed parties were to traverse his dominions in different directions; they were to kill any of the Ingcugce girls they might find unmarried, or married to men younger than the Dhlokwe regiment, and seize all the property of their fathers or guardians; the bodies of such girls as might be killed were to be placed on the paths as a warning to passers that the king could not be disobeyed. If, therefore, those unhappy girls would save themselves alive, and prevent the ruin of their relations, it behoved them to make quick sacrifice of their affections and get themselves married to members of the two regiments named, or to older men. There was no time now even for transference of their affections. There were instances of men receiving visits from women whom they had never before seen for the purpose of offering themselves in marriage. Many were not allowed the choice. Fathers and brothers were not disposed to risk the loss of their cattle to gratify what they regarded as unreasonable fastidiousness on the part of their daughters or sisters. It was desirable, in their minds, to secure the speedy marriage of those who were likely to bring such a calamity upon them. The situation was one which might, perhaps, furnish the imaginative with subjects for romance. The number of women who were actually killed was most probably not more than ten. The rest, except some few who, after romantic adventures, escaped to spend their lives with the objects of their choice, may be regarded as having married as they were required to marry; and it may further be supposed that their lives were not entirely blighted. Those still living appear little less happy and contented than other women.

The trait in the Zulu character of which it is most difficult to approve is the absence of sympathy for the feelings of the female sex. A man is almost as willing to marry a woman who hates as one who loves him. Thus many girls who were forcibly given in marriage by their fathers or brothers were subjected to much violence by those to whom they were given to secure fulfilment of their duties as wives. Yet some amongst them are possessed of strong affections. In one authentic instance a man, finding no other way of evading the edict, did so in death, which he first inflicted on the woman of his heart.

The general impression left on the minds of the Zulus by the proceeding was not one of sympathy with the women, who were the chief victims, so much as a sense of satisfaction in those who thereby acquired, and injury in those who were deprived of, intended wives. It has been useful in marking a date, the time of the "marriage of the Ingcugce" serving the same purpose to Zulus as "the year 1876" to Europeans.

Two years later another somewhat important event occurred. It was the season of the first-fruits, and the army was assembled for the purpose of the celebration. The Tulwana regiment, being that to which Cetshwayo personally belonged, had its headquarters at his Ulundi kraal, as had also the youngest, the Ingobamakosi regiment, which, though formed during Umpande's lifetime, was considered to have been enrolled by Cetshwayo. These two regiments, the proud veterans and the boastful, untried boys, were thus quartered together, although on different sides of the kraal.

Reverence for age is a prominent trait in the Zulu, and there is nothing that calls forth greater resentment in men of years than the assumption of equality with them by persons in their youth. Thus there was no reason for discord in the mere circumstance of the two regiments being quartered together. But there were causes at work which were to have a grievous issue. The Tulwana were not so numerous at this time as was desired; and, to fill up their ranks, there had been associated with them a corps of younger men called Indhluyengwe. These were not considered by the Ingobamakosi to be entitled to the respect due to their older comrades, and they made sport of the position they held amongst them. Feeling against the Tulwana was not entirely absent. Some of the Ingcugce girls had married members of that regiment to escape destruction, and in doing so had been obliged to abandon their young Ingobamakosi lovers. The feelings of the latter were sometimes covertly expressed over their early morning smoking-horns in high-pitched tones designed to reach and offend the ears of the men from whom they had suffered this injury. Eventually they assaulted the Indhluyengwe, and a fight with sticks ensued, in which the older regiment suffered considerably, and became so incensed by the insolence the boys had exhibited, that they armed themselves with assegais and attacked them, the fight thus resolving itself into a battle. Cetshwayo manifested great concern on seeing what was taking place, but could not stop the fighting. It was dangerous, indeed, for any one to approach the scene. Neither side was giving quarter; on the one the foe was recognised by head-rings, on the other by their absence. It was, therefore, difficult for the king to find a messenger who would not be marked out for destruction, and consequently to get a command conveyed to the combatants. The fighting continued till dark, by which time some seventy men were dead.

The king was sorely vexed by the occurrence. That his power was not absolute became evident from the manner in which he proceeded to deal with those who had committed so serious a breach of peace. The resentment of Uhamu, who was the chief induna of the Tulwana, knew no bounds. That boys should presume to fight with his men was more than he was able to bear. He left abruptly, and returned to his home north of the Ingome, declaring that nothing but the execution of Usigcwelegcwele, the chief commander of the Ingobamakosi, would appease him.

Some time later a story was given credence to by the king that a baboon had visited his kraal during the night. He professed to believe that it had been sent by Usigcwelegcwele, "not to injure me," he explained to John Dunn, "but to turn my heart so that I may not be angry with him. He has sent his beast because he is afraid I might kill him after what lately occurred."

Usigcwelegcwele had escaped to his own home near the Ungoye Forest in the south, and, as the simplest way out of the difficulty, Cetshwayo resolved that he should die. Messengers were instructed to request him to return, giving him assurances of forgiveness; he was to be waylaid and killed by a party to be sent along the path by which he would travel. John Dunn, having gathered this from a conversation he overheard between certain indunas, secretly sent a warning of danger, and Usigcwelegcwele found an excuse for not complying with the summons, afterwards adjusting the matter by the payment of a fine.

These were the chief events of Cetshwayo's reign. They were viewed much more seriously by the British authorities than by the Zulu people.

CHAPTER XIV

THOMAS FRANÇOIS BURGERS was elected President of the South African Republic in the year of Umpande's death, and he and Cetshwayo may be regarded, in a sense, as having commenced their rule together; they were destined also to end the careers thus begun the one soon after the other.

The South African Republic was labouring under a lamentable condition of financial depression. To guide it to prosperity was a task which the wisest ruler could scarcely have hoped to accomplish. Its resources had never been developed. Its revenue did not suffice to maintain an adequate administration. Its people lacked enterprise and industry. Spread over a vast extent of territory, each individual conducted himself according to the dictates of his own feelings. He was able, generally, to rule his own household and his native servants; he could secure at a cost of but little labour, on the farm he owned, the things needful to supply his simple wants. The need for a government scarcely impressed him; he contributed very little towards the support of a government. A sufficient revenue could not be gathered. Government securities had risen somewhat in value consequent upon the recent discovery of diamonds in West Griqualand, and of gold within the borders of the Republic, but they were still reckoned at only half their face value. It was not possible to pay salaries, much less to carry out needful public works.

Burgers during his candidature held out great hopes as to the improvements which he would be able, if elected, to secure in these respects. He promised that roads and bridges and railways should be constructed, and a system of education established which would bring instruction within the reach of all.

His efforts to carry out the promises he had made; how he attempted to restore the public credit by borrowing money on the security of land; how he spent large sums of it in the redemption of notes at par, most of which were in the possession of speculators who had acquired them at less than half the amount; how he endeavoured to raise funds for the construction of a railway from Delagoa Bay to Pretoria, and spent large sums of the money subscribed in the purchase of material which had afterwards to be sold to pay costs of transport; how his various schemes and endeavours only involved the country in greater difficulty—these subjects will have been made familiar to the reader by the many books that have been written upon this period of the Transvaal's history.

What is of special importance to the present subject is that, to crown misfortune, he became involved in a Kafir war. Sikwata, whose tribal lands were included in the territory claimed to have been purchased from the Swazi king in 1846 for one hundred cows, had been succeeded by his son, Sikukuni, and the latter was not disposed to continue acquiescence in that transaction. He asserted that the Boers had no valid title to that land, and expressed himself as prepared to maintain the assertion by force if necessary. His tribe was one of considerable power. It had grown much in strength during the thirty years of freedom from harassment by the Swazis that had succeeded the supposed cession. The fame of its fighting force had reached remote parts of South Africa. That strength had been augmented, too, by the acquisition of firearms and ammunition by those of the people who had gone to work in the diamond mines at Kimberley. They were an intelligent people, and readily attained considerable skill and precision in the use of those arms.

It became necessary to coerce him into the required submission; and, to that end, the President called out a strong force of Burghers and led them personally to war against Sikukuni. The aid was sought, also, of the Swazis, of whom a large contingent accompanied the expedition, and of whose cruelty in certain attacks that followed upon some of Sikukuni's people, much has since been said. Some preliminary engagements, in which, on the Boers' side, the Swazis appear to have borne the chief part, were successful. But when the time came for storming the chief's main stronghold the Boers would not advance to the fight. They refused, indeed, to continue the war any longer, and returned to their homes. Thereafter an attempt was made to continue operations by means of a hired army; and a kind of desultory warfare was, for some time, maintained by a Captain Von Schlikmann, with a force consisting chiefly of foreigners of various nationalities by whom he was joined from the diamond fields of Kimberley and elsewhere. No definite success was ever attained, and the commander was finally shot in an engagement with the enemy.

Not only had the Boers refused to fight; they refused also to pay taxes, and revenue was unobtainable. The stipulated salaries of officials could not be paid, and government was practically at an end.

Sikukuni had held his own; and it was a question how the more formidable danger which threatened the south-eastern border was to be met. Cetshwayo manifested a clear intention to establish the right he claimed over the territory called the "disputed." He had refrained from taking action because of the hope he entertained of a recognition of his claim through the mediation of the Natal Government, which he had repeatedly sought during a number of years. But his attitude was making it more and more apparent that he would not brook much more delay in a settlement.

THE STORY OF THE ZULUS

Matters had reached this position in 1876. The Boers attributed their difficulty to the errors of their President and his Government. They had lost confidence in him, and felt that the salvation of their country lay in a new election. They had no sympathy either with his political schemes or with the personal standard he maintained. The first they regarded as out of keeping with the condition of the country and its inhabitants, the second as vanity. They would elect Paul Kruger, one of themselves, who would understand how to govern the country agreeably to the feelings and circumstances of the people.

The view taken of the situation by the British Government was different. They considered that the weakness which the Boer Government had shown was likely to encourage a general rising of the black against the white races, and so endanger the safety of the British Colonies adjacent to their republic. The condition of this country was, moreover, an obstacle in the way of South African Federation, which it was the policy of the administration of the time to secure. The selection of Sir Bartle Frere for the position of High Commissioner at the Cape was with the special view to the employment by him of his great diplomatic experience towards this end.[1] It was thought that in the condition into which the country had fallen, the Boers might be willing to accept the protection that would be afforded by the establishment in it of British authority. Therefore, in September 1876, Sir Theophilus Shepstone (lately knighted) was commissioned by the queen to make inquiry into the origin, the nature and the circumstances of the disturbances; and, if necessary and agreeable to the majority of the inhabitants, to annex to the British Crown all, or a portion of, the territory of the republic.

He was cordially welcomed by all classes, and resided and carried out his inquiries at Pretoria: arriving at the

[1] Martineau's *Life of Sir Bartle Frere*, ii. 161.

conclusion which found expression in the annexation of the whole territory in April 1877, a step which called forth loud rejoicings from the foreign, and protestings from the Boer, section of the inhabitants. President Burgers retired into permanent privacy, receiving a pension.

The effect upon the Zulus of this event was to convert the dispute with the Boer Government into one with the British Government. Sir Theophilus Shepstone, to whom, as Secretary for Native Affairs in Natal, Cetshwayo had addressed his requests for mediation, and who had evinced some sympathy with him in the subject of his representations, was now the chief of that people against whom they had been made. His mind was to some extent impressed in favour of the Zulu contention, but the position in which he was placed was embarrassing. The section of the people of the country he governed whom it was most important to conciliate, were those who had gone into it when it was an unknown wilderness and made their homes there—the Boers. Those people were, if acquiescing at all, acquiescing but sullenly in the act by which he was at the head of their Government. Their protests were followed up by the despatch of a deputation to England to reason with the queen's Government against that act. The possibility of having to begin his administration by the abandonment of a considerable territory was unpleasant at a moment when it was so desirable that his acts should commend his rule. But inquiry into the subject set his conscience at rest, and he soon entirely set himself in opposition to the Zulu claim. He met men commissioned by Cetshwayo in October at the Blood River, including the prime induna, Umnyamana, "prepared, if it should be insisted upon by the Zulus, as he then thought it might justly be, to give up a tract of country which had from thirteen to sixteen years been occupied by Transvaal farmers, and to whose farms title-deeds had been issued by the late Government." But he

THE STORY OF THE ZULUS

was startled by the extent of land included in the Zulu claim. It was not only that claimed by the Boers to have been ceded in 1861 for the surrender of Umtonga and Umgidhlana, it included the town of Utrecht itself. The Zulu commissioners asserted this claim, moreover, in a tone expressive of their determination to have the land to which it applied. The conference proving fruitless, Sir Theophilus Shepstone took occasion, some weeks later, to investigate the grounds upon which the Republic had based its claim to the " disputed " land, and "then learned, for the first time, what had since been proved by evidence the most uncontrovertible, overwhelming and clear, that the boundary line had been formally and mutually agreed upon and been formally ratified by the giving and receiving of tokens of thanks; and that the beacons had been built up in the presence of the President and members of the Executive Council of the Republic in presence of commissioners from both Umpande and Cetshwayo; and that the spot upon which each beacon had stood was indicated by the Zulu commissioners themselves placing the first stones upon it." The sense of right was thus equally strong on both sides. Cetshwayo followed up the definite assertion made on his behalf at Blood River by a military occupation of the land, and the Boer occupants retired. The king's own claim to territory differed from that which was set forth at Blood River by Umnyamana and the indunas who accompanied him to the conference. He claimed the Blood River as the boundary up to its source, and thence the Drakensberg watershed northward; they claimed as the boundary the stream upon which the village of Utrecht is built. The situation was difficult and critical. Cetshwayo and his counsellors would not yield in respect to the boundary question. In reply to a message sent him on the subject in December, he said that he would not fight, but that he neither could nor would consent to any other boundary than that which he had described; his chief counsellors went so far as to say that the nation would fight for that boundary. The existence of the dispute, and its subject, were known to the whole people. The regiments, which were made up of men from all parts of the country, were at the royal kraal for the first-fruit festival. They clamoured as they passed in review before the king to be led to war upon the question. There was little doubt that the king was in the hands of the nation; that he had to maintain a firm attitude or be despised by his people. On the other side many Boers had taken alarm, abandoned their homes, and were living in camps until the Government should restore them.

In these circumstances there came a suggestion from Sir Henry Bulwer, the Lieutenant-Governor of Natal, that the question should be submitted to arbitration, and to this suggestion both parties agreed. The commission of arbitrators, which was appointed in the following March (1878), consisted of the Honourable Michael Henry Gallwey (Attorney-General of Natal), the Honourable John Wesley Shepstone (Secretary for Native Affairs), and Colonel A. W. Durnford (of the Royal Engineers); the referee being the High Commissioner for South Africa, the Right Honourable Sir Bartle Frere.

The claims set up by the Zulu representatives before this commission included much more land even than that which Umnyamana had claimed. The Zulu country, they said, was limited on the Natal side by the Buffalo (or Umzinyati) River up to its source, and from thence towards the north by the watershed; what evidence was available was adduced on the other side in support of the boundary based on the alleged cession in 1861.

The decision of the commission was not to be known till the end of the year, when it was to be delivered with important accompaniments.

The beginning of the year 1878 was fraught with

occurrences affecting the safety and welfare of the inhabitants of South Africa in various parts; and a feeling gained ground that a beginning only had been made of what was to be an attempt on the part of the black to expel the white races from the country. War had been waged against the Cape Government by Kreli, chief of the Galekas, living on the east of the Kei River; he was shortly joined by Sandilli and his Gaika tribe, who were subjects of that Government.

To overcome those tribes the resources of the Cape Colony were to be sorely taxed; and it was only to be accomplished after a prolonged struggle. After the annexation of the Transvaal it was hoped that satisfactory relations had been established with Sikukuni; but a change of attitude was being manifested by that chief soon to culminate in open hostilities. Captain (afterwards Sir) Marshal Clarke, the Civil Commissioner at Lydenburg, having sent a message to him complaining of a breach of the treaty he had signed, received early in March the curt reply that Sir Marshal Clarke and the English had gone the wrong way to work with him; that he would return to the Boers; that the English were afraid to fight. A struggle had to be entered into with this chief, to which the resources of the Transvaal were, for the time, unequal.

In these matters, and wherever disturbances or signs of disturbances existed, Cetshwayo was credited, rightly or wrongly, with having in some way encouraged the chiefs in their hostile attitude. In the case of Sikukuni he was very definitely blamed. Writing from Lydenburg on the 14th of January, the Rev. A. Nachtigall, a missionary, reported: " Sikukuni has again received a message from Cetshwayo wherein he tells him that his people, by strategy, have taken one of the laagers of the white people; that the remainder of the white people have escaped, and their cattle are at the Vaal River and Komati; Sikukuni, therefore, also had better begin at once, then he would easily get the upper hand."

This is the most explicit instance given in the published correspondence of the time of incitement by Cetshwayo of other chiefs to make war against the Europeans; and whether the report accurately represented a message actually sent by him must always remain a doubtful question.

It will never, perhaps, be known for certain what was the actual purport of his messages; but it is known that they ranged wide, that they reached tribes in remote parts, that intercourse was carried on with them with some regularity. He professed only to send his messengers to procure articles which could not be obtained except in those countries; it is certain that it was considered necessary, in varying circumstances, to invoke the special attributes of different chiefs or members of their tribes.

But the conviction they conveyed to the minds of the British authorities was certain, and this was expressed in a despatch by Sir Bartle Frere, dated the 5th of November, thus:

"It is not in this" (the Cape) "Colony alone, but wherever the Kafir races are to be found, from the Fish River to the Limpopo, and from the Lower Orange River to Delagoa Bay, that the influence of the Zulu king has been found at work fostering and directing this warlike spirit. It is not of late years only that this has been the case. Even before Sir Garnet Wolseley's arrival in Natal (1875) the danger was seen by most competent judges; and every month since has accumulated evidence of the reality of the danger." The disposition which Cetshwayo was thus declared to have been fostering was to "try by more or less decided wager of war whether the white man still retained his supremacy, or whether it had passed with the white man's weapons into the hands of the more numerous native races."

THE STORY OF THE ZULUS

This proud Zulu people, feared and respected throughout South Africa by the races of their own colour, had always been regarded, from the point of view of European civilisation, as so sunk in darkness that it was an important object of charity to bring them light. Missionaries from Germany had been labouring to this end since 1856. They had established some ten mission stations and expended many thousands of pounds sterling. Norway had been in the field even longer; her missionaries had been labouring since 1845; were nine in number, assisted by five catechists, and had converted about a hundred Zulus to Christianity. The Church of England had obtained a footing in 1859, but had made little expansion from the station then established by the Rev. R. Robertson at Kwa Magwaza. The number of converts shown by the Norwegian missionaries may be taken as indicating the general proportion of success that had been attained. From the first "the king could not understand the use of Zulus becoming converts," although "he tolerated it." It was, perhaps, somewhat short of justice to say that conversion had been accorded mere toleration. Such records as there are seem to show that, though few, the converts enjoyed comparative freedom from those duties which the Zulu subjects were required to render to their king. Nor do any of them appear during twenty-seven years to have suffered any of the penalties of the Zulu criminal laws. But, as was the case in the time of Dingana, the ethics sought to be inculcated were not compatible with the system by which the kingdom had been set up and was maintained.

During the last year the rule had been broken through by which the lives of Christians were specially protected. Three professed Christians were killed for the alleged practice of witchcraft or other offences, and others were threatened. The remainder, therefore, took alarm and fled to Natal. Cetshwayo had on various occasions expressed himself as averse to missionary teaching amongst his people; his aversion was now being given practical expression to, in various ways, by Zulus in different parts of the country. In February the chief Sirayo built a kraal so close to one of the stations, near to the Buffalo River, that the continuance there of the missionary was rendered scarcely possible. An appeal was made against this act to the king; but, for reply, he accused the missionaries of reporting concerning him to the Natal Government and to the newspapers, especially with writing to the *Natal Mercury* an account of the fight between the two regiments at Ulundi in December: an account in which he was personally commented upon in severe terms. Their denial was not, at the time, accepted, and the king expressed a desire that they would leave his country. He told them that he had thrown them off, meaning that he would no longer protect them. In consequence, and guided by advice they obtained from the Administrator of the Transvaal, the whole of them took their departure and had left in May.

War between Britain and the Zulus was then regarded as an event unlikely to be avoided. The minds of the European public were generally impressed with the necessity for it, although as yet no definite cause could be stated. The persons and property of such white men as traded, or carried on other pursuits, in the country were, as they always had been, rigidly respected. They were under the protection of the king, and none dared harm them. The feeling was due to the fear that had grown that the great force at Cetshwayo's disposal might some day be used for the destruction of his white neighbours. The determined steps he had taken in warning the Boers off the land in dispute between him and the Transvaal was the chief ground for such fear. In that matter he had shown a clear intention to assert his rights against a white people by force of arms unless they were peacefully yielded: if he could do so in one case there was no security against similar action in regard to other claims which events might make him feel justified in setting up. There is no doubt that to be exposed to the possibility of such proceedings, at the hands of a nation possessing so little in the nature of mercy as the Zulus did, was a condition justifying serious apprehension. Then the belief was very general that the king's system of administration was so tyrannous that his people were generally groaning under oppression; that many of them were being killed to gratify caprice or cupidity. The report in the *Natal Mercury* of the fight between the two regiments, which he charged the missionaries with having written, accused him of having purposely caused it in order to be in a position to exact fines from the combatants; Sir Theophilus Shepstone endorsed the view expressed in that report.

Much was said of his failure to carry out the changes in the system of administration which he had promised at his coronation to inaugurate.

And in July there came a violation of territory which doubtless called for serious notice, and which was to form the chief definite cause of what the end of the year was to bring forth. On the 26th day of that month there appeared before the Magistrate of the Umsinga Division of Natal a native named Maziyana, a border guard, who reported that, about six days previously, a native woman named Ka Qwelebana, had taken refuge in Natal. She was the wife of the chief Sirayo, one of the king's counsellors, who was at the time absent at the king's kraal. The cause of her flight had been an attempt on the part of her husband's chief son, Mehlokazulu, to put her to death on the charge that she had been unfaithful. Two days after crossing the border river she had been brought to Maziyana's kraal. She was suffering from the injuries she had received at Mehlokazulu's hands. She had rested there till this day, when, in the early morning, the sound was heard of horses approaching, and on going out Maziyana had found these to be ridden by Mehlokazulu and his brother Bekuzulu, and twenty or thirty other Zulus, who were then advancing towards the front of the hut. Another force numbering some forty or fifty, on foot and armed with shields and assegais, were seen advancing from the rear. Asked the cause of this visit, Mehlokazulu said he was in search of his mother, and thereupon ordered the men who were on foot to search for the woman in the huts. She was found there, dragged out and along the footpath and through the river by the ford called Nomavovo's. Another large body of Zulus was on the Zululand side of the river waiting. When the capture had thus been effected a war-song was struck up, and, the whole force having proceeded to a distance of about 800 yards beyond the river, the woman was shot dead, much firing of guns and noise following.

In seizing the woman Mehlokazulu was not charged with having committed actual violence against the inmates of the kraal in which she was found; but he was declared to have said, on remonstrance being made, that it placed him in the position of having to regard those who made it as enemies, from which they inferred that it would be discreet to say no more.

This proved to be the second case of the same kind. Two days earlier Mehlokazulu, accompanied by another member of his father's family, had seized another of his father's wives in the hut of another border guard higher up the river, under similar circumstances, and subjected her to similar treatment. The accounts furnished to the Government of these occurrences were substantially correct; all the Zulus have to say, in the way of justifying the deeds, is that the native border guards did not offer any serious objection when the surrender of the women was demanded; that they were not killed on British, but on Zulu soil. They consider that the matter was one in which Mehlokazulu was liable to punishment by his king; but the approval of his action by Sirayo would have freed him from this liability, and there can be no doubt that he had been assured of that approval before acting.

Perhaps the most important political significance that attached to the occurrence lay in the novelty of its character. Since Natal became a British Colony there had been no violation of its border by the Zulus. When their wives or daughters, or when fugitive offenders crossed the stream which marked the frontier, they had invariably been free from pursuit. These wives of Sirayo had lingered for days under a sense of absolute safety, within sight of those at whose hands they knew they would receive no mercy did not the border intervene.

The proceedings of Mehlokazulu had been without the king's sanction, but he did not regard them with any high degree of reprobation. He acknowledged that wrong had been done; but did not admit that the offence against the Natal Government had been of a very serious character. In answer to Sir Henry Bulwer's request that he would surrender those who had led the raid he offered to pay a fine of £50.

In the meantime the commission had arrived at a decision regarding the border dispute. Its reports, dated the 20th day of June, declared that there had been no cession by the Zulu kings to the South African Republic of any of the land between the Drakensberg and the Buffalo River. But having regard to long occupation by the subjects of that state; to the fact that a white government had been established in it, well known to the Zulus, and permitted if not sanctioned and acquiesced in by them; to the practical recognition of Boer sovereignty, especially in the application made by Cetshwayo in 1861 for the surrender of his fugitive brothers, when he respected it as Boer territory, they held that the sovereignty over that tract claimed to have been ceded by Umpande to the Boers in 1845 should be considered to have passed to the Transvaal. The boundary of this tract had been variously stated at different times; each successive description had extended the Boer dominions and yet left its exact position in some obscurity. The commission had not inspected the ground, and the boundary it recommended was vaguely stated as "a line stretching from the junction of the Buffalo and Blood rivers, along the latter river to its source, and thence straight to a round hill between the two main sources of the Pongolo River in the Drakensberg." They awarded to the Zulus that land which the Boers claimed to have been ceded to them in 1861.

This report had been forwarded to the High Commissioner by the Lieutenant-Governor of Natal, who generally concurred in its recommendations. But Sir Bartle Frere's mind had been strongly impressed with the belief that more serious issues were involved than that of the settlement of territorial dispute. He arrived in Natal on the 23rd of September, and on the last day of that month reported to the Secretary of State that he had found the position of affairs far more critical even than he had expected. There could be no doubt, he wrote, that the design of the native tribes to combine and resist and drive back the white man was in process of attempted execution. He regarded the attitude of the Zulus and their king as threatening the safety of the Colony of Natal, and urged the necessity of strengthening the defensive force.

The missionaries who had long resided in the Zulu country now furnished accounts of the occurrences that had come to their notice during that time. Of the reports they furnished, that of the Rev. R. Robertson supplied the most definite information.

"I have stated publicly, and offered to produce witnesses to prove it, that within a radius of eight miles from Kwa Magwaza twenty-four persons have been killed in eighteen years, nineteen of whom have been killed since the death of the late king. I believe this is not an overdrawn picture of what takes place in other parts of the country. I am writing from memory, but I think that a list Mr. Oftebro gave me contained the names of twenty-nine persons killed, to his knowledge, since 1873; and Mr. Stavem writes of, I think, seventeen in about nine years in his immediate neighbourhood. Another reason I have for believing it to be true is, that I have seen parties on their way to kill and have seen the captured cattle on their way to the king's kraal.

"No one can go to the king's kraal and listen to what goes on there, as I have done, without knowing that killing must be going on every day. The Zulus believe in witchcraft, and attribute all their ills to it. Whatever may be the matter with them or their property, they consult a witch-doctor. Some one is 'smelt out,' and then the matter goes to the indunas, and from them to the king. Many escape, of course, especially if they have not cattle, but too many cases end in the death of the one smelt out; often also of some one belonging to him." At another time Mr. Robertson furnished a list of the nineteen cases, and it is notable that the cause assigned for the killing of one of them was that he "was ill." This may be regarded as a specific case of killing for failure to discharge military duty. It has not been practicable to learn of others, and the probability is that very few suffered death for this cause.

These reports tended to confirm the impression that had been gained, that the people were sorely oppressed by the king and would gladly be freed from his authority.

The fact was not sufficiently borne in mind that they "*believed* in witchcraft," and that the prevailing feeling in regard to the killing of those convicted of its practice was that it was done for their protection. No case is known of a man having been killed by Cetshwayo for mere caprice.

The feeling gradually gained ground, both in Natal and Zululand, that important events were impending. Additional troops arriving in the Colony for its defence against possible Zulu invasion, suspicion was given rise to, in the Zulu mind, of sinister designs on the part of the British. It had been "freely talked about" in Natal "that the troops recently arrived had come to fight the Zulus." Hunts on a large scale were reported as taking place near the border, and the Lieutenant-Governor, fearing that the men thus gathering might have for their object an invasion of the Colony, caused some troops to be moved to Greytown and Verulam. Notwithstanding assurances sent by him that the troops which continued to arrive were merely for the purpose of defence and giving assurance of safety to the inhabitants of Natal, who were alarmed by the prevailing rumours, the impression steadily gained strength in the Zulu mind that there were other motives. Writing on the 15th of October Mr. Rudolph, the landdrost at Utrecht, said:

"Some time ago Gwekwana, Uhamu's confidential induna, came here under the old pretence of looking up cattle for girls. He said that Uhamu had sent him to say that Sintwangu, who has been in Natal since the Rorke's Drift Commission, came back saying that it appears that there is going to be war with Cetshwayo; that Uhamu sent him, in consequence, to me, to be informed what he is to do in the case of war, as he will not fight against the English, but will come to them, and wished to know how he should act and where he is to go when the time comes."

The sequence of this movement on Uhamu's part will required to be traced: it was to be marked by much bloodshed. The incident is noted here as the first step towards important events; it is also notable as showing that Uhamu, with the same means of obtaining information as other Zulu leading men, had at that time become persuaded that there was to be war; that it was to be begun by the English.

Three occurrences have to be noted, the first two dating about the end of September. The land upon which a small German settlement had been formed under the Transvaal Government, called Luneburg, was included in that claimed by Cetshwayo as Zulu territory. This settlement lay to the north-east of Utrecht, east of the Drakensberg. He had caused the occupation of it, in May, by a representative named Faku. Some temporary consternation was excited by the incident amongst the white population, but, as it was not followed by a more aggressive act on Faku's part than the building of a kraal for his personal accommodation, this had again subsided. But now, by order of the king, he notified to the settlers that they were required to "leave their farms and homesteads, as the lands were required for grazing purposes for the king's cattle which were being sent up from Zululand, and the garden grounds were required for field cultivation; that, as the winter was now over and there was plenty of young grass to be found at the Vaal River for stock, they (the Germans) were required to go away."

The second was held to be another violation of British territory, and an offence against two British subjects. A Mr. Smith, a surveyor in the Colonial Engineer's Department, had gone to inspect a road leading from Greytown to the Tugela River; a road which had been made some years previously by order of Sir Garnet Wolseley, but had fallen into disuse. The fear of British aggression had become so serious that the Zulus along the border river had been ordered to keep guard over the crossings. Smith and his companion Deighton, a trader, went down to the river, which at that time was very low and running close to the Zulu bank. Their presence created a suspicion that their object was to examine the crossing for the purpose of an invasion of the country, and they were seized and taken through the river by a party of Zulus. There they were detained for some time and questioned regarding their object and then released by order of a head-man who came upon the scene.

The third occurrence had the 7th of October for its date. One of the subjects of Cetshwayo was a Swazi chief named Umbilini. He was a member of the Swazi royal family, and had sought refuge in Zululand from the consequences of his pretensions to the kingship with which he had been threatened in his own country. He had proved an unruly subject to the king; had a following of men who were not enrolled in the regular army, and with whom he habitually made armed forays in various quarters. His location was near to the Pongolo River, and the facts of the occurrence of the date given were thus reported at the time by Mr. Rudolph:

"The audacious Umbilini made a daring attack on some four or five Swazi kraals at the lower Makosini kopjes, near Mozana, or Sendeling's River, north of the Pongolo River. He, with his followers, attacked these kraals before daybreak, and in the struggle four Swazi men were killed and others wounded. Umbilini burnt the kraals and made off with some ten women as captives or slaves."

The order delivered to the Luneberg settlers by Faku was never enforced, but led to the placing of a military force there to protect them.

These were ill-timed occurrences. But it must be admitted that they were not, in themselves, the cause of the conflict soon to begin. The High Commissioner was

THE STORY OF THE ZULUS

persuaded by other causes that the time had arrived when war with the Zulus could no longer be avoided. The Government in England still hoped for a peaceful settlement of the difficulties. In a despatch dated one month after the raid by Umbilini, the Secretary of State for the Colonies, Sir Michael Hicks-Beach, observed that all the information that had reached Her Majesty's Government appeared to them to justify the confident hopes that, by the exercise of prudence and by meeting the Zulus in a spirit of forbearance and compromise, it would be possible to avert war. In answer to this Sir Bartle Frere stated at length the conviction at which he had arrived and the grounds upon which it was based. In this despatch little reference was made to the overt acts of the Zulus in violation of British territory. Gradually, since his arrival on the frontier of the Cape Colony, an "irresistible body of evidence from all parts of South Africa"—evidence not at present available to the public—had convinced him of a common purpose among the Kafir races to try conclusions with the white man; that "Cetshwayo, as king of the most powerful tribe, was the head and moving spirit of the combination." It was, moreover, necessary to establish the credit of the British nation with the Boers of the Transvaal, and to justify to them the reasons which had been assigned for the annexation of that territory, that the danger which threatened it from the Zulu power should be removed. Occasion was taken in the despatch for a statement of his view of the character of Cetshwayo, by which he is made to appear in a very different light from that in which he is regarded by the people he ruled:

" It is no exaggeration to say that his history, from the first, has been written in characters of blood. I do not refer merely to the long chronicle of his butcheries, from the slaughter of his brothers and their followers early in his career down to the more recent indiscriminate and wholesale destruction of all the unmarried women who attempted to evade his order, given in a fit of caprice, that they should accept as husbands the elderly unmarried soldiers of his army; the massacre being subsequently extended to all the relatives who took away for burial the exposed corpses of the slaughtered women."

It was plainly his settled purpose to "imitate Tshaka, his uncle, who formed his dynasty on a system of indiscriminate slaughter of all his enemies, the vanquished and most submissive as well as those who resisted; of all who in any way offended him or crossed his will, and even of his own wives as soon as there was a possibility of their giving birth to an heir to the throne." He was utterly unreliable. The Secretary for Native Affairs had reported: "This Government has had ample proof that no declaration of the Zulu king made to it, at any time or in any way, however important the matter may be, can be relied on."

The troops in Natal were strengthened by "every available company," and, in time, were considered sufficient, though not so strong as was desirable; and the purpose was so generally understood to be that of settling the Zulu question that to recede would have created a dangerous impression in the minds, not only of the Boers, but of all native races.

With a mind so impressed, and in these circumstances, Sir Bartle Frere arrived at the decision regarding the disputed territory which was communicated to representatives of the Zulu king sent by him to receive it, at the Lower Tugela on the 11th day of December 1878.

The award assigned the boundary that the commission had recommended, but there were conditions attached to it which would have been troublesome to the Zulus. They were briefly indicated in the document itself, and more clearly stated in another paper in which the High Commissioner's intentions were fully set forth:

"It is intended that in this district" (that awarded

to the Zulus) "individual rights to property which were obtained under the Transvaal Government shall be respected and maintained, so that any Transvaal farmers who may now elect to remain in the territory may possess, under British guarantee, the same rights they would have possessed had they been granted holdings from the Zulu king under guarantee of the great Zulu Council."

A British Resident was to be appointed, who would see that those rights were maintained. It was the sovereignty only that was to be restored to Cetshwayo; and it was not to be sovereignty as understood by him, but subject to restrictions agreeable to the requirements of those who might become his white subjects.

But the award was an incident of merely passing interest. Half an hour after its delivery the king's deputies were again called together, and the document read to them called the Ultimatum, in which certain acts of reparation for injuries done to the British Government and reforms in his own were set forth, and required to be effected by the king, within specified times, war to be the result of failure on his part to comply with those requirements. Mehlokazulu, and those of his relatives who had aided him in the seizure of the wives of Sirayo on Natal territory in July, were to be given up to the Natal Government for trial, and a fine of 500 head of cattle paid; also a fine of 100 head of cattle for the insult to Smith and Deighton at the Tugela Drift: all within twenty days. Umbilini was also required to be given up, and such others of those who were associated with him as should be stated in a further communication which would be addressed to the king.

It was pointed out to the Zulu king that the promises he had made to the British Government at his coronation had not been kept. The indiscriminate killing of his subjects had not abated. Hundreds of them had suffered death without trial or form of trial. No man knew whether he might not be set upon at any moment and killed, and all belonging to him destroyed or taken away. The British Government in Natal had sent a representative to be present at Cetshwayo's coronation, not from any desire on its part, but in compliance with the request of Cetshwayo and the Zulu nation. It had stipulated, as the only condition, that reforms should be made which Cetshwayo, in the presence of representatives of the Zulu nation, had promised on that occasion to effect in the administration of the Zulu Government. These promises had been made, and it was due to the honour of the British nation that their observance should be required. The system of government pursued by the king was destroying the country.

All the young men, all the able-bodied men, were taken for soldiers. They were taken from their homes at an age when they were becoming useful to their parents, and kept for several years in the compulsory service of the king. They were not allowed to marry, but had to await the permission of the king, which was often long withheld. They were not allowed to labour for themselves, or to plant, or to reap, or to live in quiet and in peace with their families and relatives. They were constantly summoned up to the king's kraal as if for war, although there was no enemy, and thus they came to fight amongst themselves, and there was bloodshed and distress and moaning in the land; or they were sent out in parties to surround the kraals of those who had given offence to the king, or who were accused by private enemies, and who then, without trial, without a word, were killed, their homes laid desolate and their families and all they had carried off or destroyed. Thus the army was made an instrument for the oppression of the country, not for its protection. It served no useful purpose; there being no enemy against which it could be employed, there was no need for it.

Besides, while the king was maintaining this army, and constantly calling it together, it was impossible for the neighbouring states to feel secure. They never knew what might happen, and the British Government was obliged to keep large numbers of the queen's troops in Natal and the Transvaal in order to protect British subjects against the danger of possible aggression by the Zulu king.

It was, therefore, necessary that the existing military system should be abolished, and such new regulations adopted as might be decided upon, after consultation with the great council of the Zulus, and with representatives of the British Government. The army as it stood should be disbanded, and the men composing it permitted to return to their homes. The obligation to defend their country, when necessary, would remain with them; but they should not be called together as regiments except with the approval of the great council of the nation assembled, and with the consent of the British Government. Every man on attaining man's estate should be free to marry.

Then with regard to the promises made at the coronation, rules should at once be laid down for the trial of persons accused of offences. It was necessary that compliance with those promises should be no longer delayed. In order to secure it, the High Commissioner would appoint an officer as his deputy to reside in the Zulu country, or on its immediate border, who would be the eyes, and ears, and mouth of the British Government towards the Zulu king and the great council of the nation.

Several missionaries had settled in the Zulu country by permission of the late king. Cetshwayo had continued that permission to them. But during the past two years some of the natives residing at the mission stations had been killed without trial or form of trial, and others terrified; and thus most of the missionaries had been obliged to abandon their stations.

The High Commissioner desired that they and the natives should be allowed to resume occupation; that the missionaries should be allowed to teach, as in Umpande's time, and that no Zulu should be punished for listening to them.

A case of dispute in which any of the missionaries, or any European, might be concerned should be heard by the king in presence of the British Resident; no sentence of expulsion from Zululand should be carried out until it had been communicated by the king to the British Resident and approved by him.

The king was given thirty days within which to signify his assent to these required reforms, assuming that in the meantime the previous requirements had been complied with.

These reforms professed to be designed to ameliorate the condition of the Zulus. The message by which their adoption was required drew from one of the king's deputies the question: "Have the Zulus complained?" The chief answer to be found to that question in available documents is that contained in a report by F. Bernard Fynney, whose acquaintance with the Zulus was perhaps greater than that of most white men. One Zulu had asked him what the Natal Government intended to do about the killing, and his report proceeds:

"What Mr. Shepstone had spoken" (quoting from the Zulu) "was not spoken in the night, but in the sunshine; the king was not alone, but his people were with him, and the ears of all Zululand heard these words, and the hearts of all Zulus were joyful, and in gladness they lifted up their hands saying: 'The mouth of our white father has spoken good words; he has cautioned his child in the presence of his people, and a good sun has risen this day over Zululand.' Has the king listened? Does he hold fast these words? No! Not one. The promises he made are all broken. What does Mr. Shepstone say to this? You should stay at my kraal yonder for a few days and see the Iziza" (confiscated property of convicted

Zulus) " pass, and you would then see with your own eyes how a case is tried."

As of his own knowledge Mr. Fynney then remarks:

" When a charge is made against a Zulu the question is generally asked, ' has he any cattle ? ' and, if answered in the affirmative, there is little chance of escape. Instances of killing occurred while I was in Zululand, and, to my knowledge, no trial was allowed. An armed party was despatched on the morning I left Ulundi, and, as I was informed, to kill."

Against this it might be well to place the statement of the Zulu deputies, in reference to the Ultimatum to which they had just listened : " No one had been put to death without cause. The utmost forbearance had been shown to those guilty of witchcraft. When any one had been accused of this offence he was removed from the neighbourhood of the persons whom he had bewitched. If he was accused by those to whose neighbourhood he had gone, he was yet another time removed. But if again accused by his neighbours, his guilt was held proved and he was put to death."

CHAPTER XV

THERE is, perhaps, nothing more remarkable in the Zulu people than the great power of memory which is possessed by those of them who are accustomed to deal with important affairs. Having no writing, there has been, from time immemorial, no other record of events than the impressions upon their minds; these impressions are rendered distinct by the habit they have acquired or inherited of giving their undivided attention to whatever matter may be immediately under discussion or consideration.

Communications between the British authorities and the Zulu kings had almost invariably been conducted by means of verbal messages conveyed by natives, and there is no instance known of failure on their part to accurately deliver the words entrusted to them. There was thus nothing so remarkable as might at first appear in the circumstance that the substance of the Ultimatum now addressed to Cetshwayo was conveyed to him, not by direct reading, but, to a distance of over eighty miles, in the memory-stores of the messengers whom he had sent to receive it from the British Commissioners. It was a lengthy document, containing some 4000 words, and its practical purport was considerably involved in comment upon the state of things which it was desired to remedy. The document itself never reached him, but was left in the hands of John Dunn, near the place at which it was delivered.

His own envoys included men of considerable age, and their sense of dignity disposed them to be leisurely in their movements; and, recognising this, John Dunn sent messengers of his own, who informed the king in advance of what was required of him. In response Cetshwayo at once instructed John Dunn to write agreeing to the surrender of Sirayo's sons and brother, and payment of the fines demanded, but to ask that, if the number of days allowed should have elapsed before the arrival of the persons and cattle, action might not be immediately taken; owing to the swollen state of the rivers his envoys had not been able to return, and those whose surrender was required were at their kraals at Nqutu, distant, perhaps, two days' journey. The other demands he promised to give answer to after consulting with his counsellors. Eleven days later messengers arrived at the Tugela direct from the king with this message: "The king directed us to say that he has heard the words of the Government, but the land is great, and he has to put them before the Zulu nation, and asks for time to do so. The king directed us further to say that, in the case of Messrs. Smith and Deighton, the people accused of ill-treating them deny having come on to Natal soil at all. There are two islands on the Tugela at the point where Messrs. Smith and Deighton were, and they were on the one nearest to the Zulu side, which the king believes belongs to the Zulu nation; and he asks that His Excellency the Lieutenant-Governor of Natal will be pleased to send some one to see if it is not so."

In answer to these representations it was agreed that hostilities should not be commenced till the full period of thirty days should have elapsed; but it was made clear that the right was reserved to the general to advance across the border, should he deem it advisable to do so for military reasons, at the end of the shorter period of twenty days, unless by that time the fines were paid and surrender made of the persons named in the demand.

There is considerable evidence that some practical steps were taken in the direction of paying the fines of cattle; that they were collected for the purpose of being paid over. But, as regards the other matters, it is doubtful whether they proceeded beyond the king's personal promise, which he could not have fulfilled except by the consent of the nation through their representatives.

It must remain doubtful, moreover, whether at this time there was any serious hope on either side of averting hostilities. Evidence of its absence from the mind of the High Commissioner is perhaps stronger than that which supports the contention that Cetshwayo had abandoned it.

The conditions set forth in the Ultimatum upon which peace would be permitted to continue were such as could not be complied with except with considerable difficulty. That requiring the disbandment of the army was, perhaps, the most difficult. The organisation could not but remain while the men lived of whom the army was composed. Sir Henry Bulwer recognised this in a despatch written three years later in view of a contemplated restoration of the Zulu king. The country had by then been divided into thirteen different parts, each ruled over by an independent chief, and it had been so ruled for about three years:

"Unfortunately, the military system is not a system that has to be created. It is not a something that has to be laboriously, and with difficulty, thought out and brought into existence. The system exists already. It exists—a dormant, inactive power, it may be, at the present moment, but it exists—a perfect organisation, such as it has been from the time of Tshaka. The system which was then established has, during a period of half a century, taken deep root in the Zulu nation. It is part and parcel of the Zulu life; and its extinction would be the work of many years. The organisation is there, the material is there, the machinery is there. And, as a time-piece which has been suffered to run down and lie in disuse is silent, but no sooner is the action of its mainspring restored than, complete in all parts of its mechanism, it begins again to tell the hours and moments of time, so is the wonderful mechanism of the Zulu military system; it needs only to be touched by the master hand of whoever is recognised by the Zulus as their chief, and straightway the whole machinery is put in motion. It needs but the word to be spoken, and forthwith, as in the fabled scene where Cadmus sows the dragon's teeth, the land brings forth a living harvest of armed men. They gather at the appointed places, the regiments are marshalled, the companies are told off, the vacant places filled up, a nation stands in arms."

The nature of the new military system, by which that in existence would have to be replaced, was not indicated beyond that it was to admit of every man employing his time to his own advantage, unless occasion arose to defend his country; that men were all to be permitted to marry on arrival at man's estate. It was believed that the men composing the army would eagerly welcome a reformation conferring these advantages upon them; that the requirement would hold out a prospect so tempting as to withdraw their support from the king. In this they were misjudged. There were advantages attaching to membership of the army which, to their minds, compensated for the few hardships it entailed. They enjoyed the direct protection of the king, while those outside the army were subject to the will of subordinate chiefs; they were conscious that the nation to which they were proud to belong had been created and was supported by the system it was sought to abolish.

The proposed new system of administering justice was also one which would not, in the circumstances of the country, readily have commended itself to the minds of the people at large.

There was a good deal of discussion amongst the assembled Zulu notables at Ulundi, but of how counsel was swayed it is not possible now to obtain a reliable account. There appear, from such information as can be gathered to have been some who advocated the surrender of Mehlokazulu and others; but the feeling of the majority was opposed to it. Sirayo was a man of considerable influence and power, and his own feeling in the matter would necessarily have carried weight. Some were more strongly impressed than others with the importance of maintaining peace with the British Government.

The majority did not consider that the necessity for this lay in their own weakness. They had not had any manifestation of British superiority, either in strength or bravery. They had felt no disposition at any time to yield to threats. When defences were organised in Natal, Cetshwayo had called out a portion of his own forces to watch the border and resist possible invasion; and now, when the sand was running out, when the time within which he had to choose between yielding and fighting was fast drawing to an end, he could see nothing irresistible in the forces that were distributed along the border of his country. The display of force that had accompanied the delivery of the Ultimatum had not greatly impressed the Zulu messengers to whom the document was presented. Sintwangu, one of them, reported to the king that their number was so small that "they might be demolished like bits of meat."

The forces available for the enforcement of the demands were, indeed, somewhat scanty.

The General Commanding in Chief in South Africa, Lord Chelmsford, had arrived in Natal from the Cape Colony on the 6th of August. He had been impressed before arrival with the belief that war with the Zulus would be necessary; and, although the views of the Lieutenant-Governor of Natal were of a somewhat opposite tendency, he continued to regard the situation as demanding an increased defensive force. The war with Sikukuni was proceeding on very unequal terms. There were opposed to that chief 117 European officers and men, with 25

THE STORY OF THE ZULUS 169

horses, 100 Natal natives, and 25 who had been enlisted from the members of a local tribe. The European portion of the force was raised, with great difficulty, by the end of the month to 375, with 146 horses. Other forces were sent forward, notably the Frontier Light Horse, under Major Redvers Buller, afterwards an officer of great renown. But the season when horses could not live in the locality soon setting in, the enterprise had to be abandoned till a more favourable opportunity.

In Natal, if there were any real grounds for the belief entertained by the High Commissioner and the general that an invasion was meditated by the Zulus, the position was a serious one. The garrison of regular troops was small, and the local force consisted of some 200 mounted European police and 400 volunteers. The scheme of defence formulated by the general included the doubtful experiment of forming three native regiments of 2000 men each. Each company was composed of 13 Europeans and 101 natives; the first consisting of a captain, two lieutenants and ten non-commissioned officers; the second of an officer, ten non-commissioned officers and ninety privates. The arms consisted of guns of an old pattern supplied by the Natal Government for the native officer and non-commissioned officers, and shields and assegais for the privates. Each regiment of two battalions was placed under the command of a British officer, styled a Commandant, and the force was designated Native Contingent.

In response to urgent representations the Secretary of State despatched two additional battalions of troops to Natal, with the stipulation that they should be used only for the defence of the Colony; and, at the time of the delivery of the Ultimatum, there were four columns in the field ready to act. They were composed and distributed thus:

(1) No. 1 Column: the "Buffs," 200 Natal Volunteers, Naval Brigade, one regiment Native Contingent, and two

guns; to which was to be added one battalion of the troops expected from England, making the strength up to about 2000 Europeans and a like number of natives. This column was stationed at the Tugela Ford, near the mouth of that river, and was under the command of Colonel Pearson.

(2) No. 2 Column, under Lieutenant-Colonel Durnford, was stationed in the vicinity of the Tugela Ford called Middle-Drift, at which Smith and Deighton sustained the unpleasant experience at the hands of Zulus, and consisted of one rocket battery (two tubes), three battalions Native Contingent and five troops Mounted Native Contingent.

(3) No. 3 Column was stationed at Helpmakaar, the highlands some eight miles from Rorke's Drift. It consisted of two battalions of the 24th Regiment, in all fourteen companies; two squadrons Imperial Mounted Infantry under Major Russell; 200 Natal Volunteers and 150 Natal Mounted Police under Major Dartnell; two battalions Natal Native Contingent under Commandant Lonsdale; six guns of the Royal Artillery under Major Harness, and one half company of Royal Engineers.

(4) No. 4 Column, under Evelyn Wood, who had gained distinction in the Cape Frontier War, lately concluded, and was about to add to his renown, was stationed at Utrecht. It was made up of the first battalion of the 13th Regiment under Lieutenant-Colonel Gilbert; the 90th Light Infantry under Major Rogers; Buller's Frontier Light Horse (back from the country of Sikukuni); about 200 Native Contingent; 50 Boers under Piet Uys; six guns under Major Tremlett, and one half-company Royal Engineers.

It was designed that these columns should converge upon Ulundi as soon as the given time should have elapsed, without compliance having been yielded by Cetshwayo with the demands that had been made upon him.

On the 11th of January a general advance was made, numbers one and three columns crossing the border river at the fords opposite to which they were respectively placed. Hostilities were immediately begun. Colonel Wood had availed himself of the right which had been reserved of entering the Zulu country at the end of the shorter period of twenty days. He was encamped on Zulu soil, and rode to meet the general, who accompanied number three column, on the day upon which Rorke's Drift was crossed.

The meeting took place midway between the two camps, and on his way back Colonel Wood seized some 2000 head of cattle, reporting that the people made no active resistance, but merely expressed their surprise.

No opposition was presented at this time by the Zulus: but the general found himself confronted with difficulties greater than he had anticipated. There had been much rain, and the ground over which he had to march had become so soft that the wagons sank to their bodies. It was found that four days would necessarily be occupied in making a road across a swamp not far from where the column had crossed the river, and similar obstacles were found to exist in front. In these circumstances the general set about reviewing his original plan of campaign, and making such modifications as the unexpected condition of things rendered necessary. He would endeavour, by means of expeditions from fixed positions to be taken up by the several columns, to drive the Zulus away from the vicinity of the Natal and Transvaal borders, so as to secure these against invasion, and await a more favourable season for a general advance. Cetshwayo would thus be forced to keep his army mobilised. They would find difficulty in procuring food. If kept inactive they would become dangerous to the king; if ordered to attack they would be "playing the general's game."

When the British troops had occupied Zulu soil for five days there was still no indication of the intention of the Zulus. The general appears to have thought that his chief difficulty would be in inducing them to meet him in battle. It is difficult to understand upon what ground the opinion was formed that detached bodies of Zulu warriors might be found along the border, but it would seem that this was the form in which Zulu opposition was expected to be encountered. The instructions which Colonel Durnford received were interpreted by him to mean that he was to "operate against Matshana"; Colonel Wood was conducting attacks on other minor chiefs farther north. Seketwayo, the chief of the Umdhlalose tribe, had manifested some disposition to tender his submission to the British, and, as an inducement to carry this into effect, his cattle were seized by that officer, and their return promised when he should have done so. Writing on the 16th of January, the general said that a few days would decide whether Seketwayo would surrender or be defeated. Uhamu's early overtures had not been forgotten; communications were opened up with him with the object of securing his defection from the king and submission to the British military authorities; fear only prevented him, for the present, from doing so.

As soon as progress could be made by number three column an attack was conducted upon a party of Sirayo's men, who were in charge of some cattle between Rorke's Drift and Isandhlwana Hill. These men showed some resistance, and thirty of their number were killed and their cattle taken.

It scarcely appears to have occurred to the general, or to the officers commanding the several columns, that there might be some other cause than lack of disposition to fight for the absence of opposition to their attacks on Zulu subjects. There was soon to be a rude awakening. The men of the several minor tribes that were being attacked and despoiled were members of the army; they would fight as such and not separately in defence of their tribal lands and property. While these events were transpiring, while plans were being formulated for further harassing the border tribes, with the object of forcing the king to take action, the bulk of the men were with their regiments getting marshalled in battle order. There had been scarcity, and it was difficult to get the men to assemble on account of the hunger that prevailed. The full force of the army was, indeed, not got together for this reason. But had it been possible to view for a short time the doings at the head kraals in the White Umfolozi Valley, it would, perhaps, have been perceived that the modified plans had been made without real cause.

The number of men gathering and being marshalled there far exceeded that of the whole invading army, and was proportionately greater than any of the several columns which might be attacked separately; as was, indeed, designed.

At the end of ten days number three column had been enabled to cover a distance of ten miles. Crossing a small stream called Manzamnyama, and ascending a somewhat steep ridge on its eastern side, it passed through a neck and encamped by the south-eastern base of the hill whose name, Isandhlwana, or Isa-'Ndhlwana, "Like-a-little-house," was soon to be rendered memorable. It was the general's design to penetrate as far as the Isipezi Mountain, and there form the camp from which the expeditions that were contemplated in his modified plan of campaign were to issue. On the day upon which the column arrived at Isandhlwana—the 20th of January—he personally reconnoitred the ground towards the right front for the purpose of ascertaining the character of the reputed strongholds of Matshana ka Mondisa, who, since his escape from Natal in 1858, had dwelt with his tribe, waxing in power, amongst the rugged hills that rise on its left from the valley of the Buffalo River. Being unable to complete his examination of the locality he, next day, sent Major Dartnell with the Natal Volunteers and Mounted Police, and two battalions of the Native Contingent, to do so.

For the safety of the camp at the foot of Isandhlwana no apprehension was entertained; no steps were taken to entrench it. The position, indeed, was one which, in view of the fighting appliances and methods of the enemy, gave the idea that it afforded sufficient security. The Zulus, though to a large extent armed with guns, were not possessed of long-range rifles or artillery. There was no cover from which they could surround the camp unobserved. The steep face of the Nqutu range, separated from Isandhlwana Hill by a low and somewhat narrow neck, curved towards the left front. To approach the camp from its ridge would entirely expose the Zulus to the rifle-fire of the British soldiers long before their own smooth-bore guns were within effective distance. Towards the right front the ground was somewhat broken and stony, but capable of being swept over a considerable range by rifle fire, while the rear was in a large measure protected by the Isandhlwana Hill.

In the course of his reconnaissance Major Dartnell happened upon a body of Zulus. He reported the circumstance to the general and received orders to attack. But, later in the day, he ascertained that he was in the proximity of a considerable force, and decided to bivouac, sending to the general to ask for the support of two companies of infantry. His message reached the general about two o'clock on the morning of Wednesday the 22nd of January. On receiving it the general and Colonel Glyn, with four guns and two companies of the 2nd battalion of the 24th Regiment, left the camp to give the desired assistance. The camp was left under the command of Lieutenant-Colonel Pulleine. Colonel Durnford,

ISANDHLWANA

THE STORY OF THE ZULUS

who was at Rorke's Drift with some 500 natives, about half of whom were mounted, and two rocket tubes, was given orders to join and strengthen it. Its strength, when thus augmented, would therefore be 2 officers and 78 men of the Royal Artillery, with 2 guns; 15 officers and 342 non-commissioned officers and men of the 1st battalion of the 24th Regiment; 5 officers and 90 non-commissioned officers and men of the 2nd battalion; mounted corps numbering some 400, including mounted infantry and Natal Volunteers and Police; Colonel Durnford's force, and 1 officer and 10 men with the rocket tubes.

The Zulu army had in the meantime advanced to within five miles of the camp without having been detected or its presence suspected. According to Usibebu, who superintended the scouting, he encountered and drove in a patrol which would otherwise soon have come in view of the army: and it was probably his party that was reported by the general as having been observed by him from the ridge on the right front, on the afternoon of the day previous to that upon which he set out to join Major Dartnell. Undabuko, Cetshwayo's brother, informed the author that some scouts from what he believed to be the force that was reconnoitring in Matshana's country actually saw the army, or a portion of it, but did not apparently realise the importance of the discovery they had made. The army had advanced in the day time across open country, and ought, with proper vigilance, to have been discovered.

The 22nd of January was the day of the new moon. She was to begin her new life at eight minutes before two o'clock in the afternoon, and her "dark day" was considered by the Zulus as unfitting for an engagement in battle. It was, therefore, their design to defer attack till the 23rd. But the events of the day were destined to be guided rather by accident than by the will of those in direction. The year was one of scarcity. Many had little food to bring with them; others had travelled far, and such little supplies as they had taken with them from their homes were exhausted. Hunger prevailed amongst them, and foraging parties were early astir to gather what could be found in deserted maize fields. These parties came into collision with the British outposts; and by nine o'clock a despatch reached the general from Colonel Pulleine reporting that firing had taken place on his left front. The firing thus reported occurred at about seven o'clock in the morning. Still the presence of a large Zulu army was unsuspected. The strength of the force seen was reported to be about 400; they showed no disposition to engage in battle; they retired in all directions. Such preparations for meeting an attack as were considered necessary in the early morning had been discontinued when Colonel Durnford arrived from Rorke's Drift, shortly before eleven o'clock, and all was then quiet and orderly. Lieutenant Milne, of the Royal Navy, had been able to view the camp through a powerful telescope from the summit of a high hill, and to assure the general that nothing unusual was happening there.

Colonel Durnford did not remain in camp longer than was necessary to ascertain the position of affairs, as it was understood by Colonel Pulleine. Matters were evidently involved in some doubt which it was highly necessary to clear up. He therefore took a step which had the accidental effect of drawing on an attack for which the troops were unprepared. Sending Captain George Shepstone along the ridge to the left, with a party of mounted natives, he proceeded himself toward the left front with the remainder of that force, leaving orders for the rocket battery to follow him. He passed somewhat to the right of a small conical hill standing at the base of the ridge, and proceeded, as it chanced, directly to the Zulu camp.

The Zulu army, which has been computed to have numbered about 20,000 men, may be said to have been composed of four divisions: (1) the Ulundi, comprising the Tulwana, with its Indhluyengwe auxiliaries, and the Indhlondhlo regiment; (2) the Gqikazi, consisting of the Dhlokwe, with auxiliaries called Makwentu; (3) the Nodwengu, comprising the Dududu, Isangqu and Nokenke; and (4) the Umcitshu, or Kandempemvu, the Umbonambi and Ingobamakosi regiments. There had been much agitation in the camp, occasioned by the firing that had taken place in the morning, and restraint was becoming difficult when Captain Shepstone, having seen a foraging party driving a small herd of cattle which they had found, pursued them to within view of it. He at once hastened to report the discovery which he had made, while two divisions of the Zulu army—those numbered three and four above—thinking they were being attacked, sprang to their arms and broke away from the control of their commanders. The companies leapt forward spontaneously to join their leaders or captains. It was about this time, as well as can be gathered, that Colonel Durnford came within sight of the Zulus. Division three had streamed out to the Zulu right, along the ridge of the Nqutu range; four had started out to the left, and this he at once encountered, fighting bravely, but borne back from post to post by superiority of numbers. His rocket battery never overtook him. Attracted by the firing it had deviated from the course which he had taken and proceeded to scale the ridge by way of the conical hill. Of what it accomplished little is known, but, as he retired in the direction of the camp, he found it to have been completely wrecked.

In the meantime the Zulu commanders had been using their utmost endeavours to restrain their men until they could be seated in an umkumbi, or semi-circle, and sent into the fight in proper battle order. In this they succeeded as regards divisions one and two; the process occupying a considerable time, and resulting in important events.

M

Several companies of the 24th Regiment were sent out on the ridge to the British left to stay the Zulu "right horn," while, reinforced by Natal Volunteers, Durnford made an obstinate stand against their left in the watercourse traversing the ground towards the right front.

But neither attempt was found possible. The Zulus describe the whizzing of bullets around them as having been like to the passing of a, swarm of bees. Cannons roared and shells burst in their midst. Hundreds fell pierced by the first or lacerated by the second. But still they pressed forward till they overwhelmed the infantry opposed to their right, and drove in the artillery; till the volunteers and native troops, from want of ammunition and close pressure, had to relinquish their position and fall back on the camp. By this time the Zulu right wing was streaming past both sides of the Isandhlwana Hill and threatening to cut off the only retreat, seeing which the mounted natives made a dash for safety through the neck, over which the column had come two days previously, and down the Manzamnyama Valley to a crossing in the Buffalo River, since known as Fugitive's Drift, saving also by their example some few of those Europeans who were not too long in following it.

How the end came must be left to the imagination of the readers. It was not witnessed by a European who lived to tell the tale. After those had left who were in time to get outside the Zulu circle, and some few of whom reached Natal soil and safety, there was still a struggle that lasted for a considerable time, the living witnesses to which are those Zulus only who were engaged in it. Some idea of its concluding scene can be gathered from the declamations of some of these, as, with staring eyes and foaming lips, they recount the incidents of their own progress to the goal. Pictures are presented of Zulus falling flat on the ground on the issue of smoke from the cannon to evade the projectiles; tossing their heads from side to side as the bullets passed close to the right or left of them; of the final assault when the soldiers stood at bay, and their men were seen slashed almost in two with swords, or their skulls shattered with clubbed rifles. But the awfulness of the scene would have been beyond the powers of description, even of any who might have beheld it. The aspect of the victorious Zulus was truly ferocious. There is a question which cannot be solved with certainty one way or the other—whether the king had ordered that quarter was to be given. By some it is stated that it was offered in some cases, but that the soldiers, not understanding, replied with sword-cuts and blows. It is plain that it was not expected, and that even had it been given in individual cases, it would have been impossible to protect for any length of time, in the fury that prevailed, those it might have been desired to save. Neither fighting nor surrender would serve to avert destruction, and escape by flight soon became hopeless. Little cairns of stones mark the resting places, along the line of retreat, of many who made the attempt; but the most fought and slew until they were themselves slain. The terrors of those who fled were scarcely lessened when the closing circle of the Zulus had been passed. The track leading to the river was such as to be at ordinary times considered scarcely practicable to a horse; to abandon their mounts would render it almost impossible to reach the river before the fleet foe that was pursuing, or to ford it if reached. There was the feeling that an impassable obstacle might be encountered at any moment. The straight stalks of the many aloes that grew on the stony hills around were scarcely distinguishable, at a distance, from the bodies of Zulus, and gave the impression that these were in countless numbers in all directions. So rough was the ford, and so strong was the stream, that those who did finally reach and enter it scarcely hoped to gain the other bank; many, indeed, were drowned in the attempt.

It is a belief amongst the Zulus that the swelling of men whom they have slain will produce a like effect in themselves; and to prevent the possibility of this it is their habit to disembowel those who fall to their arms. They therefore do not leave any alive of those they wound, but proceed to the extinction of life in order to perform this act of self-protection. There were none to recover of those they had overcome. All were dead. The closing scene has been described as a "butchery." But it seems comparable with one described by Lord Roberts in his book *Forty-one Years in India*, in which British troops, and not savages, were the victors. When, in one of the operations which preceded the relief of Lucknow, the Sikandrabagh was stormed, it was found to contain 2000 Indian troops. "They were," he says, "completely caught in a trap, the only outlet being by the gate-way and the breach, through which the troops continued to pour. There could be no thought of escape, and they fought with the desperation of men without hope of mercy, and determined to sell their lives as dearly as they could. Inch by inch they were forced back to the pavilion, and into the space between it and the north wall, where they were all shot or bayoneted. There they lay in a heap as high as my head, a heaving, surging mass of dead and dying inextricably mixed."

The battle of Isandhlwana was thus fought by a portion of the Zulu army which broke away from control; the portion which waited to receive orders was able only to follow up, finding the work done as they proceeded.

Of what had occurred in the camp the general and those with him were so completely ignorant that the commander of one of the native regiments, Commandant Lonsdale, rode into it during the afternoon and did not fully realise the true state of things until he saw the blood on the spears of the Zulu occupants. The force which Major Dartnell had descried on the previous day had melted away during the night. Small bodies only were seen, who

THE STORY OF THE ZULUS 181

opposed no resistance, but retired in the direction of the Isipezi Mountain. Some of these were shot, but the day's operations had been fruitless of important incidents. The general had selected a site for his next camp, and was returning to Isandhlwana without thought of anything untoward having happened there. Commandant Lonsdale met and enlightened him. To what thoughts such intelligence gave rise it is for the imagination to conceive. But the one course open in the circumstances was bravely and instantly adopted. The column, which had been ordered to bivouac, was recalled and marched back in fighting order through Isandhlwana Field, which lay in the only line of retreat out of the Zulu country. It was seen advancing by the Zulus, who were gradually retiring to their camping ground across the Nqutu range. They had fought their fight and would do no more that day. They were, indeed, too tired for further effort. Most of them had left their bivouac without having eaten; they had covered a great distance over very rough country, and their method of fighting had imposed great physical strain. After the fighting was over they lost no time in seizing upon the provisions in camp with which to satisfy their hunger. The Zulus were extremely ignorant at that time. Being forbidden to leave their own country, they had no opportunity of gaining any sort of knowledge of the things and ways of Europeans. What they found in bottles they drank, believing that it could only have been intended for slaking thirst. Many who found wines or spirits became intoxicated; others who found drugs of various kinds died or suffered various degrees of pain according to the action of the particular preparation they had chanced upon. Such as had regaled themselves too freely, or were ill from what they had taken, were found still in the camp when the returning column arrived; but no attempt at resistance was made. The unhappy soldiers, after driving out or despatching such inmates as they found, might lie down near their slain comrades till dawn without molestation.

But in the meantime a furious battle was raging at Rorke's Drift. The Ulundi and Gqikazi divisions had not been content that their share in the day's operations should only be to see the work done by those in their van. There was still the small post beyond the river left for them to take. It has been contended by some that there was much in the attitude of Cetshwayo for which the British authorities, both military and civil, should have been grateful. Amongst other instances it is affirmed that he forbade his commanders to proceed beyond the borders of his own territory. The crossing of the border for the purpose of attacking the post at Rorke's Drift was a spontaneous act on the part of a body of disappointed warriors, and affords no proof one way or the other. But there is the authority of his own brother, Undabuko, who may be assumed to have been to some extent in his confidence, in believing that he had not issued any explicit order on the subject. Undabuko told the writer that, on seeing that portion of the army which had not been engaged cross the border, he called to members of his own regiment, the Umbonambi, to join them; but that they declined on the ground that it was necessary to return to the field of battle to attend to their wounded.

The engagement at Rorke's Drift was very remarkable on both sides. The strength of the post there was in all a little over sixty men, made up of Royal Engineers and members of the 2nd battalion of the 24th Regiment, under the command of Lieutenants Chard and Bromhead. These officers received warning from Captain Gardner, a member of the general's staff who had been in the battle of Isandhlwana and seen that the day was lost there, that they might expect to be attacked by the whole Zulu army. With this expectation

THE STORY OF THE ZULUS 183

they fortified their position with biscuit boxes and other packages, and calmly awaited what might come. Their action was remarkable in regard to the courage it displayed. The assault upon them commenced between three and four o'clock in the afternoon, and was remarkable because, instead of abandoning the enterprise after the first repulse as is the usual habit with Zulus, they persisted in it all night. Again and again they stormed the breastworks, only to be shot or bayoneted. When finally they drew off between three and four o'clock in the morning there were nearly 400 of their number dead; thirteen of the defending force having been killed and nine wounded.

Lord Chelmsford returning to Natal in the early morning, and they to their own country, regarded each other at a respectful distance, neither being disposed to engage in further battle that day.

Another battle, the memory of which has been somewhat eclipsed by that of the events described, was fought on the same day as that at Isandhlwana between number one column and those members of the Zulu army whose residences were south of the Umhlatuzi River. Colonel Pearson was advancing towards Eshowe by a wagon-road now seldom used, a more direct one having been substituted. The field upon which he fought his battle is thus seldom seen. If seen, there is little of feature by which to remember it.

The leading columns having crossed the Inyezane stream and gone some distance, a halt was called for rest and breakfast, when the advance scouts came into contact with the Zulu impi. The attack developed by the Zulus throwing out wings and advancing, under cover of the clumps of trees that studded the ground, and firing their guns, with, however, but little precision of aim. As troops became available by the gradual shortening of the column they were disposed in defensive attitude; and by half-past nine o'clock the attack, which had commenced at about eight, had been effectively repulsed with a loss to the Zulus estimated by the British officers at about 400—but the number was never definitely ascertained—and a British loss of twelve killed and twenty-three wounded. Colonel Pearson was thus enabled to reach Eshowe on the 23rd of January, where he was obliged by the events that have been narrated to make a prolonged and painful sojourn.

CHAPTER XVI

THE awe in which the Zulu power had been held by the inhabitants of Natal had, for the moment, been allayed by the military force displayed along the border. The success that had attended his operations against the Cape frontier tribes had inspired them with a profound confidence in the general. The improvements that had lately been effected in the machinery of war had led the expressions, on the subject of the approaching conflict, to turn rather on the destruction that would be dealt out to any Zulu force that might dare to attack than on the possibility of a British reverse. The border farmers continued to reside on their farms, rejoicing in the ready market for their produce which the presence of troops created.

The news of Isandhlwana came as a thunder-clap out of the blue sky, and the resultant consternation was as extreme as its cause had been unexpected. They beheld themselves suddenly exposed to the mercy of the roused Zulus. There was no longer such a force on the border as could hope to stay their armies if they should decide on following up their success by invading the Colony. The Natal Native Contingent speedily melted away. They had proved useless. Commanded mostly by officers who could not speak their language, they had been led to war by methods to which their race had never been accustomed. The manner in which they were led made impossible the rapid encircling movements, the excitement of effecting which has always been the great stimulant in native attack. They were armed with shields and assegais, which were the arms of their race, but they had never had an opportunity of using them in a conflict or otherwise. They were required to face a foe stronger in numbers, and of greater courage than themselves, and armed with guns. The natives residing in Natal were no longer a warlike people. Their courage had languished with the absence of the discipline by which the Zulu kings had inculcated and maintained it in their own subjects. They had, moreover, fought their fight on this day, and been beaten; and that part of their nature, at least, which required that they should return to their homes was still active. On the day following that of the return from Isandhlwana they were observed to be packing up their kits and departing. The general proceeded to Pietermaritzburg; complete reorganisation had become necessary. Terror spread abroad. The people became agitated by thoughts of massacres such as had characterised the invasions by the armies of Dingana. Scarcely a family in the uplands remained in occupation of their homesteads. Before many days had elapsed the bulk of the white inhabitants of the northern part of the colony were wending their way, with their stock and such of their household goods as they could place on their wagons, towards the top of the Drakensberg. Those in other parts who could not avail themselves of the mountains were seeking other refuge. Natives in remote places sought out rocky fastnesses, and for a time took up their abode in them. Lieutenants Chard and Bromhead were credited, as time went on, with having repelled the invasion by their defence of Rorke's Drift, and great was the gratitude in which they were held.

But the Zulus had accomplished that which they had set out to do, and for the time they also desired to return to their homes. They had driven from their land one of the columns by which it had been invaded and completely disorganised another. It was their intention to drive out

THE STORY OF THE ZULUS 187

the invaders and not to assume aggressive action, and there still remained within their borders the columns called numbers one and four. In due time there might be another effort made to expel these, but a time was wanted to sorrow for those who had fallen. The country was sorely stricken. Grief had found its way to the homes of the people in its remotest parts, and sore was their wailing. There was no writing in the country, and the sorrows of that time are remembered now by few besides the living of those who bore them. There was in the country one white man who made some notes of the events passing immediately around him. His name was Cornelius Vijn, and what he saw and noted was edited by Bishop Colenso, and published in the form of a book entitled *Cetshwayo's Dutchman*. He had entered Zululand on the 1st of November, and, in spite of warnings of danger, had gradually penetrated to Ulundi. He had carried on for some time a successful trade there, and then proceeded farther north until he crossed the Black Umfolozi River. He had heard much of the talk of the Zulus on the political situation, but amidst all the excitement his person and property had been rigidly respected. When the war broke out he found his safety threatened, and claimed the king's protection, which was readily given. Cetshwayo sent men with orders to place him at the kraal of his brother Usiwedu, by the foot of the Sigwekwe Hill, near to Nongoma, and to see that no harm befell him.

While there, and, as he believed, on the 25th of January, he noted: " Our attention was drawn to a troop of people who came back from the gardens crying and wailing. As they approached I recognised them as persons belonging to the kraal at which I was staying. When they came into or close to the kraal they kept on wailing in front of the kraals; rolling themselves on the ground and never quieting down; nay, in the night they wailed so as to cut through the heart of any one. And this wailing went on night and day for a fortnight; the effect of it was very depressing. I wished I could not hear it.

"The reason of this was that the head-man of the kraal, Umsundusi, a trusty person and the husband of four wives, had fallen in the fight at Isandhlwana."

Not far from where Vijn witnessed these manifestations of grief may still be pointed out a spot where a wounded warrior succumbed, and was buried, after being helped home by his brethren over the weary hundred of miles from the field of battle. Thus, helping home the wounded, returning to mourn with their kindred for the slain, or, perhaps, to convey the spoil they had taken, did the men who composed the victorious army disperse themselves over the country, leaving no such force as might have been deemed sufficient for an invasion of Natal; scarcely such even as prudence might have suggested as necessary for the purpose of defence.

There was no public recognition of individual bravery; no name has been specially remembered as that of the doer of any specially heroic deed. Not even to the chief commander, Untshingwayo, has any personal credit been given, for the battle was won by a breach of his command. It was been left to individuals to inform the public themselves, if they desire and are able to, of their deeds of personal valour. The honour of the day was to some extent disputed between the two divisions; it was generally conceded that the brunt of the fighting had fallen to the lot of that which formed the left wing. There was thus little inducement to those who had private offices to perform either to return first to the king, or to remain in the ranks, after they had done what they considered they had been called together to do.

Thus far the nation had held well together. The promises of a happier state of things that had been held out by the British authorities to such as might yield peaceful submission had withdrawn but few from their allegiance. John Dunn had crossed into Natal with his numerous family and ample herds, thenceforth to be numbered with the foes of his benefactor. This was natural. It was clear to his superior intelligence that the British arms would necessarily prevail. He found that the king was no longer disposed to accept his counsel; that he was rather inclined to suspect his good faith. He was of a disposition to follow rather that course which would conduce the best to his continued prosperity than the dictates of a sense of obligation. But the number of those who followed him was not so great as had been anticipated, and scarcely affected the power of the nation.

Uhamu had not abandoned the hope of securing the kingship for himself by secession, but he had been unable, with personal safety, to carry out his design, and obliged to employ such force as he commanded in the interests of his reigning brother.

Usibebu had had some cause to be ill-disposed towards Cetshwayo. He had lately been apprised of a design against certain of his brothers, the execution of which he had resolved to resist. The necessity to try conclusions was obviated only by the crisis created by the English demands. He had been opposed, moreover, to entering upon what he knew would be a futile war, and counselled the surrender of Sirayo's sons and those others who had given offence to the British Government. But he had not only joined in the war, when once engaged upon, but been foremost in the fighting. He had pursued the fugitives into Natal, and seized a number of cattle within the border of the colony. This adventure led to his narrowly escaping death. Occupied till late in the evening with his efforts to get the booty through the river, he had been unable to reach Isandhlwana till darkness had set in. There was no moonlight, and he was not aware of the presence of the British troops until he found himself amongst them. Being unacquainted with the ground his escape was rendered extremely difficult. But, stumbling over boulders and falling into water-courses, he picked his way to, and eventually joined, his comrades with no worse injury than a broken finger. The mark of that injury he was to retain for life; but life itself was saved, and he was destined to play an important part in later events.

The Zulus had by their victory secured the whole of the arms and ammunition of that portion of the column with which they were engaged. The cannon were intact, and conveyed to the king's kraal, but were of no service to him owing to there being none who understood how to use them.

CHAPTER XVII

WHILE these events were in progress Piet Joubert was on the road to Pietermaritzburg. He and Paul Kruger had returned from England and reported to their constituents the result of their mission thither. A great meeting had been held to hear and consider the answer that the British Government had given to their prayer for retrocession of the Transvaal. The answer had been a refusal; but it was promised that fresh instructions would be communicated to the High Commissioner. The meeting had appointed a general committee, and the committee had adopted this resolution:

"That the committee, supported by the views of the people, could not rest satisfied with the answer of Sir Michael Hicks-Beach, and resolved to continue protesting against the injustice done, and, with the people, to concert further measures towards the attainment of their object."

Joubert's mission was to convey this resolution to Sir Bartle Frere; and from the letter of his instruction he could by no means be induced to depart. He had heard by the way of the disaster at Isandhlwana. At the interview on the 4th of February Sir Bartle Frere impressed upon him the seriousness of the situation; he might tell the people of the Transvaal that if they held aloof, and did not help to defend their own border, as they would have done in former days, terrible events might happen in Natal and elsewhere, so that none of those then present might be spared to take any part in the final settlement of affairs in the Transvaal. If every British subject were driven out of Natal it would not make the slightest difference in the determination of the English people to put forth all their power for the suppression of the Zulu opposition. The feeling of the English people was entirely in favour of doing all that could be done for the prosperity and happiness of their fellow-subjects in the Transvaal. He would have Joubert to judge of their feelings if they were left to accomplish all this task of resisting the Zulus without the help or sympathy of the Transvaal people, and in a contest which had arisen more for their rights and interests than for those of the English.

Should Cetshwayo succeed in driving the English into the sea he would certainly not rest there; and the state of those who remained after purchasing a temporary peace by standing aloof, would be that of serfs under Zulu masters. The effect of this standing aloof had already been manifested. Messengers from Cetshwayo conveying to Paul Kruger and others the intelligence of the disaster to the British troops, and pointing out that the opportunity was a favourable one for the Boers to rise against the British Government, had been intercepted. The messengers had been directed to beg that the Boers would at least sit still. He did not believe that either Mr. Kruger or any other leader of the people of the Transvaal would entertain any such overtures; but the incident showed how their standing aloof was viewed by the Zulu king. Then, in tones of solemn warning, he said: "I am an old man, and worn with work, and, should I come successfully out of these Zulu difficulties, I cannot hope to work for the Transvaal many years longer; but I hope that you will carefully bear in mind what I have said, for I believe that what I have now told you is God's truth in the matter, and, should we not meet again, I hope you will remember my parting words, and that, when they find themselves standing on the brink of a precipice, the Transvaal people will at least remember that I have warned them."

But by no means could he elicit any more favourable response from the Boer delegate than that it was the unanimous feeling of the people that they should have their independence; that they would be satisfied with nothing short of it.

The Boers of the Transvaal at this time were animated with but this one feeling: they would have back their land. Joubert, who represented them, could not express sympathy which his constituents did not share, nor promise assistance out of the difficulties in which the High Commissioner found himself involved, which he knew they were not disposed to give. "We will have back our land" was their only cry; it was the only answer that could be got by the numerous individuals who attempted to argue with individual Boers on the question whether it had been for their benefit or otherwise that the Transvaal had been annexed to the British Crown. The difficulties they had experienced with the Zulus, to remove which was the main object of the war, were entirely forgotten. They would take no part in the war. Piet Uys, a son of the commandant who fell at Itala in 1838, had, indeed, joined Colonel Wood with a number of his countrymen, and was conducting a kind of warfare which partook largely of the character of raiding. There was much heard of his exploits, which on the part of the British officers it was politic to extol, and which there was a predisposition on the part of his countrymen to regard as marked by great ability. But the general sympathy of the Boers was not with him; and, when finally he died in battle, his friends regretted that he had been so foolish as to involve himself in the war at all. His monument at Utrecht was erected by British officers; and there is reason to believe that this also was suggested by motives of policy.

Colonel Wood, the fame of whose achievements at this time was spreading far, had been operating against detached bodies of Zulus composed of members of local tribes, and had not encountered any portion of the regular army. The people whom he found most formidable were those of the Swazi chief Umbilini, whose surrender had been one of the demands of the Ultimatum. He was a man of great enterprise, and commanded a considerable force, with which he acted independently. Another section of the Zulu people with whom his attention was particularly engaged were the Abaqulusi. They occupied the valley of the Bivane stream, and derived their name from that of one of the Zulu kraals named Ebaqulusini, of which the mistress was Umkabayi, a sister of Senzangakona, and which had been removed thither on the extension of the Zulu king's dominions from his tribal domains in the White Umfolozi Valley. They were, as members of that kraal, the personal retainers of the king. They were then, and have continued to be, very strongly attached to the hereditary king. They were not strong enough to oppose effective resistance to the forces brought against them, and lost greatly in life and property, their kraals being burnt and their cattle taken. Uhamu, with his people, also occupied a portion of the country over which Wood's operations extended ; but the hope of his defection, which the British commander had entertained since the commencement of hostilities, led him to treat that chief with somewhat marked leniency, a circumstance which soon led the king to suspect his loyalty.

Fear of the result of this suspicion, and the hope of a kingship, gradually led him to a decision which he carried out at considerable peril, arriving at the camp at Kambula Hill, or as the place is generally named by the Zulus, Ingqaba-ka-Rawana—" the stronghold of Rawana " —on the 10th day of March 1879, bringing with him a considerable following, and so to some extent weakening the king's fighting force.

Colonel Pearson, who had fortified himself at Eshowe,

after Isandhlwana, was in a somewhat critical position. His supplies were not great, and the prospect in the minds of himself and all other Europeans was that of death to every member of his force, either from hunger or the assegai, unless relief came. There seems reason to believe that another course would have been possible, which, however, would have involved humiliation, and was not to be thought of. In one of a series of messages addressed by Cetshwayo to the British authorities, beginning immediately after the battle of Isandhlwana, he offered the column safe conduct to the Tugela, provided that the discussion of terms of peace might be entered upon.

The apprehended invasion of Natal did not take place.

While the Zulu king was endeavouring by frequent messages, the bearers of which would appear to have met with but scant courtesy at the hands of those to whom they were delivered, to secure the cessation of hostilities and a resumption of negotiations, he was also preparing for another effort to drive the enemy out of his land. His army, which was scattered all over the country, had to be got together and something decided as to the next step to be taken. This was to occupy about two months.

In the meantime British reinforcements were arriving in great numbers. The mounted corps raised in the colonies numbered, on the 16th of March, 1033 men, and the Imperial forces in the field 7520 men. The Natal Volunteers and Mounted Police were still on active service and numbered in all 334.

By that time the British forces had suffered another disaster. On the 12th Umbilini had attacked a transport train, which was being escorted to Luneburg by Captain Moriarty with a company of the 80th Regiment, at a crossing of the Intombi stream near that village, and killed 44 of them, including the commanding officer. Yet another and a more serious disaster was to follow.

This same chief had established himself on the top of

the Ihlobane Mountain—a lofty flat summit encircled by tall cliffs, with difficult access from west and north-east. Thither he and his following had taken their cattle, which might be viewed from Colonel Wood's camp, and formed a strong temptation.

On the 28th Buller (now Colonel) was sent with a considerable force to dislodge him and take his cattle. The force which engaged in this enterprise consisted of the Frontier Light Horse; a body of horse lately raised by Colonel Weatherley (a man who had since the annexation of the Transvaal been gaining some notoriety at Pretoria, and of whom a good deal may be read in the Blue Books and other publications of the time), and detachments of other mounted corps and Native Contingent. The Boer Commandant, Piet Uys, was with it. The ascent of the mountain was made from two directions, and the cattle were secured with but little loss or opposition. The defenders were mostly in hiding amongst the encircling rocks. So far as they were concerned the expedition had succeeded. But it chanced, by a fatal coincidence, that the Zulu army had been got ready for its second great effort, and was actually near to the Ihlobane Hill on its way to attack the Kambula camp. Although Umbilini was unable himself to repel the attack he could, by means of the clear voices of his men, acquaint this force with his position. The Zulu warriors in great numbers hastened to the scene, and the British force found, while resting and taking breakfast, that their retreat was being quickly cut off. It was necessary to make all haste down the mountain, and the steep, sharp western end, where the descent was made, may be viewed from Vryheid, and continues to be pointed out to visitors by the inhabitants of that village as a place of historical interest.

All that could be attempted was to escape with life and reach the camp. Many accomplished this, and Colonel Buller greatly distinguished himself by the bravery he dis-

THE STORY OF THE ZULUS

played during the perilous retreat. But the loss was great. Colonel Weatherley perished with all his men, except one officer and a few others. The Frontier Light Horse also lost heavily, some thirty being killed. Other corps lost smaller numbers, but altogether the loss, in European troops, amounted to some 100 killed. The Native Contingent, known as Wood's Irregulars, also suffered heavily, and were so discouraged that all their survivors deserted from the Kambula camp that night. They had possibly realised, better than others did, what the real situation was and what would happen on the morrow.

On this day there occurred another instance of betrayal by a Zulu of his country, with no other object than that of personal gain. A petty chief named Umbangulana obtained access to Colonel Wood and informed him, with great exactness, of the plans of the Zulu commanders. The camp was to be attacked next day at a particular time. The army was large, and it would be necessary to prepare stout resistance.

Indeed, the position of the column was a critical one. The food supply of the country had become plentiful with the advance of the season. The men of the Zulu army were in better fighting condition than when they were called upon to advance on Isandhlwana. They were in greater number, better fed, and their successes had made them feel confidence in their powers. All the available strength of the nation was being put into this effort, under the personal command of the prime induna, Umnyamana. On the other hand, there had been much of a nature calculated to unnerve those against whom they were about to launch themselves. The only occurrence in the war calculated to inspire courage was the defence of Rorke's Drift. This had shown the great advantage conferred by breastworks, and might induce the hope that the entrenched position at Kambula, with the force it contained, would be able to resist, as was about to become necessary, the bulk of the Zulu army. There was also the consciousness in the defenders that defeat would mean annihilation.

This most important battle in the Zulu War began at the time at which Umbangulana said it would begin—at half-past one o'clock after noon, on the 29th day of March, and lasted till half-past four, or three hours.

One portion of the Zulu army was led by retiring cavalry to make a somewhat precipitate rush upon the camp. They were mown down by bullets, and those other divisions which arrived at the position later from other directions were deprived of their co-operation. The attack was, however, pressed with great determination and courage. A portion of the British camp was entered. A cattle-enclosure was seized, but could not be held. Retreat became a rout, and those who took part in the affair say that only darkness saved them eventually from destruction. They were hotly pursued by British Horse, while light lasted, and their loss was enormous. In his report on the following day Colonel Wood stated that he estimated the Zulus killed at 1000, and he was probably within the mark. The Zulus counted their losses in an imperfect way. The commanders of the different regiments, or divisions, made up an estimate from information they were able to obtain from subordinate officers. It was generally stated, as the result of the number arrived at, that the loss sustained at Isandhlwana, including Rorke's Drift, was small when compared with that of this day. It had a most disheartening effect, and subsequent fighting was engaged in with but little spirit.

The estimate made by Colonel Wood of the strength of the Zulu force which attacked him was probably within rather than without the mark. And, if 20,000 were the number, the loss as stated by him to have been inflicted was equal to one in twenty or five per cent. But the number given was that of killed alone, and the estimate

THE STORY OF THE ZULUS 199

was made from Zulus that were left dead on the field. A greater number were doubtless wounded, many of whom, though able to move off the field, never reached their kraals. They were far from home, and there was little in the way of surgical appliance available. The locality where the battle was fought was the most sparsely inhabited in the country; almost the whole of the force had come from great distances. They had no means of travelling other than what was afforded by their own legs; but few had even friendly help. The sufferings that result from such circumstances are but imperfectly appreciated by those who are so fortunate as to escape unhurt. To obtain an idea of what they were it is necessary to ask for the experience of those who received wounds. That of a chief now living, and well known, may be taken as an example. The attack had failed, and the Zulus were in full retreat. He was armed with a Martini-Henri rifle, and being still within range, he conceived and proceeded to gratify a desire to have a last shot at the camp. It chanced by coincidence that some one there also was trying the effect of long-range firing at the retreating Zulus. As he drew the trigger a bullet from an unseen foeman in the English camp struck off his thumb and smashed the stock of his rifle. He was without help beyond his own resources, and the loss of blood was rapid and gradually producing weakness. Almost unconsciously he rushed into a native hut which he chanced upon, and there, to his consternation, found himself in the presence of the commander-in-chief, Umnyamana. In this place he could not rest; but being recognised as a son of Dilikana, the chief of the Amambata, such help as could be procured was at last afforded.

There was again mourning throughout the country. The border agents in Natal reported much wailing, which could be heard across the Tugela River.

The Zulus were soon to experience another defeat.

The Commander-in-Chief, Lord Chelmsford, writing on the 25th of March, stated that, thanks to the rapid despatch of reinforcements, he felt able to advance in three days with a strong column to relieve the garrison at Eshowe, which had then been holding that post for upwards of ten weeks.

The preparations considered necessary for this advance show how differently the Zulu power had come to be regarded by that time. The force which mustered was formed into two divisions, consisting respectively of 1660 European troops and 1480 Native Contingent, with two nine-pounder guns, two twenty-four-pounder rocket-tubes and one Gatling gun; and 1680 European troops and 800 Native Contingent, with two twenty-four-pounder rocket-tubes and one Gatling gun; in all, 3340 white and 2280 native fighting men, or a total of 5620. Yet the general had some misgivings as to his ability to carry out his object if opposed by the whole strength of the Zulu army. With the view of creating a diversion in his favour he had ordered all the officers commanding the several military posts along the border to make simultaneous raids into the Zulu country. The character of the war had now changed. The action of the people in supporting the king as they had done with their arms, had led him to regard them as having so identified themselves with the war that it could no longer be regarded as directed against the king personally. When the general heard of the reverse which his forces had sustained at Ihlobane he believed that the attack upon that place had been made in compliance with the order he had issued. He was most fortunate in regard to his wish for a diversion; but the circumstance that the Zulu army was marching on Kambula while he was preparing to march to the relief of Eshowe was entirely fortuitous. That the bulk of the opposing army was engaged in the north at the time chosen by him for operations in the south was one of those accidents by which the course of the war was so conspicuously marked.

Eshowe was relieved on the 3rd day of April, five days after the battle of Kambula. The relieving force was attacked on the previous day at Gingindhlovu, one of Cetshwayo's military kraals, by such force as could be mustered south of the Umhlatuzi River. The site of the battle is traversed by the road from the railway station of that name to Eshowe. The men advanced bravely, entirely without cover, some getting within a hundred yards of the British firing lines, but were repulsed with heavy loss, the number of their killed being estimated at 700.

John Dunn accompanied the general as guide, and not only afforded valuable information and advice, but utilised his own rifle with much effect in the battle against his late fellow-subjects. The wagons had been drawn into a square for defence, after the manner of a Dutch laager. Upon one of these he perched himself, and, with the sure aim acquired by long practice on wild animals, he "picked off his men," counting at the end of the fight that he had killed some thirty.

The battle was of short duration, and the casualties on the British side were few.

The beleaguered garrison was much in need of the relief which the general was enabled by the result of the action to afford it. Sickness was rife amongst the men. Their food supply was running short, so that, even though living on short rations, their stock could not much longer have saved them from the choice between casting themselves, with such strength as they had, upon the investing enemy in the forlorn hope of forcing their way through his lines, or of submitting themselves to his mercy, a course which it was believed would be followed by the indiscriminate massacre of the whole force.

The commanding officer claimed for the column that in holding Eshowe it had contributed to the safety of Natal, because it had necessitated the employment of a large force in its investment which might otherwise have been used for the invasion of the Colony. Beyond this it is not recorded that it accomplished much. A force had sallied out in the direction of the Umhlatuzi River and burnt a kraal of the king's brother, Dabulamanzi, and shot some twelve fleeing Zulus. At another time foraging parties had gone out and taken supplies of corn-cobs from the fields in the vicinity, to the great sorrow, no doubt, of the women whose labour had raised the crops. Of even such occurrences there had been but few to vary the condition of being simply shut up within the walls of a fort during the long, weary, and anxious period that had elapsed since the column had arrived with the joyful sense of having fought the victorious battle of Inyezane, or, as the Zulus call it, of Iombane.

CHAPTER XVIII

THE third and last phase of the war was now to begin. Its development was to occupy just three months, dating from the relief of Eshowe. Its termination was to be in the destruction of the Zulu national system.

The Zulus had been disposed, since the beginning of the war, to remain within the borders of their own country. They were now so discouraged by the two reverses they had sustained in such rapid succession, that they had little inclination even to fight more. The land was filled with mourning.

A sense of security had been restored to the white inhabitants of Natal. They had been gradually resuming occupation of their deserted homes. The continued augmentation of troops had created a market such as colonists had not before experienced. Whatever they had to sell now realised prices, in cash, that were beyond the most extravagant hopes they had ever entertained. There were provident men laying the foundations of wealth, and men of the opposite tendency who were revelling in temporary plenty; an air of prosperity and happiness prevailed.

Cetshwayo made several attempts to secure the opening of peace negotiations. His messengers were not well received, the military authorities being disposed to regard them rather as spies than accredited envoys. Much difficulty was experienced in getting his representations heard by the officer who alone was empowered to deal with them. Lord Chelmsford insisted that any messenger sent on the subject should go direct to him. It was not easy for the Zulu king to become acquainted with this requirement, or to ascertain where the general was to be found when it did become known to him. It was not till the 6th of June, when preparations for another advance on Ulundi had been completed, that anything like definite communications were opened on the subject. Three messengers who had arrived at his camp on the previous day were admitted to an audience and informed by the general of the terms upon which he would be prepared to discuss proposals for peace.

The warlike preparations had been extensive. The general had under his command a force of 17,528 men, consisting of 9364 Imperial Infantry, 3957 Colonial Infantry, 1190 Imperial Cavalry, 1877 Colonial Cavalry, 755 Artillery (with 36 guns), and 385 Engineers. He had ample power to crush that of the Zulus, and was revolving in his mind a matter of greater difficulty, what new order of things should be set up amongst the Zulu people when their existing system of government should have been abolished.

One resolution had been definitely arrived at, that the Zulu power was a thing which it was necessary to crush. " I can see no alternative," wrote Sir Bartle Frere, " compatible with our duty, but effectually to crush the Zulus and govern them, as other South African races, subject to the British Crown and Government.

"It seems to me that no terms can possibly be made with Cetshwayo which can be compatible with such a result save with the indispensable preliminary of his entire submission."

With this view the general was entirely agreed. He also expressed his concurrence in the views expressed by one Charles Brownlee, once Secretary for Native Affairs in the Cape Colony, who, by reason of long experience of South African races, was credited with possessing great knowledge regarding them. Mr. Brownlee's suggestions were:

(1) That the whole of the Zulu army should be disarmed and disbanded: that each regiment, headed by its officers, and armed and dressed in regimentals, be required to lay down their arms and war-dress before an officer appointed to receive the surrender, the commander-in-chief, Umnyamana, and Cetshwayo's brother, Dabulamanzi, being required to be the first in performing this act of submission;

(2) That every article taken by the Zulu forces in the several engagements should be surrendered at the same time; that thereafter it should be held penal to possess any article, or shred of an article, so taken;

(3) That every clan incorporated by Tshaka should be made independent of the Zulus, and their government be administered independently by their hereditary chiefs;

(4) That Cetshwayo should no longer be supreme in the Zulu clan proper, but that his authority be divided between his brothers;

(5) That no execution of any kind whatever should take place without the approval of the British Resident; and

(6) That a British Resident should be appointed, with supreme authority, under the High Commissioner or Governor of Natal.

It was on the 2nd of June that Lord Chelmsford wrote concerning these suggestions that he favourably regarded them. Up to this time it is clear that he had but very imperfectly grasped the problem which final victory would present for his solution.

Its solution, was, indeed, to be placed in other hands. The course of events in South Africa was exciting grave concern in the minds of the English Government. The main object for which Sir Bartle Frere had been appointed to the office of High Commissioner—that of securing Federation—had not been advanced. The lately acquired Transvaal territory was promising serious trouble. Sir Bartle Frere had visited the camps of the disaffected and tried whether diplomatic language would reconcile them to the new order of things; but they had still the one answer only: they would have their independence. And their temper showed a disposition to seek it by other means if words should fail. There was still a lingering hope that Federation might be possible, and it was desired on the part of the Government that Sir Bartle Frere should be able to devote more time to that subject than was practicable while his responsibilities extended over so wide and troublous a field. And matters had arisen which seemed to render it desirable that there should be at the scene of action a combination of both military and civil authority in an officer of standing. A difference had occurred between the Lieutenant-Governor of Natal and the general commanding the army regarding the right of the latter to employ certain native levies outside the borders of the Colony. In addition to those natives who had been enrolled into regiments for the purpose of the operations against the Zulus, certain others had been called together for the purpose of protecting the border of Natal. The general, desiring that raids should be made into the Zulu country, ordered that these men should take part. The Lieutenant-Governor maintained that the general had no right to order such service without his authority as supreme chief over the native population; that their being so employed was, moreover, not in accordance with the understanding arrived at between them, and contrary to the purpose for which the men had been engaged. The general, on the other hand, asserted that the position taken up by the Lieutenant-Governor was an interference with his command, and expressed his inability to employ the native regiments unless his absolute authority over all the forces in the field were secured. The question being submitted to the Government in England, was answered by the appointment, on the 25th of May, of Sir Garnet Wolseley to supreme military command and as Special Commissioner for the territories of South-Eastern Africa situate to the northward and eastward of the Colony of Natal and the Transvaal territory, and not included within the territory of the Orange Free State or any foreign power; and as Governor of the Colony of Natal and the Transvaal territory, with power to supersede, at his discretion, the Lieutenant-Governor or Administrator respectively. To him, therefore, was to fall the duty of establishing the new order of things after the old should have been abolished.

But in the meantime the general in command, till his arrival, had to give some preliminary attention to the subject, because an answer had to be given to Cetshwayo's messengers. The answer which he sent partook largely of Brownlee's suggestions. "If," he said, "Cetshwayo wishes for peace he must give substantial proof of being in earnest. He must at once restore all horses, oxen, arms, ammunition and other property taken during the war. One or more regiments, to be named by me, must come under a flag of truce, and, at a distance of one thousand yards from my camp, lay down their arms as a token of submission. If this is done I shall order cessation of hostilities pending discussion of final terms of peace. Until this is done Her Majesty's troops will continue to advance."

The messengers represented the impossibility of carrying out the requirement regarding the arms and ammunition, for the reason that these were distributed amongst the Zulus over the whole country; upon which this requirement was modified to the extent that the two seven-pounder guns taken at Isandhlwana, and the oxen then at the king's kraal, would be accepted. It was required that these should be brought by one of the ambassadors to whom the ultimatum was delivered at the Tugela in December, and that he should at the same time bring a promise from the king that all arms, &c., when collected, would be given up. It was also agreed by the general that the surrender of one regiment would be accepted.

Lord Chelmsford was at this time at the Nondweni stream with the second division, commanded by General Newdigate, and consisting of 3364 Infantry, 1303 Cavalry and 300 Artillery (two batteries), and 58 Engineers.

Some miles in advance was the flying column, commanded by General Sir Evelyn Wood, who had been promoted and distinguished for his operations in the north and in the action at Kambula. He had marched from that place to join in the advance now proceeding on Ulundi. The strength of this column consisted of 2278 Infantry, 807 Cavalry, 194 Artillery and 95 Engineers, making the total advancing force up thus to 5642 Infantry, 2110 Cavalry, 494 Artillery and 843 Engineers, or a total strength of 9089 men.

Sir Evelyn Wood's march from Kambula had been marked by what has been characterised as the most lamentable event of the war. The war had excited much interest and had attracted to its scene, amongst others, the Prince Imperial of France, who desired to see active service. He had attached himself to Wood's column, and, during the march, had gone out with a scouting party under Captain Carey. The party had halted to rest at a spot in the vicinity of the Nqutu Range and near to the source of the Intshotshose stream. It was an ill-chosen spot, for not only did it command no distant view, but the ground was cut up by dongas, or nullahs, which afforded complete shelter, to within a hundred yards of it, for an approaching enemy. The party was thus surprised by a body of Zulus, who had been sent out as scouts by the local tribes from the fastnesses in which they had taken refuge. On seeing that they were about to be attacked the scant time available was utilised by the party in preparation for a retreat. Haste was necessary, and the prince's horse becoming so excited that he could not mount it, he was left no choice but to abide his death; the rest of the party, led by their commanding officer, all except two made good their escape. The most painful feeling to which the event gave rise was that caused by the apparent absence of any attempt on the part of his companions to rescue the prince from the situation in which his unruly horse placed him.

It was reckoned that the messengers leaving the general's camp on the 6th of June should be able to reach the king in time to enable him to return an answer in eight days. But they had been given a written document embodying the general's demands, and, on receipt of this, Cetshwayo, desiring to know its contents, sent for Cornelius Vijn, who was still dwelling in security at the foot of the Sigwekwe Hill, as the only available person capable of reading it. And it is characteristic of the Zulu race that not even in the extremity at which matters had arrived did dignity permit of hurry.

The distance from Ulundi to the place where Vijn resided was about thirty miles. How long it took the messengers to cover this distance in the outward journey is not precisely known, but Vijn's own account of that in which he accompanied them back to Ulundi shows how leisurely the matter was proceeded with:

"It was a rainy morning when we started. At every kraal we came to they had to supply us with food and find also food for the horses, which was readily done without a murmur. On the other side of the Black Umfolozi" (ten miles from the starting place) "we decided to pass the night at one of the kraals; we got there at 3 P.M., so that there was time to slaughter a beast, since we would gladly have something to eat. Also we were so fortunate as to find there a good quantity of beer, which was acceptable after a long ride on horseback. . . . Next morning we went on again. Our way passed through bush country the whole day, and we saw nothing but troops of Zulus going up continually to the king. . . . An hour before sunset we came out of the bush into the open, and stayed to sleep at the first kraal we came to. . . .

"Next morning the weather was quite different. The morning-tide promised a very pleasant day, and we passed on our way more vigorously to the Umbonambi, one of the royal kraals, where the king was, at the present moment, staying. About 11 A.M. I rode into the kraal."

After being provided with refreshment, Vijn was presented with the document, which was, indeed, addressed to himself, and requested to translate it. This was done by and to the prime minister, Umnyamana. Next day he was called into the presence of the king and requested to write an answer. Though never delivered to Lord Chelmsford owing, apparently, to the difficulty the king's messengers experienced in approaching the British camp, this document has been preserved in *Cetshwayo's Dutchman*. It displayed no humility on the part of Cetshwayo, nor readiness to negotiate on any but equal terms. It merely asked how he could discuss the subject of peace while the English army was in his country killing his subjects, burning their homes and carrying off their cattle.

And, indeed, while his messengers were at Nondweni delivering the king's message to Lord Chelmsford, Colonel Buller had issued from the camp of the Flying Column and was shooting and burning the kraals of the people on the western base of the Zungunyana Mountain; and, even as the king was dictating his reply to the general, the same officer, with some 250 Horse, was away in the direction of the Intabankulu carrying out operations which he thus describes:

"Soon after daylight we attacked the kraals on the east side of the Intabankulu and those in the Ulenjana Valley simultaneously. Many were completely surprised, and some in the valley had been warned of our coming and hastily left. The Zulus made but slight resistance, and we captured about 300 head of cattle, principally cows and calves, and about 100 sheep and goats, killing twelve Zulus and taking one man and about fifteen women and children prisoners. As we went up the Ulenjana Valley the number of the enemy increased rapidly: towards the head they were so many, and the country was so impracticable for horses, that I deemed it advisable to retire without burning three of the kraals at the head of the valley. In all we burned about twenty-four kraals."

It was probably from the locality of this action that the party had gone out at whose hands the Prince Imperial met his death, and the people could not claim that they were not hostile.

The method of causing diversions adopted in connection with the relief of Eshowe had been steadily pursued. When the general began this, his final movement into the Zulu country, he issued orders similar to those then issued. Thus on the 22nd of May three bodies of Native Contingent had crossed the Tugela opposite to Krantzkop and destroyed the kraals that lay within their reach, and done such other injury to the people as was practicable. It was especially provoking to the Zulus that these depredations were committed by Natal Kafirs. One of the sufferers was the chief son of Undhlela, Godide, whose kraal was destroyed by fire. Much was heard of this event afterwards; for, a month later, on the 22nd of June, a body of Zulus numbering about 1000 and guided by one Beje, a man who had removed into the Zulu country from Natal shortly before the commencement of the war, made a reprisal which formed the most serious inroad into Natal of any that had been made by the Zulus since the war began. Some twenty-two kraals were burnt and a number of natives killed, including some women and children, and captives were taken and cattle carried off. For his part in this enterprise Beje was afterwards tried, as a British subject, and convicted of high treason; and much discussion followed regarding the legality or justice of the proceeding.

These events were all that specially marked the progress, or the period, of the march on Ulundi. Another overture, accompanied by some 100 head of cattle and some tusks of ivory, was rejected by the general because it was not a complete compliance with his demands; a last one, to be accompanied by a number of cattle out of the king's special white herd and the two cannon taken at Isandhlwana, was attempted only, the warriors turning the cattle back, as they doubtless considered they were expected by the king to do, and declaring that they would die rather than submit to the English. The sword of the Prince Imperial, also sent by the king, was apparently all that reached the general.

Negotiations being thus ended, and the short armistice granted by the general having expired, a reconnaissance was made by Colonel Buller as far as the Nodwengu kraal on the 3rd of July. The undertaking was attended with great risk, and Buller narrowly escaped being cut off with his entire force, but he escaped without great loss, having chosen a site for the morrow's battle which was the most perfect possible for the method of fighting it had been decided to employ. The spot is still marked by the low breast-works that were hastily thrown up before the fight began and numerous empty cartridge cases. From all sides the ground falls gradually away, rendering it impossible to approach without being exposed to full view at a great distance. To this spot the troops marched, in hollow square, in the early morning of the 4th of July, having crossed the White Umfolozi River on the right, or south-eastern side of the precipitous hill overlooking the ford.

The conflict which ensued was called by the English, and became known as, the battle of Ulundi; but, having been fought in front of the chief kraal of Umpande, the Nodwengu, it was, perhaps more correctly, so named by the Zulus. It is curiously known also, and equally well, as the battle of the sheet-iron fort—"Ocwecweni." How this name came to be applied to it is not clearly known, but it may be assumed that the flash of the infantry bayonets, on the four sides of the square, gave the idea of four walls of tinned sheet-iron.

The storm of bullets which proceeded from the four sides of this square proved so destructive to life that the Zulus soon became convinced that approach was impossible, and broke and fled, pursued by Lancers and Dragoons who at once issued from within it. The ground was well suited to cavalry pursuit, and great havoc was wrought by them amongst the flying warriors.

Cetshwayo, after arranging the disposition of his men, had betaken himself to a kraal on the hills to the southeast, from a summit of which he either watched the battle personally or was kept informed of its progress by sentinels. Neither he nor his people had entertained any real hope of success. Kambula had practically decided the issue of the war. The hope that had arisen from the absence of a fort was quickly dispelled by the impression that one had been built of iron. The war was ended.

Many Zulus had been killed and wounded. Their number will never be known. The survivors scarcely know for what definite cause they fought. They had heard of the discussion of various subjects of difference; of various representations being made by the British authorities. But as to what the exact purport of these representations was they were generally ignorant. Some say, metaphorically, that they reached their ears in the cracking of rifles.

The result in mortality, on the British side, during the

war, is set forth on the monument that was erected to commemorate it in Pietermaritzburg:

> "In Memory of Honour
> and
> In Hope of Peace."

The number there given is 977 European officers and men, and 487 natives; altogether 1464.

ZULU WAR MONUMENT

CHAPTER XIX

THE Dragoons and Lancers were slashing and spearing the vanquished warriors as they fled in aimless despair over the plains that surround the site of the Nodwengu kraal. The king set forth to seek safety from their fury in the wilderness that lay to the east, in the valley of the Black Umfolozi River. As he descended the heights from whence he had viewed the battle there rose behind them, and him, dark columns of smoke, telling of the destruction of his dwellings that was proceeding. He had become a wanderer whose concern it would be to find refuge; who would be allowed no voice in matters relating to the restoration of peace in his country. For nearly two months he was thus to wander.

When, by a circuitous course, he reached after some days the kraal of his prime minister, Umnyamana, Ekushumayeleni, built on a mountain terrace overlooking the Isikwebezi River, he issued an order that the Zulu people were to make their peace with the victors; for he recognised that hope no longer lay in fighting. There he might also rest for a short space. Sir Garnet Wolseley had arrived and assumed command of the troops and the functions of High Commissioner. Lord Chelmsford's authority in the country had ceased. Immediately after the battle which crowned his victory he had withdrawn from its scene. For a short time there was quiet. But it was marred by the consciousness that retribution would be required. In the brief quiet which Cetshwayo was permitted to enjoy it was necessary that he should ponder this, and speculate as to what form it might take. The question occurred: What precisely was the wrong he had committed to bring this ruin upon him? His attitude towards the missionaries?—these had been very troublesome people. His refusal to permit his soldiers to marry?—he would no longer withhold this from any but the youngest of his regiments. He would cause a letter to be written praying that, for pity, he might be permitted to retain the country of his fathers; and would promise to surrender all his cattle when these could be got together. Cornelius Vijn was with him, in the retreat he had been carried along: he would write that letter.[1] He did not yet know the decision arrived at after the battle of Ulundi to accept nothing from him short of personal and unconditional surrender.

After a sojourn of some two weeks he repaired to the kraal of his brother, Usiwedu, on the Nongoma Ridge, and there the intelligence reached him ere long that the British troops had returned to the vicinity of Ulundi. News came also that he was threatened with an inroad of Swazis from the north. It was necessary to do something. He sent Umnyamana to the Commander-in-Chief with an instalment of cattle, and Vijn to say that the remainder were being collected and would be handed over. The first of these messengers, on arrival at his destination, was regarded as having come to treat on his own behalf; the second agreed for a sum of money to induce the king to surrender. He came back, not with any answer to the message he had borne, but offering that personal advice, compliance with which would have secured substantial pecuniary benefit to himself. In this he was disappointed. His advice was not accepted, but he was at once sent back with a definite proposal of terms. This time for answer there came a force of cavalry, numbering some 500, and, at their head, as guide, rode Cornelius Vijn, still hoping to gain his reward by showing them where the king was.

It was, therefore, necessary again to fly. The kraal

[1] *Cetshwayo's Dutchman.*

THE STORY OF THE ZULUS 217

at which Vijn had left him was that of Zonyama,[1] on the heights west of, and overlooking, the Umona stream. It was forty miles from Ulundi. The road lay across broken, stony and wooded country. The night was dark, and the progress of so large a body of cavalry was necessarily slow. Before the Nongoma Ridge could be reached the sun was high in the heavens. Notice of their approach was forwarded by the people who perceived it, and, when Zonyama's kraal was eventually reached, an hour after noon, Cetshwayo was not there. He had crossed the deep and steep valley to the kraal of his relative, Unkabonina, on the opposite hill, where dwell the Hlabisa tribe. Thither the weary pursuers had to follow. The path descends by the south side of the Undunyeni Hill, and the few who may chance to travel by it will realise to some extent the experience of those jaded cavalrymen. It was not to be expected that they would find the king awaiting them on the opposite side; but, if the scent could be renewed there, something might be gained. There was, however, in the people at this place much of the kind of sentiment which so conspicuously characterised the Highland Scotch when, in like plight, Prince Charles Stuart sought refuge from his pursuers amongst their hills, and which has so enriched their songs since that event. They could not be induced by threats, or any other means, to disclose what they knew of the course the king had taken. Not till a considerable time had elapsed could a clue be found, and this led down the steep hills, in a southerly direction, to the valley of the Black Umfolozi River, near where the Umona stream joins it, amid a profusion of trees, cacti and various tangle, and where, more hopelessly baffled, the troops formed detached parties and wandered wildly, ending in a sorrowful and disappointed return to headquarters. They had, at times, nearly come up with the object of their pursuit, who had ascended the valley.

[1] Nephew of Sotobe.

Other parties went out with no better success. But, although the sentiment of loyalty was strong, it is a quality in the Zulu upon which too much reliance should never be placed in time of adversity. The places at which the king, or, as termed by them, the shadow of him, had been seen began ere long to be whispered. Guides were found to conduct parties to such places or localities. Gradually information became more definite, till at last, on the 28th of August, a party of Dragoons under Major Marter were able to make sure of his hiding. At a kraal on the southern slope of the Ingome Range, some way west of the Ibululwana stream, and near to a detached portion of the great Ingome Forest, he was surrounded and taken. By whom his retreat was definitely pointed out has remained a secret, except for a suspicion that has attached to Umnyamana. It is certain that it could not have been discovered except by the aid of some of the king's own people. He was tired and travel-worn. Neither he nor any of his men made any attempt at resistance. He was hurried away to the coast and sent by ship to Cape Town, there, for the time, to be confined in the Castle.

The incidents of his wandering have been well remembered by the Zulus. The paths he trod and the places where he took rest or shelter are pointed out and regarded with interest.

To the removal of his person there could be no opposition made: but it was soon to be found that the suppression of the influence he had gained over the minds of the people was a matter of much greater difficulty.

The task set Sir Garnet Wolseley was to establish a new order of things in which the king was to have no share; to divide the country into a certain number of "states or principalities," each under an independent ruler, bound by engagements directly with the Imperial Government. The number of these principalities was eventually fixed at thirteen. Sir Garnet Wolseley was at Ulundi settling the details of this arrangement. It must be left to doubt whether the notion of reviving the clans that were incorporated into the Zulu nation by Tshaka was seriously considered. There were few of the hereditary chiefs that could have been found to assume the position from which their fathers had been deposed, and perhaps fewer still of the clans they ruled in anything like an organised condition. The Zulu element had entirely pervaded the nation. Such chiefs as there were, were either related or owed their position to the king. There was but one clan which had maintained anything like an unbroken existence, the Umtetwa. Its chief, though not of direct descent, was of the family of Dingiswayo, by whom the example of kingship was set which Tshaka perfected. But he had married a daughter of the Zulu house, and in this now lay his chief distinction. Umgojana was a grandson of the Ndwandwe chief Zwidi, and occupied the hereditary lands of his tribe; but he also had married a sister of Cetshwayo, and for his restoration his father, Somapunga, had been, as has been seen, indebted to Tshaka. Of the people who had composed the clan but few were with him.

That these two men were chosen would indicate that the idea was not entirely lost sight of; but of the other eleven chiefs appointed one was an Englishman, one a Basuto who had never resided in the country, two members of the Zulu family and others were indunas, or descendants of indunas, of the Zulu kings.

With some exceptions, these men would scarcely have been prepared to undertake the duties imposed by their appointments but for the feeling that the British Government would afford them practical support. The people, feeling that their defeat had been complete, were prepared, for the time being, to acquiesce in any arrangement which the conquering power might make. They also did not fully realise that the power which had beaten them was being withdrawn from any share in their control.

The country was duly divided, and the limits of the portion assigned to each of the thirteen chiefs were marked with beacons, which long continued to form useful landmarks.

The settlement became known as that of Sishwili, the name of the plain in front of the Ulundi kraal upon which it was concluded.

It was destined to last some three years, and to effect important changes in the condition of the people. There was to be a good deal of blood spilt during that period, but, on the whole, the people were to enjoy privileges that were new to them and which they highly prized. It was to be terminated by the substitution of another, under which more blood was to be spilt and the country thrown into a state of greater confusion.

CHAPTER XX

EACH of the thirteen chiefs promised as a condition of appointment that he would not permit the existence of the Zulu or any other system of military organisation within his territory; that he would permit all men to marry who desired to do so; that he would permit men to go to Natal and the Transvaal, or elsewhere, to work for wages; that he would not allow the lives of his people to be taken except by sentence passed in council and after a fair and impartial trial and the hearing of witnesses; that he would not tolerate the employment of witch-doctors; that he would not sell or alienate any of the land of his territory; that all people desiring to leave his territory would be permitted to do so freely; that all arms found in the possession of his people would be handed over to the British Resident, as also all cattle that had belonged to Cetshwayo; that he would not permit the importation of firearms into his territory; that he would observe and respect the boundaries of his territory and not make war upon any other chief without the sanction of the British Resident; that in all disputes in which British subjects were involved he would abide by the decision of the British Resident, and that he would not hold any trial upon a British subject without that officer's consent. The nomination of his successor should be in accordance with the laws and customs of the Zulu people, and subject to the approval of the British Government.

As to the people, all that was required of them was that they should yield due submission to the chiefs in whose territory they elected to reside. But that which constituted due submission was a matter the definition of which had in a large measure to be left to the chiefs, and, in some cases, there were to arise serious differences on the point between them and their subjects.

With the appointment of these chiefs the British Government transferred to them such sovereignty as had been acquired by the conquest; for the right to exercise any sort of influence over the affairs of the country it depended on compliance by them with their promise that in certain matters they would be guided by the advice of the British Resident.

To this latter office was appointed Mr. (afterwards Sir) Melmoth Osborn, till then, since the annexation of the Transvaal, the Government Secretary in that territory, and previously well known amongst the Zulus and other South African natives. His task was one of great difficulty, how difficult will perhaps never be fully realised. His position was one in which it was difficult to obtain credit for the trouble he prevented, because of the large amount of trouble that occurred.

In a general sense the new order of things made a satisfactory beginning. The privileges it brought to the commonality were highly appreciated by them. All men under forty years of age were still unmarried; they lost no time in availing themselves of the general permission to marry which was now given. No shield-bearing Zulu had been permitted to leave his country; the young men now hastened to places where they could earn that by means of which they could acquire herds. The men rejoiced in freedom from the hunger which military duty had entailed.

But in some other respects their feelings were not those of entire satisfaction. They, at first, regarded the change as having made them British subjects. They were surprised only that no form of tribute was required of them. They made preparation to pay tax. They were

Sir Melmoth Osborn

imposed upon by, and made payments to, adventurous natives from Natal and the Transvaal, who represented themselves as messengers from the British Government. They regarded the appointed chiefs as indunas of the British Government rather than as independent rulers. But gradually they realised the true state of things, and a disposition grew to resent the uncontrolled authority of those under whom they found themselves, who were, moreover, not always the chiefs they had been accustomed to obey.

Hlubi the Basuto chief was followed from his own country, west of the Drakensberg, by a considerable number of people of his race; but of the original inhabitants of the tract of which he was made the ruler the number was far greater than that of these, and between him and them there was no common feeling; neither did they feel any affection towards him. His territory included the lands of Sirayo and Matshana. The objects of his appointment were the reward of his services during the war and the security which his presence at that part of the border, with a Basuto following, would afford to Natal. He was sufficiently strong to control the people over whom he was placed, and sufficiently intelligent to grasp the principles of the justice which he undertook to administer, so that, as time passed, he gradually overcame the difficulty of race in a large measure, and little fault was found with his rule either by his subjects or his critics. He imposed a tax of fourteen shillings on each hut and applied the proceeds to his own purposes; but this payment may be regarded as having appeared to him as a necessary token of the people's submission to his authority.

On the south-east his territory was adjoined by that of John Dunn, which extended along the Tugela River and the sea-shore to the Umhlatuzi River. He had held a high position under Cetshwayo, but had not widely ingratiated himself with the people. When the country had fallen into trouble he had left it and joined those at war with it. As a reward for this act he was given ascendency over chiefs who had previously regarded him as their inferior. These included several of the ex-king's brothers (the principal of whom was Dabulamanzi), and Mavumengwana and Godide, sons, the latter the chief son, of Dingana's chief induna, Undhlela, both of whom had held high rank in the Zulu nation. The territory assigned to Dunn was the most extensive of the thirteen, and its inhabitants were more alien to him, and more divided in their affections, than those of the territories of any of the other twelve chiefs. He also imposed a tax on the people placed under him, part of which he devoted to the administration of justice and to public works. He appointed and maintained three European magistrates, whose decisions were subject to appeal to himself as final judge.

In the north Uhamu, whose secession during the war had secured to him exception from the principle that had been proposed of excluding all members of the Zulu family from a share in the ruling of the country, was given an extensive territory, including within its boundaries the land occupied by Umnyamana, with his numerous following, and the Abaqulusi. Umnyamana, when the selection of chiefs was made, shared the impression which had induced Uhamu's secession, that the latter's reward would be the kingship; and, believing that he would thereby the best serve his personal interests, he expressed his willingness to be subject to him. The Abaqulusi, having been members of the king's personal kraal, were, perhaps, purposely left out when sentiment was under consideration.

The territory lying to the eastward of Uhamu's was assigned to the hereditary chief of the Ndwandwe tribe, Umgojana. It consisted almost entirely of land occupied by the Umgazini tribe, which had been formed by Umpande's chief induna, Masipula. It excluded Umgojana's personal kraals, and he wisely interfered but little with its government.

Usibebu was placed over the territory lying to the south-east of this. Although his personal kraals and following were within its borders there were also others who had never been subject to his authority. These included Cetshwayo's brother and half-brother, Undabuko and Usiwedu, who had both occupied a high place in the king's, and the nation's, estimation.

South-east of this again, and along the 'coast, lay successively the tracts assigned to Somkele, the chief of the Umpukunyoni, and Umlandela, of the Umtetwa tribe. These two were the recognised chiefs of the people over whom they were respectively placed; and, as far as they were concerned, it might have been supposed that no difficulty would arise.

Of the remaining chiefs little need be specially said. They were characterised chiefly by the weakness which was soon detected in them, and taken advantage of, by the people they were set to govern; they did nothing during their short reign that made a lasting impression.

In some parts of the country missionaries were enabled to resume their labour, and, except for the reluctance of the people to relinquish those social habits held to be incompatible with Christianity, the obstacles in the way to success were not so serious as in the past.

Altogether, at first, there was no reason to regard the prospect as unpromising.

But a change soon began to take place. It is not easy to ascertain how, precisely, it received its first impulse, but it may be regarded as having originated with Undabuko and Umnyamana. These two men smarted under the sense of the altered position in which they found themselves. The first, who had ranked next to the king, was now a mere vassal of Usibebu; the second, who had held the highest place among the commonality, was in a like relationship to Uhamu. Undabuko felt himself to be, and the people regarded him, in the absence of the king, as the representative of the throne. The heir, Dinuzulu, was a young boy and under his guardianship. It only required a lead to secure to him the reverence of a very large portion of the Zulu people. He and Umnyamana resided near to each other ; their feelings spread and found sympathy amongst the people around them, and a combination was formed which gave rise to serious concern in the minds of the appointed chiefs. Undabuko proceeded to Pietermaritzburg with the ostensible object of paying his respects to the Governor. His real object found expression in a request that he might have Cetshwayo's bones, a metaphor the meaning of which has already been explained. In taking this course he incurred the serious resentment of Usibebu, while in the course of his journey he met with much sympathy and support. That Umnyamana was a party to the movement was apparent to those concerned, and Usibebu and Uhamu proceeded in the manner which appeared to them to have been rendered necessary by the circumstances to secure the submission they considered their due from those chiefs.

The British Government, as has been seen, had required that the appointed chiefs should collect, and hand over, all royal cattle and the guns in the possession of the Zulus. This requirement furnished a pretext for the action which suggested itself. Many men had yielded to their natural desire to retain their guns. Many others, who had been lent cattle by the king, had possessed them so long, and depended upon them so much for the subsistence of their children, that they had come to regard them almost as their own, and to view the loss of them with much dread. They naturally tried to evade their loss.

While Uhamu was escaping to the British camp also, Umnyamana, acting on behalf of the king, had captured certain of his cattle, and these, owing, perhaps, to the unsettled state of matters, had remained amongst the latter's own herds.

Uhamu now required repayment of these, while both he and Usibebu manifested much zeal in the collection of guns and royal cattle from those whose disaffection they suspected. Those in whose possession either were found were punished for their concealment by confiscation of their own herds; those suspected were required to asseverate, by means of the payment of a cow, that the suspicion was unfounded; those whose cattle were seized on unfounded suspicion were able to get them back only by the sacrifice of one or more of their number to their captors— an exaction which had long been common, and was metaphorically called a fee to the person who stabbed for withdrawing his spear (Kok'umkonto).

The pursuit of these measures tended to gratify the natural desire of Zulu rulers to add to their herds, but was scarcely calculated to secure the affections of those whom they desired to subordinate. It was hoped that they would have the effect of checking agitation; that hope was also to be disappointed. That agitation was stimulated, rather than otherwise affected, by the efforts of the chiefs to suppress it. Complaints began to be made to the British Resident of oppression. It became necessary to take notice of these complaints in order to avoid a conflict. Umnyamana was prepared to resist his chief by force of arms, and a serious fight was imminent. The seizure of cattle in this case had amounted to over 2000 head, mostly for but slender cause, partly without any. The parties agreed to accept arbitration in the matter, and Sir Evelyn Wood, in Natal at that time administering the Government, since the death of Sir George Pomeroy-Colley on Majuba, and arranging, with other Commissioners, the matters relating to the retrocession of the Transvaal, was urged by the Resident, and agreed to arbitrate.

A revolution arose in the Umtetwa tribe. A man from Natal, named Sitimela, came representing himself to be the grandson of their great chief Dingiswayo. He pretended that his father, a son of that chief, had been expelled by Tshaka; that he had himself been born in the Transvaal; that he had been kept out of his right by the Zulu kings who had placed his tribe under a chief not of the direct line. The tradition of Dingiswayo was still strongly impressed on the minds of the people. The story gained credence, and his adherents rapidly increased, largely owing to the lavish generosity he displayed when he had succeeded in seizing a portion of the chief Umlandela's herds. He also succeeded, by means of a judicious distribution of these presents, in gaining a considerable amount of sympathy outside the tribe to the chieftainship of which he aspired. Old Umlandela was forced to fly, and took refuge with John Dunn. It was feared that, like the chief whose grandson he professed to be, Sitimela would attempt to extend his dominions. He professed great power as a magician, and his fame rapidly spread. He induced the belief that those who fought against him would be attacked by reptiles of such kinds and ferocity as had never before been heard of. He had collected a considerable army, and to have allowed him to retain the position he had gained in the Umtetwa tribe would, it was feared, have led to general insurrection.

Mr. Osborn was, therefore, instructed to visit the district over which Sitimela had assumed authority; to persuade him, if possible, to disperse his following and take his departure, and if he should decline to do so to advise other chiefs to assist Umlandela in his expulsion. The latter course was the result. Mr. Osborn, having warned Sitimela of what would happen if he failed to disband his following within a given space of time, departed from the locality, leaving it to John Dunn to see that the warning was obeyed. Dunn's own account of

THE STORY OF THE ZULUS

what followed, which was an accurate statement, exhibits a good example of how Zulu battles were fought:

"As I wrote to you on the 31st of July, Sitimela's men chased and killed ten of Umlandela's, and wounded one, running them to within a mile of my camp. I at once saw that if I delayed, and allowed a single day to pass, his cause would have been strengthened; so I mustered my force, allowing Sitimela's men time to get back to their headquarters, which were sheltered by a high ridge of hills about 1500 yards from the kraal. I then followed up and divided my force, which was about 2000 strong, and made for the kraal right, left and centre. As soon as we showed on the top of the hill we saw all his men collected 'gwiyaing' and making a great noise in the kraal at their success. As soon as they saw us they came out of the kraal and formed in fighting order. I then, myself, fired three shots into the middle of them, killing one man. This caused a commotion, and the whole of the force broke and made for the top of a high hill at the back of the kraal. My men followed up sharp, which caused a panic amongst the rebels, and they broke and fled after five or six shots had been fired at them. The loss on my side was only three or four killed and four wounded; it would be difficult to tell the loss of the rebels, but I should say over 200."

The slaughter was great, occurring almost entirely in the merciless pursuit which followed the rout.

Thus ended the pretensions of Sitimela. As to whether he was the rightful heir to the chieftainship of the Umtetwa tribe no inquiry is reported to have been made, and to this day there exists no evidence. He disappeared when his forces dispersed, and has not since been heard of. The operation by which his object was defeated was scarcely different from what it might have been under the king. The two victorious chiefs added largely to their private herds by the spoil they gained. For the people on either side little advantage resulted. Of general result there was little. The agitation throughout the country was not checked. Only about two years had elapsed since the king's overthrow, and already there had occurred a more sanguinary conflict than any during the period of his actual reign. And it was to be followed within two months by one more sanguinary still. The Abaqulusi had not yielded that submission to Uhamu which he regarded as his due. They had assisted in the building of his kraals and the planting of his crops, and paid such demands as had been made upon them. But their submission was not of that free character that should mark the conduct of willing subjects. They were, no doubt, in active sympathy with the agitation, now assuming formidable strength, for the restoration of the king. Their chief head-man had informed Uhamu that he was precluded from formally transferring his allegiance by the circumstance that he had been the custodian of the king's medicines. An alliance was forming between Uhamu and Usibebu, who perceived that they would sooner or later require to defend their positions against a formidable combination; for, whether or not Cetshwayo were restored, it was plain that the control of the Zulu people was rapidly passing from the chiefs who had been appointed over them. The combination under Umnyamana and Undabuko was becoming so strong as to seriously threaten the security of those chiefs against whom their efforts were chiefly directed; and it was desirable that he who would continue to rule should take steps to remove disaffection from within his borders. Usibebu having for this reason expelled Undabuko and Usiwedu from his territory, offered assistance to Uhamu to expel the Abaqulusi. He refrained from sending a force for this purpose only because the British Resident would not sanction it.

Complaints to the Resident became frequent and

urgent. Uhamu charged the Abaqulusi with lack of submission and they accused him of causeless oppression. But, as the Resident's powers were limited to the giving of advice, he was unable to effect a settlement of the matters in dispute between them. Both Uhamu and the Abaqulusi had armed forces in the field, and seizures and destruction of property, as an inevitable consequence, soon took place on both sides. A conflict became unavoidable, and the first to be killed were three women of the people of Uhamu. They were put to death by members of his own force, who probably believed at the time that they belonged to the disaffected. The mistake, though discovered, was not acknowledged, and Uhamu, in order to justify the steps that were maturing, represented to the Resident that the Abaqulusi had done the deed. Matters culminated on the 2nd of October 1881. The two hostile forces met on the right bank of the Bivana River. The battle, as usual, was short; the pursuit which followed was, as usual, merciless. Many hundreds of the defeated Abaqulusi were killed, only those escaping who were able to gain and cross the Bivana River, which formed the border of the Transvaal territory. The people were thus driven from their homes. They were refused permission to return except on condition that they delivered up all the cattle they had driven to the Transvaal for safety, and yielded submission.

These were the only two serious conflicts that actually took place under the settlement of 1879. Others of a more serious character were averted by the intervention of Mr. Osborn. But it was perceived that the arrangement as it stood could not endure. A system under which a greedy chief might destroy and confiscate the goods of such sections of the people within the territory under his authority as did not, in his judgment, yield him due deference could not be tolerated. Some supreme authority was necessary by which the action of the chiefs might be controlled. John Dunn proposed himself for the position of supreme chief; but, for the present, nothing was done beyond acknowledging the necessity for central authority. Sir Evelyn Wood had visited the Residency at Inhlazatshe, and held a meeting of chiefs there on the 31st of August. He had delivered awards in the matters in dispute between Uhamu and Umnyamana, and Usibebu and Cetshwayo's brothers, Undabuko and Usiwedu. He supported the chiefs in their authority, but found that they had made excessive seizures. Uhamu was required to pay back 700 head of the cattle he had taken from Umnyamana, and Usibebu one-third of those he had seized from Undabuko and others, who were directed to quit his territory. He proposed certain measures to the chiefs for the better administration of their territories, which included the imposition of taxes and the appointment of residents, leaving it to them to consider the expediency of those proposals.

The support he gave to the chiefs had the effect of allaying active resistance to their authority, and the condition of things had improved as the year closed.

But it was only a superficial improvement. Important events had occurred. In July of the year following the Zulu war a general election in Great Britain had resulted in a change of Administration, the Liberal Party, under the leadership of Mr. Gladstone, coming into power. The Ministry in power at the time when the war was embarked upon had never been very clear regarding actual facts justifying it. During the election those who had now succeeded to office had condemned it as an unjust war; and, being elected, it was necessary that they should evince some sympathy with those who had suffered by it.

The members of the new Cabinet had also adversely criticised the annexation of the Transvaal; shortly after their appointment they had to face a Boer insurrection in that country. These people, after much futile petitioning, had taken up arms to regain their independence. They beleaguered the towns, and opposed the advance of British troops at the Lang's Nek Pass of the Drakensberg. So stout was the fight they maintained, and so general was the rising, that the Government determined to abandon the country rather than enforce its rule on an unwilling people. When the retrocession had taken place the Settlement of Zululand was condemned by the Boer Government that became established in the country.

In a minute, dated the 25th of October, it urged the release of Cetshwayo and his restoration "to his rights" in order to prevent further bloodshed in Zululand.

This representation was made on the recommendation of Piet Joubert, then Superintendent of Native Affairs. The bloodshed to which the communication had special reference was that which had occurred in the conflict between Uhamu and the Abaqulusi; it was dated twenty-three days after that event. But it urged also that the peace of South Africa would be endangered if the restoration did not take place, thus directly contradicting the view by which Sir Bartle Frere had, in a large measure, justified the war. It was a remarkable contradiction of that view, coming as it did from the representatives of those people whose safety was the main consideration which led to the overthrow of Cetshwayo's power.

Cetshwayo, on his own behalf, was most importunate. His letters to various persons in high authority were frequent and eloquent. He soon began to produce the desired impression. On the 15th of July he had addressed a letter to Lord Kimberley, the Colonial Secretary, in which he said that continued banishment might induce him to take away his own life, and begged that he might be taken to England in order to state his case and clear himself of the wrong-doing of which he had been accused; a telegraphic reply came on the 14th of September by which he was informed that the Government were disposed to favourably consider his application.

In Zululand his cause was very strongly advocated by those who were disaffected to the appointed chiefs. Indeed, some of the appointed chiefs themselves joined in the movement in favour of his restoration.

In April of the following year a party proceeded to Pietermaritzburg to make formal application for this through the Governor. It was headed by his brother, Undabuko, numbered some 800 men, and was highly representative of the Zulu people, being composed of notables from all parts of the country. It represented also a very extensive disaffection to those of the appointed chiefs who desired to retain their positions, and the suppression of the movement was a matter which could not be looked forward to except with dread.

It was becoming plain that some change would be necessary; to those acquainted with the facts there could have remained little doubt that Cetshwayo's cause would in some degree prevail.

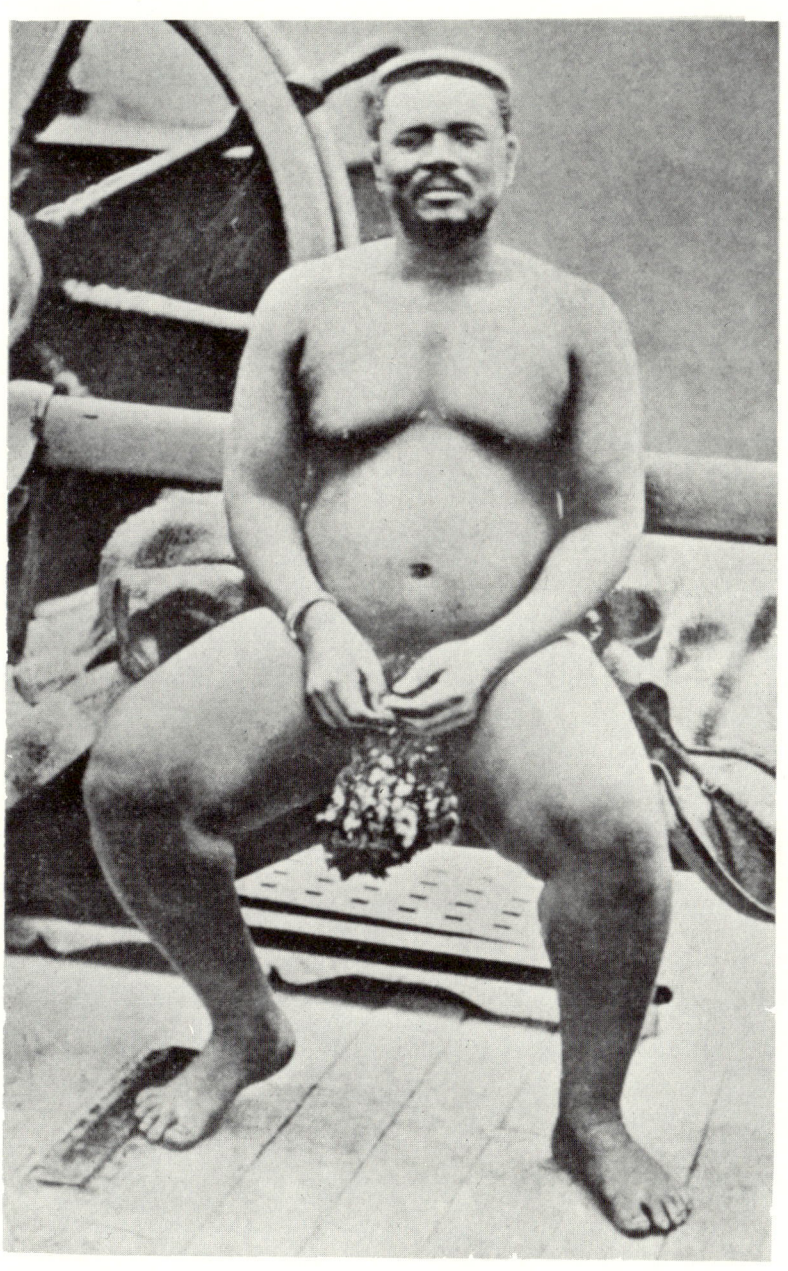

CETSHWAYO ON BOARD SHIP

CHAPTER XXI

MATTERS did not proceed with great rapidity. It was not till January 1883 that those who had from the first watched for the king's return were rewarded by the sight of a "mast-head appearing over the waves."

Cetshwayo had been to England, and seen and spoken to the great English Queen. He had been much impressed with the magnificence of her surroundings, as well as by what he saw generally of English civilisation. He had also not failed to impress with agreeable feelings regarding himself those to whom he had gone to present his petition. As he appeared in London he was of handsome presence; his intelligence and rich metaphoric form of expression were striking.

There had been much opposition to his restoration, and much general expression of opinion as to what might result from it. Sir Henry Bulwer was now again Governor of Natal and Special Commissioner for Zululand. His desire to do right was very strong; the pains he took to inform himself correctly in respect to the position of affairs were very great. The varied and voluminous correspondence which took place is interesting, and contains much detailed information which is useful. But it would not be safe to accept as entirely correct its exposition of the causes that were at work in producing the complications which it was sought to unravel.

The various reports and arguments had been considered, and the outcome was the anchoring of Her Majesty's ship *Algerine* at Port Durnford, near the mouth of the Umlalazi River, on the 9th of the month, with preparations proceeding for the landing there of Cetshwayo on the following day. Feeling had run high, and this somewhat precarious landing had, perhaps, been chosen for that reason in preference to the safer harbour of Natal. An important experiment was being tried; doubt prevailed amongst the Zulus, no less than amongst those less capable of judging, as to what would be the result of it.

The question of restoring Cetshwayo had involved serious considerations. There was the question of Natal's safety; whether the old danger, the belief in which had contributed so largely to the reasons for which the war had been waged, of a Zulu invasion of the Colony would not be renewed with the restoration of the Zulu kingdom. There was that of the appointed chiefs; whether the circumstances justified their being deprived of the rights that had been conferred with their appointments. There was the question of the protection of private individuals who had done such things during the king's absence as might have rendered them liable to punishment if done during his reign. There was the question of how a better administration could be secured than that by which Cetshwayo's previous reign was considered to have been characterised.

The consideration of these questions had led to important restrictions both in regard to the territory and power to which he was about to be restored. His territorial dominion was to be reduced on the south and west by those tracts which, in the settlement of 1879, were assigned to the chiefs John Dunn and Hlubi. These were to form a Native Reserve under a British Resident Commissioner, and to be a place to which such Zulus might remove as might be unwilling to accept the rule of the restored king.

On the north-east Usibebu was to retain his independence and territory. He was distinctly unwilling to subject himself again to the rule of the Zulu king; in his exercise of authority he had committed himself to an attitude which would have created difficulty in the way of his being accepted as a subject. But an alteration was made in the boundaries of his territory. The expulsion of Undabuko and Usiwedu from the Ivuna Valley had been a somewhat serious matter. It was felt to be desirable that they should be enabled to return to their former homes under the restored king; and in order to admit of this Usibebu's boundary was removed from the Ivuna Stream to the Nongoma Ridge. By an easterly line it was also sought to exclude from his domains the lands of the Hlabisa and Umdhletshe tribes, under the chiefs Umbopa and Umsutshwana, who had been very unwilling subjects, and had constantly supported the agitation, the effect of which was now ripening. The loss of territory which this alteration involved did not seriously affect Usibebu, the people occupying it never having been his personal adherents, and being of a disposition to oppose rather than to support him. It was, moreover, to a large extent uninhabitable land. But in area it was extensive, and it was thought to be due to him that he should receive some compensation for its loss. This it was resolved to effect by pushing his northern boundary from the Umkuzana and Umkuzi streams to the Pongolo River. Umgojana had never occupied the territory assigned to him between those rivers, but remained at his own hereditary sites on the south of it, and he could therefore have no objection to its transference to Usibebu. The circumstance that he had refrained from attempting to exercise authority, owing to a sense that it would be impracticable to do so, over the powerful Umgazini tribe, which occupied it, does not appear to have been appreciated.

The chief of this tribe was Maboko, the son of

Umpande's prime induna, Masipula. His name appears on the list of those chiefs who proceeded to Pietermaritzburg to petition for the restoration; it should have been plain from this circumstance that his affections were with the king and not with Usibebu. The assignment of his territory to that chief, in the circumstances, was indeed in effect merely an authorisation to him to conquer it. Sir Henry Bulwer does not appear from the correspondence to have had full information on the subject.

Cetshwayo had been required to sign conditions by which he undertook to be guided in the position to which he was being restored. They were in terms almost identical with those by which the thirteen appointed chiefs had promised to be bound, but varied by the undertaking that he would respect, specifically, the territory of Usibebu and that reserved for occupation under the British Resident Commissioner, and in no way interfere with the people living on those territories; that he would leave unmolested any of the girls of the royal household who might have married during his absence, and make no claim whatever in respect to them, or their husbands, parents, or guardians; that he would hold no one criminally, or otherwise, liable for any acts committed during his absence. A British Resident would be appointed to see that the conditions he had agreed to were faithfully observed.

The feeling in the country was mixed. There were those in the several territorial divisions who desired, and those who did not desire, to have the king back. Many were in a condition to be influenced by the tide of events rather than by sentiment. Those possessed of a considerable following were little disposed to resign their authority and resume a subordinate position; the men who supported such chiefs were disposed to be guided in their affections by the course that would best ensure their own comfort and safety. It was difficult so to gauge the probabilities as to justify an immediate selection. There was danger of becoming compromised by declaring openly for the king, as there was in definitely espousing the cause of such chiefs as might have contemplated refusing to subject themselves to his authority. Those chiefs who resided in the territory reserved by the British Government, might enjoy a larger measure of independence by remaining there than would be allowed them if they left it and placed themselves under the king; but it was doubtful whether there was that in their circumstances which would satisfy the ambitions of the followers on whom their positions depended. Usibebu alone of those outside the land restored to Cetshwayo, had so assured himself of the integrity of his people as to be prepared to resist any attack that might be made upon him. The others, if they could retain their people, and thus their power, might perhaps feel secure under the protection afforded by the British Government; but if their people should elect to acknowledge the king's authority they also would naturally have to seek his favour.

Uhamu's territory was included in that restored. His position was not a pleasant one. If he should elect to submit, he could not fail to be affected by the circumstances that he had destroyed the Abaqulusi and incurred the enmity of those who had led the agitation for the restoration. He had a strong personal following, and the land which he occupied was favoured with strongly defensible positions. He might refuse either to submit or to leave. There was an element of uncertainty in the position of things that might well inspire uneasiness in the mind of the returning king.

The shores presented no conspicuous demonstration of welcome. It was, indeed, not within his own dominion that he was to land. It was within the Reserved territory, the administration of which had already been placed, for the time, in the hands of John Shepstone, whose illustrious brother, Sir Theophilus, was on the beach to receive the king on his landing, as he did, in a somewhat dazed condition, by means of a surf-boat. There was also a strong detachment of the 6th Dragoons, by whom he was to be escorted to the place at which he was to be reinstated. But of his own people there were not many. His first message to them was sent by a young man in the employ of the Government.

It was just ten years since his first progress to his royal seat; now began the second, but in altered circumstances. The singing of the multitude, the exultant cries of the hunters over their quarry, the clamorous shouts of loyalty that rent the air during the journey of 1873, were absent on this occasion. It was perhaps fitting, as Sir Theophilus Shepstone said when addressing the meeting at the installation some days later, that a portion of the army which had captured and carried him into exile should accompany him on his return. The escort of Dragoons was doubtless necessary and gratifying. But of his own people, whose presence would have been more gratifying and reassuring, there were singularly few. As the procession wended its way up the valley of the Umhlatuzi and over the Inkwenke Heights to the northward it was visited at intervals by men and women, the first giving loud expression to joy and wonder, the second to wonder only. All were impressed with the desirability of saying such things only as would be pleasing alike to the returning king and to those in whose hands he still was. Much uncertainty hung over their immediate future; it behoved them to be wary lest in some way they should bring trouble upon themselves.

Arriving at Mtonjaneni on the 17th of January, he still found little to dispel misgivings. Below and in front lay the broad valley of the White Umfolozi; some few miles away to the left were the graves of many of his ancestors; within sight was the Makeni where Masipula, ten years before, had proclaimed him king of the Zulus; he was near to, and within sight of, his ancestral home, and about to be again invested with the kingly office, because events had made it appear good that it should be so, in the interests of the Zulu people. But of these people few were to be seen. Umnyamana, by whom his loyal subjects were led, had not arrived; days passed and yet he did not arrive. He was, indeed, known to be coming; but Uhamu, by whom he had been accompanied on the first occasion, would not be with him on this. Usibebu came, but alone, and to greet Sir Theophilus Shepstone, not the returning king. As he rode into the camp he was execrated by the women. Umfanawendhlela, whose dominion, as one of the appointed chiefs, had included the royal sites, also came; but he brought an offering to the British Commissioner, not to Cetshwayo. His bearing towards the king was, moreover, in marked contrast to that of former days. In approaching the royal presence he had then crawled on the ground, now his servant carried a chair, upon which he seated himself for the interview. He was again to be a subject, with residence near to where the king was to reside, but his attitude promised only partial submission. Days passed, and yet the representatives of the nation by whom the king expected to be welcomed did not present themselves. It became apparent that considerable numbers of armed men were gathering in the valley; it began to be whispered that there might be a purpose to accomplish what Usibebu had almost attempted at Makeni, forcibly to seize the king and avoid having to receive him at the hands of those by whom he had been brought into their midst. Matters were, therefore, discreetly pushed forward; and, with due speeches and ceremony, the reinstallation was effected on the 29th of January, and the commission with the escort withdrawn, without loss of time, across the Umhlatuzi.

Mr. Osborn's duties as British Resident were ended.

He had done what could be done in a difficult position. His place as British Resident was now taken by Henry Francis Fynn, whose father had been associated with the founder of the Zulu nation and witnessed some of the important battles by which it had been built up. It was now to be his lot to witness some of the events attending its final downfall. The reports he wrote of these events are instructive and interesting.

The situation was not long in developing. Umnyamana was in his old position as prime induna. His tribe or following, called the Butelezi, formed the most considerable section of the king's supporters. He was now in a position which promised an opportunity to turn the tables on his late oppressor, Uhamu, to whom in his turn the two alternatives presented themselves, of yielding due submission or of quitting the land upon which he dwelt. Feeling secure in his alliance with Usibebu, now sufficiently established, he was resolved to do neither the one nor the other. The second section of Cetshwayo's supporters were mixed people, classed generally as the Usutu party, while the third consisted of the Umgazini tribe, headed by Maboko, who by territorial division were made subjects of Usibebu. There were those besides Uhamu occupying land within the territory restored to Cetshwayo who were unwilling either to remove from it or yield him submission; in the Reserve there were many similarly disposed towards the power ruling there. Pressure was brought to bear upon the latter by the Resident Commissioner to declare what they would do. It was not a question which they felt that it was safe to decide hurriedly. The previous policy of the British Government had not been such as to assure them of the permanence of the new arrangement. Sir Henry Bulwer himself had misgivings on the subject. He had stated with emphasis that the main principle in the Reserved Territory should be the establishment in it of British authority and protection; the Secretary of State had directed the withdrawal of the second term on the ground that its use might detract from the inhabitants' sense of obligation to protect themselves. The number of Imperial troops left in the Territory was but small, and these were soon to be relieved by a small force of Zulus raised and brought into discipline by Commandant George Mansel, and called Carbineers. For the main purposes of defence the Resident Commissioner was to be dependent on disorganised levies of natives whose loyalty to him had not been proved.

For the greater part the chiefs declared themselves in favour of remaining under the British Commissioner in the Reserve, but a minority expressed a contrary intention. In the meantime, as their crops were standing in the fields, neither the latter nor such as might elect to leave Cetshwayo's territory were required to do more than signify what they intended to do. The actual removal, either way, would have been a serious matter. It would have involved the abandonment of land that had been enriched by long occupation for that which would probably be found unfruitful for some years. Much of the land on the hill-sides of Zululand is of very poor quality. Cereals will not grow upon it without artificial fertilisation. The Zulu method of manuring is most primitive. When their huts have stood for a certain length of time, with the cattle-pen within the circle which they form, it becomes necessary for sanitary reasons to remove to fresh ground. The abandoned site is then planted, and, however poor the soil may have been, yields a good crop. The value of a locality to the occupiers increases with the number of these fertilised spots, and migration often entails a period of scarcity. The inducement to migrate would require to be very strong, and that of sentiment would seldom, in itself, be sufficient to cause a people to risk the prospect of hunger by following their chief. There was very strong hope amongst the chiefs and people generally that the necessity for removal would be obviated. Cetshwayo hoped that a general expression by the people of their affection towards himself might induce the British Government to restore that portion of the country to him which had been professedly reserved for the disaffected. With the object of eliciting such an expression he gave them to understand that the reservation was only a temporary measure. They, being uncertain whether to believe these assurances or the contrary from the Resident Commissioner, endeavoured for the moment to secure the favour of both. While to the latter they stated their preference for British rule, they excused themselves for it to Cetshwayo by the pretence that they had been in doubt whether it was really he who had returned. The popular form of salutation thus became the question and answer: "Is it he? Verily it is!" The difficulties that were to beset the Resident Commissioner did not promise to be light; but those to which Cetshwayo was to be subjected were the first to manifest themselves. Scarcely had he taken up his position when news came that the Abaqulusi were making reprisals for what they considered past oppression by killing and plundering the people of Uhamu. He could scarcely afford to alienate the affections of this section by causing reparation to be made to the man, or the people, to whose action was mainly due the part it had taken in the agitation for his restoration, especially as he felt he had strong reason for disliking and distrusting that man and those people. He felt little disposition to take steps in regard to the complaints that reached him. The occurrences of disorder, he said, were merely a continuance of what had obtained during his absence.

It was necessary that he should cultivate his own party, and this consisted mainly of those who had looked for redress of their grievances through his return. Those of them who had dwelt on the borders of Usibebu's territory had been the strongest advocates of his restoration, and were the most expectant of redress. The object at which Sir Henry Bulwer had aimed had been in but a small measure realised. He had intended that the new boundaries should exclude these from Usibebu's dominion. There were a number of sections, or clans, of them, and they were styled by him Ultra Usutu. He was under the impression that his wish in their regard had been given effect to. But this had only been the case in regard to the sites of Undabuko and Usiwedu and a portion of those of the Hlabisa tribe under Umbopa. The others were still subject to Usibebu, to whose unwilling subjects had been added also, as already mentioned, the Umgazini tribe under Maboko.

Cetshwayo was not long in sounding a warning as to what would be the outcome. On the 6th of February, eight days after his reinstatement, he caused Mr. Fynn to intimate to Sir Henry Bulwer that he was keeping those chiefs with him because he feared there might be disturbance if they returned to their homes. The most important of them were Mahu, the son of Usibebu's uncle, Tokotoko; Umsutshwana, chief of the Umdhletshe tribe; Umfinyeli, the Xulu chief; and Haiana, a brother of Usibebu, who had shared expulsion with Undabuko. None of these would yield submission to Usibebu; and there was an obvious resolution of the people, which doubtless Cetshwayo felt no desire, and which it would have endangered his position, to check, to regard any attempt on his part to assert his authority over them as an act of war.

An error prevailed in the minds of the British authorities at this time in the belief which they entertained that the will of the Zulu king was absolute in all matters affecting the people he governed. To some extent this was justified by the assumptions of some of Cetshwayo's predecessors; but the fate of these showed plainly that only those governed securely who governed according to the will of the generality of the people. Tshaka was assassinated with the approval of the nation he had formed, Dingana's subjects rose in rebellion against him and sought, at the risk of losing their country, the aid of the Boers in ridding themselves of his oppression.

It was impressed upon Cetshwayo that he was personally responsible for the keeping of good order, but it must remain doubtful whether he possessed the power to control the development that was in progress. It is certain that, had he done so, he would have sadly disappointed the expectations by which those were actuated who had prayed for his restoration.

The Ulundi kraal was rebuilt near to the site upon which it had formerly stood. It was, said Mr. Fynn, about 500 yards in diameter, and capable of accommodating a large number of people. The king's household was established at the head of it, as before, and the general circumstances of kingship restored. In reality, however, its restoration was never to take place.

Its first rude shock was to be received just two months after the reinstatement at Mtonjaneni. Usibebu had not been blind to what he would have to face. He had perceived that an armed defence of his position would be inevitable. With the dogged courage that marks his character he awaited events, committing no act himself to which exception could be taken by the British Government. Not only did those of the Usutu party who dwelt within his boundary fail to yield submission to his authority, but they committed acts of violence against his loyal subjects. These acts he contented himself with reporting to the British Government; but from the tone of those reports it was plain that he regarded hostilities as imminent. He resolved on a step which could not in his circumstances be well avoided, but which he doubtless knew would bring matters to an issue. He assembled a large force, led it into the land of Maboko, and demanded the submission of that chief.

In the course of the expedition his army, as is usual, supported themselves by taking of the crops standing in the fields. The effect was electrical. His force was withdrawn on the 23rd of March; on the 30th Usibebu was face to face, in the valley of Umsebe, with an army which outnumbered his own by about three to one. A force composed of three divisions, the Usutu, the Umgazini, and the Butelezi, had hastened to his destruction. Cetshwayo had not, as it was supposed he would do, reorganised the latent regimental system. It may, indeed, be regarded as true that he bore but little personal part in the organisation or sending of this expedition; that it was scarcely within his power to prevent its being sent. It was an effort on the part of those who had petitioned for his restoration to right a condition of things which they considered that event would have afforded a means of righting. Even if he had possessed the power to do it, he could not have prevented the movement except at the cost of disappointing the whole of his supporters.

The army assembled according to its tribal divisions. It was very loosely handled; but it was large, and presented a formidable appearance as it marched across the open ground from the Inhlopenkulu to the Inxongwana Hill, beyond which was the Inkungwini, one of Usibebu's chief kraals. It met with no opposition, so far, although far within the boundary of his territory. It numbered, as well as can be gathered, about 5000 fighting men; its strength was made to appear much greater by the numerous baggage-boys who accompanied it. Some small bodies of the enemy were seen, but quickly retired, giving the impression that it was regarded as irresistible. The Inkungwini kraal, when reached, was burnt, and there the army was fired upon by a small force of Usibebu's mounted men, who then retired precipitately in a northeasterly direction, towards the Umsebe Valley.

The name Umsebe will long serve to fix a date, for the

battle fought there on the 30th of March 1883 was memorable. There is no conspicuous landmark by which it can be recognised; but the mouldering bones of the slain may still be seen.

Of the reasons which induced Usibebu to select the ground upon which he had decided to make a stand it would be difficult to obtain an explanation; but the conditions which favoured it are easily discernible after the event. There was no lofty point from which his position could be viewed. The slopes of the valley's sides are not abrupt; they are ribbed by the action of surface water; the curve of the ridges between the channels thus formed renders it impossible to see any great distance. At the time of the event the grass was long enough to conceal a crouching man; much cover was also afforded by scrub and mimosa trees. That the invading force was badly informed regarding Usibebu's position, and the disposition of his men, is evident from the circumstance that they went into action while still accompanied by the baggage-boys, who are usually left in a position of safety. Usibebu's line was stretched north and south near where the wagon track to Ubombo traverses the valley. The advancing force moved upon it still in its tribal divisions. When it had come sufficiently near, Usibebu personally rode along his line of men setting them on. Fighting was scarcely begun when wavering was perceived on the side of Cetshwayo's army. Owing to the nature of the ground they could see little of each other; word passing along their ranks that portions were in flight created a panic in the whole force. Despair overtook them. Men were heard crying, "Oh, my children!" It was early in the day. There was no cover along their line of retreat. The pursuit continued till dark. Some few eluded pursuit by running down the valley; the rest, trusting to their speed alone, made their way across the fifteen miles of open country that lay between the field of battle and Nongoma.

Their course is still marked by the bones of those that were overtaken. They might have been expected to walk (for running had soon to be abandoned) as fast as those by whom they were pursued. Spread widely over the flats, it might have been supposed that many would defend themselves in single combat against the individuals who overtook them. It is curious how completely hope is abandoned by the Zulu when once defeated in the field of battle. Of Usibebu's men only some ten were killed; but a small proportion of the invading force escaped. The wide expanse over which skulls may still be found proves how great must have been the number that fell. Once overtaken they were as defenceless as sheep. A curious scene is described by one of those who pursued as having been witnessed by himself. A man was flourishing his shield and stabbing wildly at the air as if engaged in a fierce conflict. Despair had so deprived him of reason that while thus engaged one of the pursuers advanced and despatched him without meeting with any resistance or apparently exciting any consciousness of his presence.

Two men were captured and their lives spared— Usiteku, a brother of Cetshwayo, and Undulunga, a son of Umnyamana. To the rest no mercy was shown. When night interrupted the slaughter, the victors, and those that remained alive of the vanquished, had reached the place where the Nongoma Magistracy now stands. The pursuit was resumed next morning, but the broken character of the country now made escape more easy. Few were killed on that day; but the course of the victors was marked, as far as the Umfolozi River, by the flames that rose from the habitations of the people. Probably in no battle had the Zulus ever suffered greater loss of life.

CHAPTER XXII

In the result of the matters related in the last chapter Cetshwayo suffered both the calamity and the blame. It was felt by the Special Commissioner that he had sent the force against Usibebu in wanton violation of the solemn promises he had made as a condition of reinstatement; that in repelling the invasion Usibebu had acted entirely within his rights. Neither could he find much fault with the latter because, in the heat of pursuit, he had followed the invaders across his own boundary. But he counselled Usibebu to keep within the limits of his own territory, and reproved him for an act of retaliation he committed subsequent to the invasion.

Having regard to the small extent of his territory, comprising, as it did, only a portion of what is now the Magisterial District of Ndwandwe, and the comparatively small number of its inhabitants, Usibebu's performance had been marvellous. It could not but excite admiration even in his enemies. But any admiration was necessarily mingled with the feeling that it would not be possible for him to hold his own for long.

The calamity that had befallen Cetshwayo was serious indeed. Of the men that had gone forth, the greater number had been slain, and those remaining were sorely discouraged. On the other hand, Usibebu had overcome such difficulty as sentiment might have placed in the way of waging war against the king. The success which had attended him in the first encounter had astonished his own warriors as much as those against whom they had fought. He was greatly angered by the feeling that he had been unjustly attacked, and little disposed to be merciful if placed in a position to exact vengeance. Such fighting strength as he possessed had not been reduced by the conflict that had taken place, no appreciable loss having been inflicted upon him. He could no longer be regarded as a mere annoyance; he had become a serious danger. One result of his success was to render active the alliance which had subsisted between him and Uhamu. That chief now felt that he might with some degree of safety oppose active resistance to the authority of the restored king. It became necessary, if he were to be reduced to submission, that coercion should be applied, and in this task the reinstated prime induna, Umnyamana, willingly engaged. The grudge he owed his late chief was in no wise diminished. The cattle he should have received under Sir Evelyn Wood's award had not been paid, nor had he obtained any redress for the various other injuries under a sense of which he laboured. His turn was now come. He might now, without the restraint which the British Resident had imposed, try conclusions with his oppressor; and he had under his command for this purpose all Cetshwayo's available forces. The task seemed not a difficult one, but experience soon belied anticipations. Uhamu betook himself to the fastnesses of that rugged region where the Sihlenge Stream joins the Umkuzi River, whose precipitous ravines have been called Ingotshe —gorge, or that which swallows—and could not be dislodged. There was fighting and killing and burning of homes and seizure of cattle and food; but, on the whole, the advantage remained with the besieged. Uhamu was sometimes helped by Usibebu, but this help was scarcely needed for the mere purpose of defence. Usibebu had a difficult position of his own to maintain. The Umgazini tribe had not yielded him submission, but cast in their lot entirely with the king's party. Any invasion of their lands they regarded as invasion of the king's territory.

They met and fought with any force sent by Usibebu to exact submission, and such attempts as he made against them were not successful. The Swazis, too, and farther east the Amatonga, were suspected of being in alliance with Cetshwayo, so that, with the powerful Umpukunyoni tribe, under Somkele, on his south-east, he was regarded as entirely encompassed by the enemy. At any time he might be attacked from any quarter, and he was kept in a state of constant expectation of a combined movement against him by reports which reached him from all sides. That such an attack was contemplated there can scarcely be a reasonable doubt. His position was regarded by the Special Commissioner as hopeless. That the position was one of his own choosing was the only consolation that Sir Henry Bulwer could derive to himself from the circumstances.

There was much confusion in the country, and there appeared no hope of issue except in the shedding of blood. Nor was there such shaping of affairs as to indicate the conclusion towards which war might lead. The little territory that had been the country of the Zulus was divided into three parts and placed under three separate rulers. The people, according as their sentiment or interests might divide them, were required to support these rulers, if need should arise, against their own countrymen, perhaps against their own kindred. The success of either ruler had to depend upon how sentiment or self-interest should divide the people, and the chances of native warfare.

In the Reserve it was no less so than in the other two territories. The people who resided there were not all willing to accept the rule of the Resident Commissioner. Some professed their willingness, but their visits to the king created a doubt as to the sincerity of their professions; others expressed their preference for the king, but evinced no disposition to remove within his boundaries.

Cetshwayo continued to believe, or to profess the belief, that the object of the establishment of that separate territory would cease if it could be shown that the people were generally well-disposed towards him. He became impatient of the oft-repeated advice of the Resident to keep within his own boundaries; to permit those to go who desired to leave and find a place for those who desired to come to him. He did not see, he said, why people should be expatriated because they were his people.

And at this time there came to him one who was more prepared to prophesy things that were agreeable to his feelings and aspirations. He reposed his confidence in William Grant, of Durban, who visited him shortly after his misfortune, although how recommended it is not practicable to ascertain. On the 14th of June he appointed Mr. Grant "to be his resident adviser and counsellor, to confer with him on all matters affecting the constitution of his country and the government of his people, and to act as a medium of communication and faithful representation between himself and Her Majesty's Government, with the view to the restoration and maintenance of peace and good order within his borders."

The hope of attaining that which was aimed at was strengthened by the advice given to Mr. Grant ten days later by Natal's leading lawyer and politician, Harry Escombe, who said: "Bear in mind that whilst Cetshwayo wants the Reserve back the Crown has no interests in retaining it; England will be glad to be free of Zululand; Natal does not covet any portion of it. As between the two Governments, the one in the Reserve, the other in Cetshwayo's district, the fitter will absorb the other."

Cetshwayo therefore endeavoured to secure the affections of the people in the Reserve territory, and they were filled with misgivings as to the wisdom or safety of opposing themselves to him. The principal chiefs continued to reside at Ulundi, notwithstanding their repeated recall by Mr. Osborn, who had assumed the office of British Resident Commissioner in the Reserve. There was no circumstance to justify those who might prefer the rule of the Resident Commissioner in believing that greater security lay in that rule than in making their submission to the Zulu king.

Cetshwayo's weakness will, perhaps, be apparent from what has already been said. Usibebu and Uhamu were ranged against him. The second, though within his own territory, was supported in his resistance of authority by the first. Both, and together, they had successfully battled with his forces. Before he could hope to carry out his aims in regard to the Reserve, it was necessary that he should vanquish the one and exact submission from the other; if Usibebu could but be overcome the rest might be easy.

That he designed attacking Usibebu he himself declared to Mr. Fynn. The operations against Uhamu were pressed with less vigour, although the main force was kept in his immediate neighbourhood; and Usibebu maintained his army in a state of readiness to resist the expected attack, chafing somewhat under the delay which occurred.

The strain became great; but eventually the spell was broken on the 14th of July. The forces of Cetshwayo that were stationed at the Isikwebezi River proceeded in the night, in two divisions, to the Itokazi Hill, a considerable distance within Usibebu's territory, and uniting there, swept back, killing a number of people whom they surprised, and carrying off their cattle and other property. What gave immediate rise to this movement cannot be precisely ascertained, but it was natural in the circumstances.

The incident was seized upon by Usibebu as justifying a movement on which he had resolved some time previously, and for which he had been making preparations. He was now joined by a contingent furnished by Uhamu, and began assembling his forces at the Ekuvukeni kraal on the eastern slope of the Nongoma Ridge.

USIBEBU

Although rumours of his designs were brought to Cetshwayo they were not credited, and the bulk of the force remained at the Isikwebezi with Umnyamana. Very many of the notables and old men of the nation were residing at Ulundi, and went to rest on the night of the 20th of July unconscious of danger, having no thought of what was in store for them on the morrow. No one believed that so audacious an enterprise would be embarked upon as an attack upon the king at his capital. But as sleep came upon them, the Mandhlakazi, by which name Usibebu's followers were known, with their allies, were filing down the steep and stony sides of the Qonqo Hill and, crossing the Black Umfolozi River, were heading by a bee-line for the heights overlooking Ulundi on its south-east. At their head rode the resolute little man whose personality nerved them for the enterprise which lay before them. The road lay through a wide mimosa-clad valley, whose only inhabitants were wild beasts. The distance to be covered during the night was over twenty miles, but there would be nothing to take alarm at their approach except an occasional antelope or wild cat. Nothing would oppose their march till Ulundi itself should be reached; but woe to them if they should waver before the enemy to be encountered there! Tired with their long night march, there would be little hope of retraversing the wide expanse by which they would be separated from their homes before the fury that their audacity would have evoked. Usibebu must be regarded as one of the most remarkable of the Zulus. It is impossible to see his face without recognising those qualities that will dare much. But though the enterprise was daring it had not been rashly embarked upon. He knew what was practicable in the circumstances. The men he was going to fight were still unnerved by the recollection of their hopeless flight across the Umona Plains; their preparations for battle were incomplete; and they were made to feel weak by the absence of so large a portion of the army to which they belonged. They would not stand before a determined attack, and he knew he could trust his men to attack with determination.

As the day dawned he concentrated his men upon a narrow neck some five miles from the Ulundi kraal, and having assigned to each company the place it was to occupy in the action, the march was continued in file by a footpath till the heights were reached. Then each section fell into its place and the encircling movement began. Not till it had got within sight of Ulundi was the approaching army detected. Then the available force was called to arms and sent out to meet it; but to meet it was all that these defenders of the king were able to do.

Unprepared for fighting, the Usutu turned and ran as soon as they received an impression of the resolution which animated their assailants. Fynn was an eye-witness of the scene. "About eight o'clock," he says, "on the morning of the 21st of July 1883, I saw the forces proceeding from Ulundi towards the south-east. They had proceeded about a mile when they spread out in detachments, apparently in irregular form, on the knolls east of Ulundi, and appeared to become disconnected. About 8.30 they became scattered like a swarm of bees and were running, and passed the entrance of Ulundi in their flight, when I observed the huts on the right-side of the entrance to be on fire, and could hear gun-shots amongst the scattered people running and covering the country westward of Ulundi. The fire in Ulundi spread until the whole kraal was in a blaze (I estimated the number of huts to be 1000 or more)."

So for the second time did that ill-fated kraal ascend in smoke, while its owner and defenders sought escape in flight. The king himself was perhaps in less danger at the hands of the present attacking force. The men composing it had been his subjects and knew him and held his person in a high degree of sacredness. Not less appalling, even

THE STORY OF THE ZULUS

in the ranks of the enemy, would be a deliberate attempt on his life than was the reported declaration of Oliver Cromwell that "if he met the king in battle he would fire his pistol at the king as at another."

Cetshwayo had left at an early stage of the proceedings, and, mounted on a somewhat sorry horse, betaken himself in a south-western direction. But before proceeding a great distance he took shelter in a clump of trees, where he was presently discovered by a party of Usibebu's force, led by one Ralijana, a son of Somfula, the chief of a section of the Hlabisa tribe, who cast their assegais at him, two of them wounding him in the thigh. Upon his remonstrating with them, however, for stabbing their king, they desisted, explaining that they had mistaken him for his brother, Usiwedu. He was thus enabled to escape. As for Ralijana, he could no longer dwell with the chief for whom he had fought, so serious was the resentment he incurred by injuring the king's person.

For others there was no respect or mercy shown. Mr. Fynn prepared a list of the principal chiefs and notables who were slain. The list gives the names of fifty-nine of them. They were from all parts of Zululand, including the Reserve territory. The list includes the names of Seketwayo and Ntshingwayo, who had been appointed chiefs in the settlement of 1879, and the latter of whom commanded the Zulu forces at Isandhlwana; Godode, the chief son of Dingana's adviser and victim, Undhlela; Sirayo, whose son had given the immediate cause for the Zulu war; Umbopa, the Hlabisa chief, the same man who participated in the assassination of Tshaka, whose aunt was the mother of Umpande, and whose name, Songiya, may still be heard in asseverations; Nkabonina, brother of Umbopa, who had been prominent in sheltering Cetshwayo when pursued by the troops in 1879; Dilikana, the chief of the Amambata; Haiana, the brother of Usibebu, whose disaffection had been fruitful of much

R

trouble, and others of less note, perhaps, but who nevertheless had filled important places in the nation. The destruction of old men which occurred on this occasion rendered it difficult afterwards to find those in the country who could supply from memory accounts of the incidents of the nation's progress.

The slaughter was very great; in the wake of the victorious invaders there remained nothing but blackness and desolation; the flames of grass fires sped over the hills; the homes of the people were burnt, wherever found, and their cattle and food taken, and their women made captives.

In Usibebu's service, and assisting him in these proceedings, were five Englishmen; and he was possessed of, and carried into use, a considerable number of guns which he had acquired, although in what way it is not clear, after the general disarmament which followed the war of 1879.

He was become a terror, and, sweeping round by the Inhlazatshe Mountain, he soon made Umnyamana's position extremely precarious.

The country was in worse confusion than ever. For days Cetshwayo was believed to be dead, and Mr. Osborn had instructions, on verification of this belief, to proceed to his territory and endeavour to restore order. But verification was not forthcoming, and contrary rumours soon began to circulate.

CHAPTER XXIII

RUMOUR was soon found to have spoken truly. By the 6th of August it was clearly established that Cetshwayo not only was alive but that he was at the kraal of the chief Usingananda, in the vicinity of the Inkandhla bush, and within the Reserve territory. And it soon became evident that a strong disposition existed amongst the people there to treat him rather as their own king than as a fugitive from his country. On the strength of this disposition a good deal had now to depend. The maintenance of the Reserve depended upon that of those people within it who were opposed to Cetshwayo's rule; the question seemed likely to arise: What number were prepared to fight for the king or for the white ruler? Mr. Osborn, while expressing his confidence that those on his side were both able and willing to support him, urged the importance of sending a body of troops into the territory he ruled in order to impart confidence as to the determination of the British Government to maintain the position in the country which it had assumed. As for Cetshwayo, his attitude did not clearly disclose his intention. Hearing of the approach of troops towards the border, he expressed his willingness to place himself under their protection. But he evaded seeing Mr. Osborn, who visited the locality in which he had taken up his abode, and declined to proceed to his seat of government at Eshowe. He accused Mr. Osborn and the British authorities in Natal of favouring those who sought his destruction. He declared that Usibebu had been supplied with guns, and that he had been encouraged in the proceedings he had taken. The circumstance that that chief was assisted in his recent operations by European subjects of the queen was proof, he said, of the correctness of the accusation. It soon began to be said that he was holding communication with the Boers in the Transvaal. He denied this; but it is clear, at least, that those people were already regarding the condition of affairs as holding out a promise of addition to their territory. Indeed, an independent party of Boers was already establishing a settlement near to the Ihlobane Mountain, and measuring off farms and appointing a committee of management.

Usibebu continued active. About the middle of August he led his forces to the coast and attacked Somkele, forcing him to take shelter in the Dukuduku Forest, and seizing large numbers of his cattle. Just before the attack Sokwetshata, now chief of the Umtetwa tribe, instigated by Usibebu, and emboldened by the general demoralisation under which Cetshwayo's adherents laboured, attacked, with the same result, some minor tribes on the immediate south.

In these acts Usibebu had proceeded in direct opposition to the injunction of the Special Commissioner, who had hastened to request, on hearing of the attack on Ulundi, that he would discontinue warlike operations pending such decision as might be come to by the British Government. Finding that this injunction, which had been sent to all chiefs, had been disobeyed in these instances, messengers were at once sent to repeat it.

A story told by one of these, who visited the domains of Somkele immediately after the departure of Usibebu's impi, may be interesting for its similarity to that of Jael and Sisera, as well as showing how the killing of those opposed to them in war was regarded by the Zulu race. Arriving at a kraal, there the messenger beheld the inmates engaged in a dance of the kind which celebrates the performance of some heroic deed. Prominent amongst the dancers was a young woman. She was decorated

THE STORY OF THE ZULUS

with Iziqu—threaded bits of wood worn by those who have slain an enemy—which had been lent for the occasion by her brothers. She leaped wildly while her praises were vociferated by the assemblage. One of Usibebu's men had lost his way in the bush. He had wandered hopelessly for several days without food or water. Eventually he had emerged where the heroine of the scene was employed in her garden, and, confiding in her, begged a drink. She told him to hide while she fetched water, promising also to bring food. When presently she returned, however, there were with her two stalwart brothers, armed with assegais, and they laid hold of him and held him fast while she stabbed him to death with one of those weapons. It was for this act of heroism that her praises were being celebrated.

Cetshwayo continued at the Inkandhla bush. A number of armed men had accompanied him from his own territory, and there gathered round him also some from amongst the people of the Reserve. His attitude was regarded by the Special Commissioner as extremely unsatisfactory. He neither acknowledged himself to be a fugitive from his own dominions nor complied with the imperative demand of the Resident Commissioner that he would disperse his armed following and proceed to the Residency.

On the 24th of August Mr. Osborn telegraphed announcing his determination to "call up the loyal tribes and coerce him without delay"; and again on the following day that he meant to "push coercive measures rapidly." It thus seemed as if the question who was to govern them was again about to plunge these unhappy people into a sanguinary conflict; the one party, on this occasion, having the support of the British Government. But caution prevailed. Circumstanced as the Resident Commissioner then was the issue would have been very doubtful. It would have depended upon the result of the first encounter;

and the chances of success were not favourable to him because of the strong position held by Cetshwayo's forces. The state of the people was such that one failure would have entirely discouraged them. British troops were urgently appealed for in order to give "moral" courage to the loyal tribes. These did not arrive till a month later. In the meantime frequent communications were exchanged without giving any hope of a peaceful settlement. William Grant, acting on the appointment he had received at Ulundi, had joined Cetshwayo at Inkandhla and advised him to stay there until he should receive a reply to voluminous representations which he had made on his behalf to the Secretary of State. Sir Henry Bulwer's solemn warning as to what would be the result of a continuance to disregard the request that Cetshwayo should proceed to Eshowe failed to produce any effect; and by the beginning of October there appeared to be no course open but that of the application of force.

But the hopelessness of his position was beginning to impress itself upon Cetshwayo's mind. Usibebu had gauged the situation. He had perceived that his own safety lay in the failure of Cetshwayo to re-establish himself. It was apparent to him that the position of the Reserve was critical. He had, therefore, assembled a large force, made up partly of men supplied by Uhamu and the chief Umfanawendhlela, and marched to the Ibabanango, a point on the border stream, the Umhlatuzi, opposite to the position occupied by Cetshwayo in the Reserve. This was a strong moral support to the people of that territory who might be disposed to fight against the king, but of a character which had necessarily to be repudiated by the British authorities.

The necessary instructions were issued and preparation made to enforce the demands with which Cetshwayo had failed to comply; but Fynn, the British Resident at Ulundi, having been recalled, volunteered on his arrival

THE STORY OF THE ZULUS

at Eshowe to convey personally a final message of warning, and to use his personal influence in persuading Cetshwayo into compliance. He was successful. His persuasive eloquence was palpably supported by the proximity of Usibebu; but the important result attained was that he was able to return to Eshowe on the 15th of the month bringing the fugitive king with him.

The place at which Cetshwayo took up his residence there was near to the spot which was occupied in 1839 by the Gqikazi kraal, from which his father, Umpande, proceeded on the enterprise which resulted in his becoming king of the Zulus. As for him, his kingship and life were shortly to end there.

The state of the country was, indeed, a sad one. That portion which had been given back to Cetshwayo was without a ruler. Usibebu was walking rampant over it, seizing the cattle and food of the people. Large areas were depopulated, the places where the people had dwelt being marked by the ashes of their dwellings. The planting season had come, but there was no planting. The question what should be done to end so unhappy a condition was greatly perplexing the British authorities. Should Cetshwayo be reinstated? Against this it was argued that he had so violated the conditions of his restoration that he could not be trusted to abide by such requirements as it would be necessary, in the interests of law and order, to stipulate; that he had abandoned the territory assigned to him and could not return without the support of British troops, which might thus become involved in such lawless acts as he might commit; that by the attitude he had assumed in the Reserve he had forfeited all claim to such support. Should Usibebu be recognised as by right of conquest? This would be unjust to those Zulus who were opposed to him, and would put him in a position in which he would have to assert and maintain his authority by the spear. Should the country be left to itself? The result would be harrowing. Should the principles of the Zulu Native Reserve Territory be extended over the whole of it? This course the Special Commissioner believed would best secure the welfare of the people, but its success could not be secured unless Cetshwayo were sent out of the country. Should Dinuzulu, the then only son of Cetshwayo and a minor, be established in the place of his father, with a British Resident and Council of Regency composed of Zulu head-men? This was believed to be practicable if Usibebu's authority were extended to the Black Umfolozi and Cetshwayo removed.

Of these alternatives the only one which in any sense commended itself to the Secretary of State was the last. This he was prepared to accept, provided that it could be ascertained to be acceptable to the people by whom Cetshwayo's territory was occupied. It had been perceived by Sir Henry Bulwer that it would not be acceptable to Uhamu at least. The object which he had in view, when he made the proposal conditional on the extension of Usibebu's border, was plainly to bring Uhamu under the authority of that chief. He assumed, perhaps, that as these two chiefs were in alliance there would be no objection on the part of the one to the rule of the other; there would have been a danger in acting upon this assumption. The object of the alliance had been to secure independent rule to each; the arrangement would, without doubt, have set them at war with each other. The bulk of Umnyamana's lands and tribe would also have fallen to Usibebu, as also the Umpukunyoni under Somkele. The circumstances precluded almost all hope of a peaceful adjustment.

Cetshwayo had entirely lost even the little to which he had been restored. Those chiefs within his territory who had yielded unwilling submission to his authority now thought they saw in the state of things a prospect of being able to throw it off again, and regain independent authority over their own tribes. Conspicuous amongst these was Umfanawendhlela, the Zungu chief. So satisfied had he become that the desire, which he had not disguised from the first, was about to be realised, that he actually afforded assistance to Usibebu in his operations against Cetshwayo. There is evidence that he had an understanding with the former before he made the attack on Ulundi on the 21st of July; it has been seen that a number of his men were with him at the Ibabanango at the time when the question was presented to Cetshwayo whether he would go to Eshowe voluntarily or under compulsion. He expected that a speedy settlement of the affairs of the country would be arranged by the British Government, and shaped his course in the way which seemed to him most likely to secure him favour at the hands of that Government. His proceedings had early attracted the attention and called forth the resentment of the king. Soon it became known that an attack upon him was comtemplated by the king's partisans, and he betook himself with his people for safety to the territory of Usibebu. Thinking, however, that nearness to that chief would afford sufficient protection, he returned with his own family to the south of the Black Umfolozi River, to a kraal he had built in the mimosa bush there. In the meantime Mankulumana, a son of the Ndwandwe chief, Somapunga, was gathering an impi for his destruction; and early on the morning of the 14th of December he was awakened by its arrival. There was no mercy in that impi and no way of escape.

This was the most serious breach of the peace that had occurred for some time. There were other fitful raids and reprisals; but generally the injunction of the Special Commissioner to all to remain quiet, till they should hear of the decision to be arrived at, had been observed. Usibebu had been restrained by this injunction from further harassing Umnyamana. Though in constant expectation of attack, the people of that chief were generally able to go into the fields to plart.

Such quietness as prevailed was, however, of but a temporary character. Something had to be done by the British authorities to give permanent peace. Sir Henry Bulwer prepared exhaustive expositions of the prevailing condition and strove to indicate a remedy. But, as has been seen, there was little that was promising in his suggestions. The Zulu country and its affairs formed, perhaps, the most perplexing and distasteful of the subjects with which Mr. Gladstone's Government had to deal.

A period was given to the course of events on the 8th of February 1884, on the cause and effect of which were despatched and received these two telegrams, both dated the 9th of the same month, the one from Sir Henry Bulwer to the Earl of Derby, Secretary of State for the Colonies, the other in answer to it: "Mr Osborn has telegraphed, under date the 8th instant, to say that Cetshwayo died in his hut about 4.30 P.M. on that day, and that Dr. Scott, who saw him after death, was of opinion that death was due to fatty disease of the heart." "Circumstances are now altered; have you any new suggestions?"

CHAPTER XXIV

THERE was in reality but little alteration in the circumstances. When Cetshwayo was dead his brothers went to Mr. Osborn and made a report which surprised him and in a higher degree surprised Sir Henry Bulwer. Both had been led to understand that his death had occurred suddenly and unexpectedly. Now it was formally announced to them that he had called the members of his family together and told them that he felt himself to be overtaken by death, but that he would not altogether die, inasmuch as he had a son, Dinuzulu, who would succeed him.

That he had actually done this was seriously doubted; but it mattered little whether or not, since those who made the announcement were the same to whom the dying words were supposed to have been addressed, and it was their design to be guided by their purport.

The king had been placed in a position in which he could afford little help to the party which supported him. That party could be little worse off with a king who was still a minor, but who was free to act as might be necessary. Therefore they were resolved to recognise Dinuzulu as the successor to Cetshwayo and, with his uncle Undabuko as regent, to set about the business of getting out of their difficulties. There at first appeared no clear way to that end. The quarrel with Usibebu had become so serious a matter that conciliation was not possible; he was grown so strong that they could not live in his proximity except by his permission.

Sir Henry Bulwer made his recommendation. It was

that the dominion of Usibebu should be extended to the Black Umfolozi River from the north, and British authority, as established in the Reserve Territory, from the south. The Usutu party would thus be apportioned between the Resident Commissioner and Usibebu. It is not necessary to mention this proposal except to show that the condition of affairs had become such that no remedy could be found that would not involve bloodshed. It was rejected by the English Government, a telegram, dated the 16th of May 1884, announcing their purpose to "adhere to their decision not to extend sovereignty or protection over Zululand."

By this time there had been fighting in the Reserve, and important movements were in progress out of it.

Events had been carefully watched by certain Boers, and they perceived that the time had arrived when the object which they had in view might be gained. There were two of these whose names had already become familiar to the Zulus, and have ever since been remembered, not without bitterness, by the party for whose benefit it was their policy to manifest solicitude. The first was Jacobus Van Staden, known to the Zulus as Kontshi—a mis-pronunciation of Kootje, the Dutch diminutive of his Christian name; the other Conrad Meyer, a Boer emissary of old standing. These men first proceeded to Umnyamana, but finding that, with his characteristic caution, he would not commit himself by countenancing their proposals, they set about searching for Dinuzulu, who was a mere boy; but whose position they knew would render their offer a tempting one. They came with offers of Boer help to secure him in the succession. They desired him to accompany them to Wakkerstroom, where arrangements would be made for placing him on the throne, as had been done in the case of his grandfather Umpande.

By the 3rd of April he had left Inkandhla, where he had been resident at the time of his father's death, and proceeded to join Umnyamana at his Ekushumayeleni kraal for the purpose of considering this offer. There was much misgiving in the minds of the Zulus. They suspected some design to take their land, and intimated their fear in that regard. But the most emphatic assurances were given to the contrary. The Boer emissaries "made a heap of stones and put a stick in it as their oath. One of them took off his hat and placed it on the heap of stones swearing that they wanted neither cattle nor land."

Their mission was successful. Dinuzulu accompanied them. And the necessities of the circumstances thus created added to the disposition of those of the Usutu party who resided in the Reserve Territory to withhold that submission which the authority there considered its due. The principal Usutu chief residing within the borders of that territory was Dabulamanzi. His attitude was such that the Resident Commissioner felt it to be necessary to reduce him by force to submission or to expel him. Accordingly he mustered what he could of the men well affected to himself, about 3000, and, with the Zulu Carbineers under Mansel, was at the Inkandhla early in May. He summoned the Usutu there to answer for molestation of loyal natives, of which they had been accused, and, no response being vouchsafed, he ordered the seizure of their cattle. A slight conflict ensued, with a few casualties on both sides, and, in the early morning of the 10th of the month, Dabulamanzi attacked his camp with a considerable force. It was fortunate for the Commissioner that he had the disciplined and properly armed Carbineers, for the other native force which he had brought would plainly not have withstood the attack. Dabulamanzi was repulsed with considerable loss; but the situation was still so discouraging that Mr. Osborn decided on a retirement to Eshowe, and concluded that he would be unable to maintain his position without the aid of troops, which aid was authorised a few days later, some regulars being soon despatched to Eshowe.

But of serious attack or armed opposition he was, for the time being, in little danger. The attention of the Usutu party was engaged in the main enterprise in which the help of the Boers had been secured.

By the 7th of May some 400 Boers, armed as for war, were in central Zululand, and matters proceeded with considerable rapidity.

It was still the profession of the Boers that they were actuated by motives of solicitude towards the Zulu people. They desired, they said, to make an end to the strife which was destroying them; to give them peace. They sent assurance of friendship to Usibebu, and invited him to attend the ceremony of Dinuzulu's installation as king. They affected a hope that friendly feeling might be reestablished between these two chiefs by this means.

In some measure they would appear to have believed that the object they professed was their real object. But that at which they aimed could not be attained by friendly intercession, and the pretence, whether to themselves or to others, was not long maintained. They were marching against the man who had proved himself so formidable a foe to the Usutu that they could no longer trust in their own strength to prevail against him.

In vain Usibebu applied to and supplicated the British authorities for help in his extremity. He had no fear of the Usutu force by itself: but, aided by this considerable European army, he realised that he would be no match for it. He was resolved, nevertheless, to face the odds that were advancing against him. He elected to make his stand where the Umkuzi Stream enters the gap in the Lebombo Mountain, through which it has found its way to the sea. The spot is some fourteen miles to the northeast of his principal kraal, the Banganomo. It is still marked, after sixteen years, by the bones of those that fell

THE STORY OF THE ZULUS

in the battle that ensued, and has an interest to the few who travel in the remote locality in which it lies. When those bones have finally returned to their elements the scene of the battle will possess a sufficient interest in its own physical grandeur and beauty. The mountain on the southern side of the gap forms a lofty peak of bald rock, called by the Zulus Itshana, or the little stone, which has become more widely known for the battle that was fought at its base. On the north it is less abrupt, so that it has been found possible to make a road by which vehicles may be drawn to the magistracy at the top. It is clothed with wood and a profusion of vegetation, and presents a landscape the beauty of which largely compensates for the fatigue involved in the ascent. Tall trees and various luxuriance of heat-loving plants fringe the stream at the bottom.

Usibebu placed his fighting men between the Itshana and the stream, and those who could not bear arms in places of security on the brow which faces the south.

The position was obviously chosen with the view of escaping in the event of defeat, while if success should attend him the invaders might be pursued to destruction across the fourteen miles of waste level which they had traversed before reaching it.

The invading army was advancing. The Boers were mounted and were a serious difficulty, as, by conducting a running fight, they would render but partial any success the defenders of the position might attain. Usibebu perceived this, and made a disposition by which he hoped to destroy their horses at the beginning of the engagement.

An accidental shot betrayed this intention.

The Boers had, as when they went to war on behalf of Umpande, designed that the Zulus should do their own fighting. They placed them in front, undertaking to support them if necessary with their rifles.

The collision took place on the 5th of June. The

Usutu army was strong, but experience had led it to respect the foe it had to encounter. The Boers took up the best covering position the ground would afford; it was the sense of their presence that induced the Usutu to advance to the attack. Their formation was as usual, but the ground was ill-adapted for an encircling movement, the space between the Itshana and the stream being narrow and wooded. The right wing was the first to encounter Usibebu's force near the base of the hill. The shock it received forced it back in some confusion on the main body. Then the Boers' rifles came into action. They were unable to distinguish between friend and foe; many of both fell to their fire. But it had the effect of checking the retreat. The Mandhlagazi, being unable to face the shower of bullets that rained upon them, turned and fled; the Usutu also turned, partly for the same cause, partly because their pursuers had turned. The battle was over. The pursuit was active and unsparing. The stream, sluggish in parts, with its tangle-grown banks, seriously impeded retreat, as is testified by the number of bones to be seen there. The battle of Etshaneni has been well remembered, and may be referred to for the purpose of fixing a date.

Usibebu was at last vanquished and driven forth. Dinuzulu was recognised as king of such Zulus outside of the Reserve as would yield him allegiance; those who would not had, perforce, for the present to seek other dwelling places or the shelter of rocks. Usibebu, and those of his people who could get there, took refuge in the Reserve, as did Sokwetshata and his Umtetwa people. Uhamu maintained a kind of resistance in his own rocky country; he and his people were destined to find themselves tenants on Boer farms, into which his land was soon to be converted.

As for the Usutu, it was now required of them that they should make payment for the help they had received,

Itshana, or Etshaneni Battlefield

THE STORY OF THE ZULUS 273

and the claim was a heavy one. A farm was demanded for each Boer who had joined in their service. Report of the expedition, and the prospect it held out, had spread far, and the Boers claiming reward were found to number some 800. To provide each with a farm would require a quantity of land that would very seriously diminish the little country that still remained to the Zulu kingdom.

In vain the Usutu repudiated any agreement to give land, or offered what to their minds would be sufficient for the service that had been rendered them, or protested that they had not engaged so large a number of Boers. "If," said one of the latter, at a meeting to discuss the matter two months after the battle, "the Kafirs don't want to give the land we must take the land and bring the Kafirs to their senses"; and he thus gave expression to the view of the matter which prevailed amongst his compatriots.

William Grant was with Dinuzulu exercising the functions of "representative and adviser of the Zulu nation." His appointment was at first verbal, but afterwards, for the satisfaction of the British authorities, it was reduced to writing and signed by Dinuzulu, Undabuko and Umnyamana. The written appointment was dated the 11th of September. Already, on the 16th of August, Dinuzulu as King of the Zulus and Grant in the capacity named had signed a document granting to the Boers the full reward which they had demanded; consenting, apparently, while they protested that they would never consent. As to how this came about, the statements of Mr. Grant are entirely opposed to those of the persons he represented. While he declared on the one hand that he was empowered to sign the document and that its contents were understood, the men who were supposed to give him that power declared with great emphasis that they had neither understood it nor authorised its signature.

It "granted a certain number of South African farmers

S

in Zululand, for their free use and as their property, a certain portion of Zululand, bordering on the South African Republic and the Reserve Territory, in extent, more or less, 1,355,000 morgen, with the right to establish there an independent Republic called the New Republic"; and further proclaimed that from its date the remaining portion of Zululand and the Zulu nation should be subject to the supervision of the said New Republic.

On the strength of this document the measuring of farms was proceeded with. It continued until the sea was reached, and there remained little for the Zulus beyond what had formed the territory of Usibebu.

CHAPTER XXV

MATTERS continued in this condition until April 1886, when the Zulu authorities resolved on asking for the intervention of the British Government on their behalf. The message on the subject was conveyed by Undabuko and Tshingana, and was represented as from Dinuzulu in the capacity of Zulu king. He was generally regarded as possessing the kingly quality. The Boers had declared him king, although possibly with the same mental reservation as has been claimed on behalf of their forefathers in the case of Umpande, whose kingship they are said to have intended to affect the people and not the land.

It was nearly two years since the assumption by the Boer community of sovereignty over territory, the limits of which were to comprehend farms of a specified number and acreage; they had also during that period exercised such supervision over the whole of the country that had been under Zulu rule as amounted to the assumption of complete authority over it. Dinuzulu and his council had never, on their part, shown any disposition, whatever may have been their understanding of it, to abide by the terms of the document he and Mr. William Grant had signed, and by virtue of which the Boers maintained their sovereign rights as a community and title to ownership of land as individuals. They consistently repudiated the construction placed upon that document by the Boers, declaring that they had understood it to have reference to a piece of land on the north-western side of their country, limited by a line from the Inkandi to the Zungeni Hill; that it was designed to reward about a hundred Boers, which number only had actively helped them in their operations against Usibebu. In their view of the subject their minds would appear to have gone back to the territorial dispute which preceded the Zulu war; and they were willing, for the help they had been afforded, to surrender the land which had formed the subject of that dispute.

As the result of their representation to the Governor of Natal in his capacity as Special Commissioner for Zulu Affairs, communication was opened between that officer and the authorities of the new republic at their capital town of Vrijheid.

There had been established a Volks Raad there under the presidency of Lucas Johannes Meyer, who was destined to command the first attack upon the British forces in the Boer war at Talana.

In response to an invitation, he and other Boers forming an authoritative deputation proceeded to Natal, and met the Special Commissioner in Durban with the object of endeavouring to arrive at some agreement; but there was no result. The Boer delegates declared themselves unable to accept the basis of negotiations laid down by the Special Commissioner. This contained the conditions that the land to be acquired by the Boers should be bounded on the south-east approximately by a line drawn from the Ibabanango Hill to the Inhlazatshe Mountain, and thence in a northerly direction to the Pongolo River; that the Boers should abandon all claim to a protectorate over Zulus residing outside that boundary, called the Zulu nation, and leave them in undisturbed possession of what remained of their country; that they should guarantee within the land to be acquired by them the rights derived by missionary bodies, of whatever nationality, from Cetshwayo and his predecessors.

THE STORY OF THE ZULUS 277

The negotiations were broken off and the Boer deputation made a statement of their case to the Press. They had found it impossible, they said, to consider the question of accepting the boundary stipulated by the Special Commissioner. They required 2,260,600 acres to provide farms for 800 Boers; the boundary he had indicated would deprive them of 250 farms, leaving provision only for 550. The deprivation of 250 Burghers would cause dissatisfaction and imperil the young republic. It would moreover reduce the area of their land so greatly as to render it incapable of supporting a government.

The deputation returned to Vrijheid and the administration of the republic proceeded as before. The chiefs and people were made to realise that they had become subject to the rule of the Boer invaders; that their position had become that of tenants, subject to the same conditions in that respect as members of the native race in other parts of South Africa which were under European occupation. They had to render personal service to their landlords, and found this exacted in some cases by means of bodily coercion. In their own exaggerative words, "in all the country where there was a Boer, their people were beaten; they were tied up and beaten, men, women and children; they had wounds on their heads and wales on their backs."

On the 4th of the month succeeding that of the abortive conference, Dinuzulu and his councillors addressed a long and pathetic appeal to the Special Commissioner, setting forth these troubles and complaining particularly that the graves of his ancestors, Makosini, were being desecrated. Then on the 12th of October came three other messengers, Siziba, Zeyize and Umlulwana, to report two occurrences to which great importance was attached, and to reiterate the prayer for intervention by the British Government. The first of these occurrences was the death of Dabulamanzi. He had been arrested by a Boer field-cornet on the 21st of September for declaring the rights of Dinuzulu to the land, and, escaping on the following day into the Reserve territory while being escorted to Vrijheid, and there claiming British protection and refusing to proceed, was shot by his guard. The second was the burning by the Boer authorities of the Ondini, or Ulundi kraal, which Dinuzulu had caused to be built at Inhlazatshe.

In the meantime there had been a renewal of correspondence with the authorities of the New Republic. The Special Commissioner had assumed a more imperative tone on the subject of the desired settlement. On the 6th of September he had addressed a letter to the president, in which, while expressing a willingness still to negotiate, he intimated that it might become necessary in the event of negotiation being declined, to send a commissioner into Zululand to fix a line of demarcation in such a manner as might seem expedient after inquiry on the spot; and it had been agreed that another meeting should take place between him and a Boer deputation on the 18th of October.

The meeting was held at the appointed time, and attended on behalf of the New Republic by President Meyer, R. J. Spies and D. J. Esselen; the Zulus were unrepresented except in so far as they may be regarded as having placed their case in the hands of the Special Commissioner.

The negotiations proceeded upon the basis previously laid down, except in regard to the question of boundary; the Special Commissioner had found it necessary to admit discussion of that which he had previously indicated.

On the fourth day (22nd October 1886) an agreement was arrived at. The Boer deputation undertook, subject to the approval of the Zulus, to abandon all claim to protection over them as a nation, and gave the required guarantee in respect to missionaries. Approval of the agreement by the British Government was to carry with it the recognition of the New Republic as an independent state. These questions involved little difficulty, but the matter of boundary was different. In regard to this a very considerable departure had been made, in favour of the Boers, from that which had been proposed by the Special Commissioner at the earlier meeting. The one agreed upon was to leave the Ibabanango and Inhlazatshe far to the west, and instead of reaching the Pongolo River by a northerly line from the latter mountain, it was to proceed from a point on the White Umfolozi River over the Idhlebe and Ceza mountains, and by way of the Umkuzana and Umkuzi streams and the ridge of the Lebombo Mountain. Then a large tract of country lying still to the eastward was made subject to the proviso marked " B," " that all settlers having received allotments " therein " might continue to occupy and possess such allotments ": the additional land thus made available for Boer occupation, and of which they were to become the absolute owners, extended to a line drawn from the Hlopekulu Mountain, some ten miles below the Ulundi Drift of the White Umfolozi River, straight towards the Hlokohloko Mountain, as far as to the Umhlatuzi River, by which the territory was to be further limited. The wagon road from the upper Umhlatuzi to the Ulundi Drift completed the boundary of the New Republic. This excluded from what remained of Zululand that portion of the country "described as the 'cradle' of the Zulu nation, in which are situated the sites of the royal burial places," which under a misapprehension the Special Commissioner reported that he had secured to the Zulus.

And before twenty days had elapsed there came another deputation from Dinuzulu and his councillors, in the persons of his uncle Tshingana, Sibamu, and Umtshupana, the latter being a well-known induna of the old prime minister Umnyamana. They had heard of the Ibabanango-

Inhlazatshe boundary which the Special Commissioner had at first proposed, and sent this deputation to protest against it as ceding too much land to the Boers. They said they had been led to expect, and still expected, that they would be afforded an opportunity of discussing the question with the Boers in the Special Commissioner's presence. This deputation caused a letter to be written to the queen in like terms, and requested the Special Commissioner to forward it. But by this time the agreement had been approved by the Secretary of State, and it remained only to intimate its terms to the Zulu deputation, and to convey through them the request to the Zulu authorities, that they would appoint a commissioner to represent the nation at the demarcation of the boundary shortly to be proceeded with by the Resident Commissioner of the Reserve territory, Mr. Osborn and Colonel Frederic Cardew on the part of the British Government, and commissioners representing the New Republic.

The Boer deputation had objected to the boundary first proposed, on the ground that it would deprive individual Boers of their allotments. Any alienation of country to them necessarily affected individual Zulus in the same way. The boundary which had been agreed upon deprived whole tribes of all rights whatever, and made them liable to summary removal by those who had come into ownership of the land they had dwelt upon for generations. Amongst the tribes so affected were the Umgazini, that of Uhamu, the Umdhlalose, the Abaqulusini, and the greater portion of the Butelezi under Umnyamana. These derived no compensating benefit from the agreement. It was only theoretically possible for them to come within the land secured to the Zulu nation. In the course of his interview with the Zulu deputation the Special Commissioner threw out the suggestion that a large tract had become available through its abandonment by Usibebu, but how far this promised practical relief will be seen as this account proceeds.

The commissioners duly proceeded with the work of demarcation. A beginning was made on the 4th of December 1886. The expected Zulu Commissioner, Umeni, did not arrive; it transpired that his horse had fallen with and injured him. An educated native Christian named Martin Lutuli, who acted as interpreter and writer to Dinuzulu, was present with the British Commission, but merely as a spectator. On the 12th of the month the old man Kwabiti presented himself, the work having been in progress in the meantime. He was a man of distinction derived from long life and important experience. His memory extended back to the days of Tshaka, whom he remembered to have seen; amongst other experiences he had been present at the death and received the dying words of Dingana. But as regards the powers conferred upon him on this occasion, these appear to have been very limited. He announced to the British Commissioners the desire of Dinuzulu and Umnyamana to be accorded an interview in order to protest against the partition of the country. He did not accompany the commissioners to the points upon which beacons were to be erected, but contented himself with receiving reports from Martin Lutuli. Eventually he ceased to attend, and to a question as to the reason of his absence, Umnyamana replied that he did not know that it was necessary for a condemned man to appoint any one to witness his execution. Martin Lutuli continued to attend, taking no part in the proceedings. At a meeting held on the 3rd of January 1887, the chiefs, including Dinuzulu and Umnyamana, protested personally against the demarcation, and refused to admit that a final decision had been arrived at on the subject by the British Government. They also refused to entertain the question of accepting a British Protectorate, which was suggested to them, and denied willingness, which they were reported to have expressed, to come under the Government of Natal.

The work of demarcation was completed on the 15th of January, but there remained the question, which seemed of some urgency, what was to be done to secure the safe settlement of the Zulus upon what remained of their country. Mr. Osborn had been charged with the duty of solving this question. He remained in camp at the Idhlebe Hill when the other members of the Commission dispersed, in order to seek a solution; and was able to report on the 8th and 10th of February the decision he had arrived at and the attitude towards it of the Zulus, an attitude which scarcely seems from the reports of the proceedings to have been so definitely favourable as it was subsequently held to be.

Mr. Osborn had held meetings with those in charge of the affairs of the Zulu nation, the chief of whom was Umnyamana, and impressed upon them the hopelessness of the situation in which they had been placed by the events which had culminated in the work just completed by the Commission. It was impossible for them, he said, to continue as a semi-independent people in presence of the dangers by which they were beset.

From those dangers nothing could free them but British protection. He asserted, and they admitted, that the queen might, by virtue of her existing sovereign rights in and over Zululand, extend such protection without consulting them. The object of discussing the subject with them was to convey to their minds a true understanding of the situation, and thus enable them to fully appreciate the great benefit which the queen was graciously pleased to confer in the offer to place them under the protection and supreme authority of the British Government. He invited them to express their views on the subject, intimating that the British Government would disclaim all responsibility for any trouble that

THE STORY OF THE ZULUS 283

might overtake them from within or without their borders if they should delay in availing themselves of the proffered benefits. They asked for time to consider, but days passed without manifestation on their part of a disposition to come to a decision. When urged to resume the adjourned meeting they pleaded illness. Mr. Osborn thought that he perceived the reason underlying this attitude, and that it was favourable to his proposal. He reflected that they were precluded by their laws and traditions from expressing acquiescence in any surrender of sovereignty or alienation of territory, although they were capable of understanding the necessity of yielding to conquest or submission to what circumstances might render inevitable. He construed their omission to refute his statement of their case as a tacit admission that he had correctly stated it.

He therefore resolved to take the initiative into his own hands, and notified Umnyamana, the principal members of Dinuzulu's family, and other chiefs, on the 5th day of February 1887, that "British Protection, carrying with it the supreme authority of Her Majesty's Government," was extended over Eastern Zululand from that date. He assumed at the same time the duties of Resident Commissioner in that territory. The answer of the Zulus was awaited with some anxiety, but when it came it was of a somewhat indefinite nature. It did not recognise any change in their relations with the British Government. The Zulu house, it said, had belonged to the English since the day when Tshaka sent Sotobe to the king across the water. They desired to be permitted to take Dinuzulu to Pietermaritzburg to see the Special Commissioner and urge him to make some further endeavour to get back the land which the Boers had taken.

At the request of the Special Commissioner the effect of what had thus transpired was construed by Mr. Osborn, and also by Sir Theophilus Shepstone, whose valued advice upon natives and their habits of thought and ways of acting was still available at this time. To the first he put the specific question, "Is it understood by the Zulus that the assumption of the Queen's authority is *Annexation to Empire* or *Protection?*" The answer as to the question of understanding by the Zulus was vague, but Mr. Osborn recommended annexation on the ground that the Zulus would not be able to understand protection. Sir Theophilus Shepstone's observations were also of a general character. He characterised the assent given by the Zulu authorities as half-hearted, but attributed the cause to past vacillation on the part of the British Government. It could not be expected, he said, that the Zulus would give an express approval to a proposal by which they might be embarrassed in the event of failure to give it definite and permanent effect. Only the royal family had been dealt with in the matter, who had personal interests to serve, and against whose views the people would not venture to speak. Those personal interests were, however, opposed to the quiet of the country and the happiness of the people; and it was a reproach to the British authorities that they alone had been consulted in the past. The members of that family would doubtless feel that the step was adverse to their personal ambitions, but the generality of the people would hail it with gratitude. He appears to have assumed that annexation was contemplated.

When Sir Arthur Havelock reported acquiescence by the Zulus in the action taken, he was still undecided as to the degree of authority he should assume. The question was resolved by the Imperial Government. The decision was telegraphed on the 11th of May 1887. By that telegram the Secretary of State authorised the Special Commissioner, whom he at the same time appointed to be Governor of the new territory with power to legislate by proclamation, to declare the whole of what remained of Zululand, including the Reserve Territory, to have become a British possession, under the name of Zululand. The proclamation giving effect to this decision was issued on the 14th of the month, and made operative from the 9th day of May 1887.

The request of Dinuzulu and his advisers for permission to visit Sir Arthur Havelock in Pietermaritzburg had resulted in the arrival of a deputation there on the 19th of April. Dinuzulu excused himself for not having gone personally by the fact that certain of his relatives had recently died, including Dabulamanzi and Uhamu, the death of the latter having occurred during the previous February. The message which the deputation bore was a protest against the giving of the country to the Boers, and a request for an inquiry, to be attended by representatives of the New Republic and of the Zulu nation; but to all such representations the answer given was that the settlement was a final one, and that no further discussion could take place upon the subject.

CHAPTER XXVI

THE proclamation of the 14th of May was followed by a second, declaring the laws in force in the Colony of Natal to be extended to the territory of Zululand, so far as they were applicable to its circumstances, and promulgating certain special laws and regulations, based upon those of the Protectorate of Bechuanaland. By these laws and regulations there was no special status recognised as belonging to the heir to the Zulu kingship, or the members of the Zulu royal family. They contemplated equality of authority in all chiefs, and were silent as to who were to be recognised or appointed as such. Such as were to be regarded as entitled to the office were given jurisdiction in all civil causes between natives of their respective tribes; and in criminal matters their powers were limited only by certain classes of crime involving capital punishment under Roman Dutch law, and cases of pretended witchcraft and faction-fighting. Their decisions were all to be subject to appeal, first to the magistrates of their respective districts, and thereafter to the Chief Magistrate, an office which was combined with that of Resident Commissioner.

The Royal Commission appointing the Governor of Natal to be Governor of Zululand and the annexing proclamation of the 14th of May were read at Eshowe by the Resident Commissioner in presence of a large concourse of chiefs and people, who saluted the flag when hoisted at the conclusion of the ceremony and expressed no dissent. Afterwards, on the 7th of July, the ceremony was repeated at Inkonjeni, where the members of the royal family were expected to be present. Dinuzulu did not personally attend, but his uncle Undabuko, who was virtual regent during his minority, was there, and also the prime induna Umnyamana, and Tshingana, and various others associated by office with the royal house, the whole gathering numbering some 600 men. These also saluted the flag, as they were required to do. Copies of the proclamation and of the laws and regulations were sent to Dinuzulu, but he refused to receive them.

The precise extent of the change that had taken place in Dinuzulu's position would perhaps have been somewhat difficult for him to realise, but he appears not to have recognised any change. The question cannot be definitely answered, how far he exercised his personal authority, but either he or his uncle and guardian Undabuko continued to administer the affairs of the people who adhered to him in the same manner as had previously been the practice. A man named Umfokazana, residing near to where the Isikwebezi joins the Black Umfolozi River, was found guilty, through the instrumentality of a diviner, of having practised witchcraft and thereby procured the death of several persons. He was condemned to death and confiscation, and a party of men was despatched to execute the sentence. Umfokazana was found to be absent, but his wife was put to death and his cattle were taken. A quarrel took place between two brothers named Umkosana and Zonyama, residing near the Undunyeni Hill, overlooking the Umona valley, which was regarded as having taken the form of a faction-fight; this Dinuzulu also dealt with by seizure of cattle. The magistrate who had been appointed over the district in which he had established his principal ("Usutu") kraal, and where he resided, required that the cattle should be restored in both cases in order that such offences as might have been committed by the persons accused might be dealt with by lawful authority. Dinuzulu declined or failed to comply with this request, and the Resident Commissioner proceeded to the Inkonjeni, where the magistracy had been temporarily established, in order to obtain an explanation. He summoned Dinuzulu and Undabuko to meet him there on the 3rd of September, and as they failed to attend personally, he imposed upon the first a fine of 30 cattle. Neither these, nor those the restoration of which had been demanded being delivered, a force was sent to seize a sufficient number, this being effected without resistance.

In the meantime a large meeting had been held at the Usutu, and a resolution arrived at to appeal to their late allies at Vrijheid in respect to the proceedings of the British authorities in taking the country and deposing Dinuzulu from the kingship. Dinuzulu proceeded personally to Vrijheid to give effect to this resolution. He was accompanied thither by Undabuko, another uncle named Mahanana, the chief Maboko of the Umgazini tribe, Bantubensumo, chief of a section of the Butelezi, and other representative chiefs and head-men. Tshanibezwe, the chief son of Umnyamana, also went, but according to evidence he gave later, his father did not authorise him to express agreement with the object of the visit.

There had not, up to this time, been a definite expression on behalf of what had been called the Zulu nation, of that approval subject to which the authorities of the New Republic had abandoned their claim to a protectorate over it, and the latter understood, or affected to understand, that what took place at the meeting between their president and this deputation amounted to an assertion by the Zulus of their right to be protected against that of which they now complained. The Governor regarded the proceeding as amounting to treason, and

THE STORY OF THE ZULUS 289

demanded an explanation through the Resident Commissioner, who was still at Inkonjeni. To this demand, though frequently repeated, no compliance was yielded, and the Resident Commissioner's messengers reported that they were treated with indignity, one being actually assaulted by an irresponsible individual without visible intervention by the chiefs. Finally, on the 14th of October, an answer came from Undabuko referring generally to the subject of complaint. Dinuzulu, he said, had taken cattle from his own people, in his own country; Dinuzulu had never agreed to the annexation of the country by the queen; as regarded the request that they should personally attend before the Resident Commissioner, they were prevented by the recent death of the mother of Usiwedu and the illness of Dinuzulu. The messengers reported that the latter was not ill, that they had seen him ride out upon his horse.

It was to secure himself in the kingship that Dinuzulu had embarked on the proceedings which had culminated in the annexation, and the terms of the annexation deprived him entirely of the kingly office. He resented the action by which he found himself thus deprived; it appeared contrary to the nature of the help he had asked the British Government to afford him in his trouble with the Boers. It was his policy to avoid any act of acquiescence in the measures which the British Government had adopted. It was to avoid what might be construed as a manifestation of acquiescence that the surrender of the cattle which he had seized, and payment of the fine that had been imposed upon him, were so obstinately neglected.

The objection to the new state of things was not very general. It was entirely from sentiments of loyalty to Dinuzulu as heir to the kingship that any objection existed at this time. The majority of the people accepted the change cheerfully, and especially those who had for

T

some years experienced a modified form of British rule in the Reserved Territory. By the settlement it had been arranged to pay stipends to certain chiefs, principally members of the royal house, and these had been accepted, except by Dinuzulu and Undabuko. Umnyamana was showing signs of a disposition to secede from the royal cause.

The Governor felt that it was necessary to take serious notice of the conduct of Dinuzulu and Undabuko, especially in respect to their mission to Vrijheid, but also of their attitude towards the Resident Commissioner and their treatment of his messengers. He summoned them to meet him at Eshowe, being resolved to cause their arrest and trial on the charge of treason in the event of a failure on their part to comply with his summons.

The question had in the meantime been under consideration, whether Usibebu should be permitted to return to his tribal lands, from which Dinuzulu, with Boer aid, had expelled him in 1884. His misfortune on that occasion had been viewed by the British Government as a matter in which its obligation did not extend beyond that of affording him a haven in the Reserve. There he had been residing with those members of his tribe who had accompanied him since the time of his expulsion. A considerable number of his adherents had sought other refuge. His chief induna, Usikizana, had gone with a considerable following to Swaziland; his brother Hlomuza, with others, had remained and yielded submission to the victorious Zulu house. Other tribes and tribal sections who had been expelled by him in the circumstances which attended the restoration of Cetshwayo had returned to the sites of their old homes, and Dinuzulu had signalised his assumption of authority by causing a personal kraal to be established in his late territory. In his exile, when importuning the British Government for restoration, he based his appeal on the question, what wrong he had done.

THE STORY OF THE ZULUS   291

He had, he affirmed, obeyed all orders and injunctions which the British authorities had addressed to him. It was due to obedience of such instructions in evacuating Cetshwayo's country after he had been forced by the aggressions of that king to conquer it, that his misfortune had been brought about.

The latest of these representations had been made on the 26th of April 1887, just before the annexation, but after the announcement of protection and the assumption of sovereignty. Upon this, inquiry was made and advice sought; the advice which resulted was unanimously in favour of granting his request. Sir Theophilus Shepstone, Mr. Henrique Shepstone, then Secretary for Native Affairs in Natal, and Mr. Osborn, the Resident Commissioner in Zululand, wrote memoranda strongly recommending it. In their view restoration was an act due to Usibebu in consideration of the loyal attitude he had maintained towards the British Government ever since the settlement of 1879. Omission to restore him might alienate his affections from the Government, and at the same time the influence and energy he was capable of exerting on its behalf. There might even be difficulty in restraining him from spontaneous action in returning to his lands. His presence in the Eshowe district, in the lands of John Dunn, was embarrassing. If restored to his own domains by the hands of the Government, and his affections thus secured, his presence in the eastern portion of the country would exercise a salutary effect upon any disaffected persons. It was believed that the fear his warlike operations had inspired in the past would be a sufficient safeguard against any attack upon him, and that his loyal disposition was a guarantee against any aggression on his part. Upon these views, which Sir Arthur Havelock heartily endorsed, he "earnestly begged," in a despatch dated 3rd of August 1887, "to be entrusted with authority to arrange for the repatriation of Usibebu, at such time and in such manner as circumstances might render convenient," and his request was acceded to by the Secretary of State in a despatch dated the 12th of September.

By the energetic persuasion of the magistrate, Dinuzulu was induced to obey the summons of the Governor, and, having been preceded by Undabuko, they both appeared in his presence on the 14th of November, and had their altered position strongly impressed upon them. "The House of Tshaka," the Governor declared (he might perhaps more correctly have said the House of ZULU), "is a thing of the past; like water that is spilt." He had other things to say little less unpleasant. He had resolved on fining each of them fifty cattle for neglecting to obey the summons and directions of the Resident Commissioner. Then he had to tell them of the decision that had been come to in regard to Usibebu. That chief and Sokwetshata, of the Umtetwa tribe, were to return to their tribal lands. The case of the latter was counted of little importance. He had vacated his tribal lands about the same time as Usibebu, his alliance with that chief having rendered his situation unsafe when the change of fortune occurred. But, beyond the dislike in which he was held by the neighbouring tribes, there was nothing in the way of his reoccupation of his old sites. The case of Usibebu was different. Everything had been hazarded to secure his expulsion, and everything had been lost. The bare satisfaction of having driven him out was all that remained; now even that was to be taken away.

The decision was given immediate effect to. In ten days after the announcement the two chiefs had started. The reason for such precipitancy is perhaps scarcely to be learned from the public statements of the time upon the subject. Those statements cannot be regarded in themselves as justifying it. It was summer, and the crops were growing in the fields. There had been no warning against planting issued to those occupying the lands that had been Usibebu's. On the contrary, the Resident Commissioner had expressed his surprise at a question asked by Dinuzulu on the 21st of September, whether the people might proceed with the planting of their crops. It was the duty, he said, of every one to do so, and the chiefs were to do nothing to prevent them. There can be no doubt that the people referred to by Dinuzulu's question included those in the territory that had been Usibebu's. That chief was now launched amongst these with the "male portion of his tribe," an army of some 700 men entirely unprovisioned, the inhabitants being expected to make way for him, and nothing being said about their standing crops. Perhaps the extent to which the land was inhabited had not been realised, or possibly such consideration as the question might otherwise have deserved was held to be outweighed by the circumstances of the country. The garrison of Imperial troops in the territory and the Zululand Native Police numbered less than 1000 men, in widely distributed detachments. The authority of the Government depended in a considerable measure upon the strength of the well-affected people. It was believed that the presence of Usibebu with a fighting force would overawe disaffection in a somewhat critical locality.

The seat of magistracy was now changed from the Inkonjeni (a lofty plateau between the White and Black Umfolozi rivers, deriving its name from one of Langazana's kraals which once stood upon it) to the site which had been chosen for it beyond the Ivuna stream, known later as Nongoma. There had been two other magistrates appointed for the added territory; the two sub-commissionerships in that which had previously been styled the Reserve were also changed to magistracies, the officers occupying the posts being given the additional office of assistant commissioners. The Eshowe district was also created a magistracy.

When "Mr. R. H. Addison, the Assistant Commissioner and Resident Magistrate of the Ndwandwe district, accompanied by 50 men of the Zululand Police (by which title Mansel's Carbineers were now designated) under Sub-inspector Pearse," arrived at his new seat of office at Nongoma on the 18th of November 1887, he found himself almost immediately beset with difficulties. Usibebu with his 700 hungry followers reached his district on the 3rd of December, and the initial note of trouble was sounded on that day in what had once been the domains of Umbopa, and which had since Usibebu's absence been reoccupied by his son Umtumbu.

Those troubles, which it is the principal object of this chapter to sketch, became the subject later of much acrimonious comment and elaborate inquiry. The papers referring to it, and presenting the views of the responsible officials and those affected by their acts, as well as the comments of partisans, are numerous and voluminous, including much sworn evidence. These documents are attainable only by a few, while those who might be willing to devote to them the time and energy necessary to determine the question of blame, to which so much importance was attached at the time, would doubtless be fewer still. The primary official aim was to establish British sovereignty over the people, and to eradicate affection for that which had been declared extinct. This was a condition, in their view, necessarily precedent to the fostering of an improved state of social life, and it was a condition necessarily somewhat difficult of attainment in presence of the man in whom the supposed extinct sovereignty had been embodied, and the varied and uncertain sentiments towards that man, and opinions as to whether the kingly quality had in fact gone out of him. It was hardly to be expected that he would desire to be regarded as so bereft, or that the people as a whole would desire him to hold himself divested of that which gave them title to be called a nation.

There had been but little time to arrive at an understanding of the condition which it might be thought desirable to improve. The personal power, daring, and obedience to British authority and later misfortunes of Usibebu, had by the prominence they attained become well known, but of the effects of his acts upon the minds and fortunes of those who had been opposed to him an imperfect grasp had been obtained. The Hlabisa tribe, amongst which Umbopa had attained chief importance by reason of the office he had held under the king, had long occupied the lands surrounding what has become the seat of the Hlabisa magistracy. It has been seen that Cetshwayo took temporary shelter at his kraal when he was being pursued by the military in 1879, and that his loyalty was strongly manifested on that occasion. His family was highly distinguished in the sentiments of the nation because of the fact that the mother of Umpande was a member of it. The family had now become divided into two sections, Umbopa being the head of the one and his cousin Somfula that of the other. The latter claimed by the law of primogeniture to be the chief representative of it; the former was ranked higher in the popular estimation because of the distinction his father had enjoyed under the king. Somfula had submitted to Usibebu and shared exile with him; Umtumbu, who had assumed charge of Umbopa's family affairs after the latter's death at Ulundi in 1883, had continued faithful to the royal cause and been driven out. Somfula was amongst those now to be restored with Usibebu, Umtumbu being found in occupation of the locality in which his father had dwelt, the absence of Usibebu since 1884 having enabled him to return thither. It was in that locality that the first note of trouble was heard. Umtumbu had accompanied Dinuzulu to Eshowe, and brought back intelligence of Usibebu's impending advent. Either from Dinuzulu or in his name a warning quickly pervaded the people that any one succouring the latter would be destroyed. A Mr. Galloway, who officially accompanied Usibebu, reported on the 1st of December that the people were all up in arms against him, declaring that they would not permit him to reoccupy the district; that his followers were nearly starving, and there was difficulty in restraining them from seizing the inhabitants' stores to satisfy their hunger; according to evidence given at Dinuzulu's subsequent trial stores were pillaged. Two days later, when the Umsebe Valley had been reached, the same official reported that Usibebu had not met with a single friend, whereas he had expected that all the members of his former following would have hailed his return with delight and hastened to join him. His brother Hlomuza, who had sent friendly greetings to him while he was on the way, now declared that he did not know him. Usibebu, "with about 700 men, was in the midst of thousands of enemies, without food, and yet tied by the order of the Government not to help himself." It was "absolutely necessary that he should be supported by an armed force." Dinuzulu's "Usutu" party regarded, or affected to regard, Usibebu's advent as a hostile invasion, which their own safety rendered it necessary that they should prepare to resist.

The magistrate found the condition of things much confused. In his district there had been no express recognition or appointment of the chiefs by whom the jurisdiction prescribed by the laws and regulations was to be exercised. Certain individuals were considered to be chiefs by virtue of the rank they had held in the Zulu nation, but there had been no arrangement as to the people or territory over whom or which they were to rule. By the laws and regulations they were given authority over "their respective tribes," but that might have been construed to mean several things. In effect it could hardly have

gone beyond such people as might have been willing
to submit to the authority of any particular chief. The
clan-name could have been of little help, because of the
people who composed the respective followings of chiefs,
the fewest were members of their own clans. The term
"tribe" practically meant a party rather than a clan, and
the integrity of each party depended upon the degree
in which the chief had secured its affections. In many
cases the attachment of the people had resulted from
sudden and temporary causes, and was easily broken
by any reason of inconvenience. There had been no
territorial limits assigned; the people, though divided by
affection, were intermixed by residence.

It was imperative that territorial limits should be
assigned to Usibebu at least, and the magistrate was
placed in the position of having to do this after he had
taken possession. There had been two definitions of his
territory, but the permission he had now received from
the Governor was to return to his "old tribal lands," and
the extent of these had never been ascertained. The first
delimitation had been effected in 1879, the second in anti-
cipation of Cetshwayo's return in 1883. Both had been of
an arbitrary kind and based upon political considerations.
His right to land under the Zulu kings had been regu-
lated by the extent of his personal occupation, and the
Governor's desire and expectation was that he should be
repatriated on this basis. It was of course intended that
those who had been driven out with him should go
back with him. The subject was one which needed
careful inquiry.

Mr. Addison effected a provisional settlement by partially adopting the boundary laid down in 1883. He cur-
tailed Usibebu's territory thereby limited, by drawing it in
somewhat at the north-western corner, and added largely
to it by extending it to the Black Umfolozi River on the
south-east, and towards the sea on the east. Those within

the boundary thus assigned who were in occupation of sites that had belonged to Usibebu or his adherents, as well as those who were not in occupation of such sites but refused to submit to Usibebu's authority, were required to move out. Some did so; others had to be forced. The number of persons who thus sought new homes was officially stated to be about 800; from the Zulu account it would appear to have been much greater. The people had stored their previous year's crop in pits underground, and that for the coming year was standing in the fields. The former they were permitted to remove; for the latter it was decided that they should receive compensation according to assessment.

These proceedings met with sullen protest, but not with active resistance, although a considerable number of Dinuzulu's adherents armed and assembled at his kraal. The magistrate visiting him on the 14th of January 1888, found some 2000 men there, being members of two young regiments. They "looked very thin and half-starved." The impression conveyed to his mind of what he saw was that there was a resolution to attack Usibebu. Undabuko and Dinuzulu "complained most bitterly about the standing crops." It seemed plain that the proceedings of the Government were regarded by Dinuzulu as having created a situation in which he might have to assert his own position by means of his own force.

The Governor relaxed somewhat the imperious tone in which he had emphasised the fact of the chief's altered state in November. He now required that the magistrate, whom he designated as the representative of the Government in the district, should " repeatedly and personally visit both Dinuzulu and Undabuko, especially the former, and thus obtain, by personal discussion with them of the questions underlying the prevailing unrest, direct opportunity of explaining to them any matters which they might consider grievances through not properly comprehending

THE STORY OF THE ZULUS 299

them." This instruction implied considerable deference to those chiefs.

Irritation and dissatisfaction continued to prevail. Usibebu was pressing for the removal of all Usutu from his land; the Usutu chiefs were crying out against the hardships they alleged they were being subjected to by the incidents of his return. They refrained generally from acts of violence, but the rule was broken in March. A headman of the Unzuza tribe named Unkowana, who had been removed to make room for Usibebu, with one or more companions attacked and killed two of the latter's men at the Umtatube Stream, some three miles north of the magistracy. They removed a portion of their victims' bodies, as if to prepare medicine for the purposes of war. They were, however, apprehended and subsequently brought to trial.

Respecting the boundary, Dinuzulu made a strong representation to the Governor in this month (March 1888), and it appeared to the latter, and to the Resident Commissioner, that there were grounds for his contention, that it gave more land to Usibebu than he required and more than had ever belonged to him as a tribal chief. Mr. John L. Knight, the magistrate of the Mtonjaneni district, was accordingly appointed to revise it. He began his investigation, the disputing parties being present, on the 16th, and on the 20th he completed the work, having made no alteration which improved matters for Dinuzulu's party. He declared his decision to be authoritative and final, but the Governor reserved signification of his approval for six months to admit of appeal.

There had been reason to hope from the circumstances attending Usibebu's arrival, that it might be practicable to replace Somfula upon his old sites without disturbing the other section of the Hlabisa tribe under Umtumbu. The sites were said by the latter to be vacant, except one, of which Somfula's son Umkonto had remained in occupation when the tribe removed to Eshowe. But Usibebu applied for the removal of the people on the ground that they were antagonistic to him, and this was decided upon. Umtumbu was furnished with a reference to the magistrate of the Lower Umfolozi district, and ordered to remove thither with his following. He threw away this reference, repaired to the Usutu kraal, and declined to respond to the magistrate's summons to appear before him and explain his conduct.

Mr. Osborn had gone to Nongoma at the same time as Mr. Knight. The Governor had suggested that he should do so in order to be in a position to facilitate on the spot settlement of any complicated question which might arise. The context indicated that the complications anticipated were in connection with the resettlement of Usibebu. Six days after Mr. Knight's decision, Mr. Osborn resolved upon an important step (26th April 1888). He had already caused the seizure of a balance due of the cattle which Dinuzulu and Undabuko had been ordered to pay as fines. He now resolved to deal with another difficulty which had presented itself. Umtumbu could not be prevailed upon to appear. Three other men had failed to answer the magistrate's summons, two to plead to civil claims, one of which had been preferred by Usibebu; the other to give evidence in a civil cause. Warrants were issued for the apprehension of these persons, who were known to be at the Usutu kraal, and Sub-inspector Osborn proceeded thither with 80 men of the Zululand police, starting during the night and reaching the kraal at dawn. There he found a Zulu force which he estimated to number 1000 men, and this was immediately called to arms and presented such a front as to cause the abandonment of the attempt to arrest the men required; they were demanded, but not delivered up. Undabuko was present at the Usutu kraal, but Dinuzulu had been absent since the 3rd of May visiting friendly tribes in the New Republic.

THE STORY OF THE ZULUS 301

The Resident Commissioner urged the need of troops to support the magistrate's authority, and a squadron of the 6th Dragoons under Colonel (afterwards Sir Richard) Martin was advanced to a point north of the Ivuna Stream, and about seven miles from the magistracy. There the Colonel established himself upon a low apex to which the ground gently and evenly rose from all sides. He regarded the position as possessing very high defensive qualities, and took some credit to himself for its selection, as a result of which his friends playfully called it Fort I.

The expedition was not otherwise commemorated.

Some communications were still interchanged between the Resident Commissioner and Undabuko, but on the 13th of May the latter betook himself with an armed following to a fastness, while the families of his party abandoned their homes and sought safety in distance from the scene of expected trouble. Dinuzulu returning from the New Republic with some 500 men whom he had enlisted in his service there, the forces were united, and encamped on the lower edge of the bush which partially encircles the summit of the Ceza Mountain.

The question what Dinuzulu's motives and hopes were in the action thus taken will perhaps always have but a speculative answer. On the one side it was asserted that he deliberately defied the Government by the attitude he took up; on the other, that oppression and fear of Usibebu had driven him to adopt the course he did as a forlorn hope. He always ridiculed the notion that he had been so presumptuous as to contemplate war against the English queen. He likened what he did to the scratching which a cat might attempt if trodden upon by an elephant. The men he assembled on the date given have been computed as numbering only some 1500; they were drawn largely from tribes residing in the New Republic. It was plain that the feeling against the new settlement was not so general as to justify him in hoping that he might be enabled to overthrow it. The local Government was manifestly supported by Imperial troops. Dinuzulu was acquainted with the nature of the Governor's office and had already appealed to him in respect to what he represented as oppressive measures by the officials; he had, however, started for that visit to the New Republic from which he had just returned without waiting for an answer to that appeal. It is scarcely credible that he in fact feared an attack from Usibebu. Usiwedu and Umnyamana, whose enmity towards that chief had been as strong as his own, had held aloof from the enterprise on which he was embarked, thus showing that danger was not seriously apprehended. These chiefs realised, and it is difficult to doubt but that Dinuzulu realised, that the question was no longer one between him and Usibebu, but a question between him and the Queen of Great Britain. Umnyamana propounded a simile at this time which has often been quoted. He said it was an act of aggression to strike a dog which the owner was leading by a string. It seems incredible that it could have been regarded as possible for the Government to observe neutrality in respect to renewed war between the Usutu and Mandhlagazi parties. But the actions of the Bantu people are seldom supported by a clearly ascertained or logical basis.

The army of 1500 men was encamped at Ceza; its leaders had made it clear that they were not amenable to the authority of the Government, and it was necessary to decide upon some course of action by which that authority could be established over them, or the menace removed which their attitude and position formed. The need for this was soon accentuated. The maintenance of so large a body of men in a camp was necessarily attended with some difficulty in regard to food supply. The old method of cattle-raiding had to be resorted to, and the first victims were Umnyamana and Usiwedu. From the former 103 cattle were taken; on the 22nd of May 1888, on a boisterously windy night, a party carried off a considerable number from the latter and his adherents residing some miles south of the magistracy on the Nongoma range.

A report having reached Umnyamana that there was a design to assassinate him, he had placed himself under the protection of the troops at Inkonjeni; but there was some uncertainty as to how many of his followers might adhere to him or join Dinuzulu's party.

Up to this time, except for the contumacious acts for which they had been fined, it was felt that Undabuko and Dinuzulu had not offended in a manner so definite as to justify the taking of criminal proceedings against them; but these raids were regarded as necessitating their arrest for cattle-stealing. Warrants were accordingly issued for that purpose, and arrangements made to have them executed by the Zululand police with the support of Imperial troops. Communication with Dinuzulu had ceased, messengers expressing themselves afraid to go to him.

Mr. Osborn had moved to Inkonjeni on the 21st of May, the day before the second raid. From there a movement was made on the 1st of June to attempt the arrests that had been decided upon. The main force marched to the store of Dirk Louw at the Umfabeni Hill, about half-way to the objective, and slept there. They were joined by some more Zululand police commanded by Sub-inspector Pearse, and accompanied by the magistrate from Nongoma. Next morning some 400 of Umnyamana's men joined the force at the Insugazi kraal, some miles farther on.

The regular troops were commanded by Captain Pennefather of the 6th Dragoons, and consisted of 3 officers and 81 non-commissioned officers and men of that regiment, and 43 and 35 non-commissioned officers and men respectively of the Royal Irish Fusiliers and the 1st North Staffordshire Regiment, as mounted infantry, with one officer from each of those regiments. The Zululand police under Mansel numbered 66 men, 17 of whom were mounted. The whole force, exclusive of native levies, numbered about 208. It reached the house of Piet Louw at the base of Ceza Mountain at about 11 o'clock. Dinuzulu's camp was in full view and about two miles distant as the crow flies. There, while at breakfast, they saw the Usutu impi form up in semi-circle for the purpose of being addressed by those in charge of it, or of being assigned its disposition for the purpose of battle. They concluded that the latter was the purpose, but it is not clear from later inquiry that the Usutu commanders had formed any definite intention. Prayers were said by a native Christian, but no definite orders followed. Soon, with what object it is not clearly known, the impi was marched through the encircling bush towards the summit of the mountain, by two paths some distance apart, the one ascending the south-western side, the other by a spur on the north-east. A small portion of the open ground beyond the bush was on the British side of the boundary, but both the paths by which it could be reached lay partly within that of the New Republic. The position of the boundary was not clearly known to those in charge of the expedition. While Commandant Mansel with his 17 mounted men proceeded in line with the lower edge of the bush towards the south-western path, Captain Pennefather took up a covering position within the New Republic by that on the north-east. A number of the Usutu lingered about where that path enters the bush towards which Mansel was advancing, and as he approached they presented a front which he held to justify him in opening fire. This was immediately returned, and a charge begun which made it necessary for Captain Pennefather to afford active protection. The

THE STORY OF THE ZULUS 305

sound of battle brought back many who had ascended the mountain, and it was soon held to be necessary on the part of the Government forces to withdraw from the position altogether. Umnyamana's men had declined to advance, in which they were probably justified by the circumstances. The Usutu felt that they had been victorious, and pursued the retreating troops till the evening, but were prevented by the fine handling of his cavalry by Captain Pennefather from getting within effective distance. The losses on the side of the Government were two men of the regulars killed and two wounded. The whole force returned to Inkonjeni next day, having made an unsatisfactory beginning in the enforcement of authority. Dinuzulu was present during the action and accompanied the pursuers.

The magistracy at Nongoma being weakly protected, Usibebu had been directed to assemble his men there to protect it; he and they could see from their bivouac on the northern base of the Undunu Hill the smoke from the volleys on the Ceza Mountain, and the result of the conflict was soon heard. But it was not thought that the Usutu would be so audacious as to attack him there.

The tension which precedes the first blow usually produces unreasoning violence when that has been struck. Unpleasant occurrences quickly succeeded each other. On the next day raiding parties pervaded the domains of the nation's old adviser Umnyamana. He had definitely separated himself from the Usutu cause, and taken up arms against it, and that party felt no disposition to spare any of his partisans who might fall into its power. Most had fled into rocky fastnesses, but it fared ill with one family who had ventured home. The head of it was named Butshelezi; his kraal was close to that of Umnyamana's brother Santinga, in the vicinity of the Umfaba Mountain. He had accompanied the expedition to Ceza; it was on the morning of the third day after that event that a raiding party found him at his kraal. There

U

were with him three men, three women, and two young boys. Of these there were killed, besides himself, two of the men, one woman, and a small boy, the others escaping, except the elder of the boys, who was taken captive and thus lived and afterwards declared as an eye-witness that Dinuzulu had been of the party and personally killed his child-brother by running him through with an assegai. Upon the same day as the affair at Ceza, Dirk Louw was shot dead near to his store. He had believed himself to be on such friendly terms with the Zulus generally as to be free from danger of injury at their hands. On the 5th his son Klaas met the same fate at his store at Ivuna. Upon that date also two of Usibebu's men were killed at their kraal on the western side of the Iwela Stream, near the road leading to Inhlwati. This was the act of certain young men of the Umdhletshe tribe on hearing of the result of the attack upon Ceza. Their chief Umsutshwana manifested disapprobation of the deed, and endeavoured to convey a report of it to the magistrate at Nongoma, but was unable to induce his messenger to go there on account of the presence of Usibebu's impi. On the 7th another of Usibebu's men, travelling by the road, was attacked and killed by Hlabisa people, and on the 9th the kraal of Somfula's son Umkonto, who had now rejoined Usibebu's party, was raided by another party of the Umdhletshe tribe. This party took certain of the cattle there seized to Umsutshwana, who was residing temporarily at a kraal on the edge of the forest on the eastern side of the Inhlwati Mountain, and left them there, although the chief expressed strong disapproval of their act.

In consequence of the occurrence at Ceza, the Resident Commissioner had instructed Usibebu to patrol the district; that chief now (10th June) set out with 350 men, with the declared object of carrying out these instructions in the locality in which these acts of lawlessness had been committed. He informed the officials that his objective was Umkonto's kraal, but did not go there, as he afterwards explained, because of intelligence he received after setting out. He divided his force, despatching one portion to the kraal of Unkowana, a brother of Umsutshwana, who with a section of the tribe occupied the land lying along the head of False Bay near the coast; he with the other portion arrived at the kraal where Umsutshwana was at dawn on the 12th of June. There were afterwards diverse accounts of the personal part he took in the proceedings which followed, but an important result of the visit was the death of Umsutshwana and some women and a child. The cattle found at the kraal were taken away, and amongst them some of those that had been raided from Umkonto's kraal were recognised.

The advance party attacked Unkowana's kraal later in the morning, killing a woman and carrying off cattle. Other kraals were also visited in that locality and persons killed and cattle and captives taken, the patrol returning to the magistracy on the 13th of the month.

A brief lull followed, but intelligence of what had occurred was quickly conveyed to Dinuzulu at Ceza, and probably added definiteness to such design as may have been in the course of formation. And the stillness of the evening and night of the 22nd (of June 1888) was broken by the significant and awe-inspiring clatter of assegais in the hands of a long file of warriors descending by a narrow path the steep hillside from the mountain to the valley of the Isikwebezi; up the other side to the Mahashini plateau (deriving its name from that of a kraal Dinuzulu had established there at which to keep his horses, on account of its comparative healthiness); down again into the Ivuna valley, and finally, after being marshalled into battle order, at the dawning of the 23rd up to the seat of magistracy at Nongoma. It was a long and toilsome march, and the last ascent alone would have proved in no small degree fatiguing to an ordinary pedestrian.

Mr. Addison had returned to his magistracy some days before. He had with him a force of native police numbering in all some 50 men under the command of Sub-inspector Osborn, son of the Resident Commissioner, who had constructed a circular fort of turf, large enough to accommodate that number of men. Between him and Usibebu's position was a deep, swampy ravine; it was about half a mile distant.

The Usutu impi, which was estimated to number about 4000, appeared at the head of the ravine and divided into two bodies, the one coming over the round hill upon which the courthouse has since been built and heading towards the fort some 700 yards distant, down the ridge; the other moving in an easterly direction towards Usibebu's bivouac on the edge of the scrubby bush on the Undunu Hill. The alarm being given, the magistrate with his small force repaired to the fort, and there awaited what might befall; Usibebu marshalled his men and advanced to meet Dinuzulu's left wing, soon coming into conflict with it. The opposing forces ran towards each other, and for a short space engaged in mortal combat, fighting hand-to-hand with assegais. Then Usibebu's men turned and fled, seeing which the right wing swung round to its left to intercept any who might attempt to cross the ravine to the fort. As they did so fire was opened upon them from there, inflicting some loss. Many of Usibebu's men met their death in the swamp at the bottom of the ravine. Many others, who trusted to their speed to afford them escape testified with their dead bodies that the pursuit was active and sustained, notwithstanding the distance the attacking impi had marched during the night. Usibebu lost some 200 of his small force in killed, and the fort was made melancholy as the morning advanced by the arrival at it of wounded persons of both sexes.

Amongst the slain was the Ndwandwe chief Umgojana one of the thirteen appointed by Sir Garnet Wolseley in

1879. His career had since then been one of vicissitude and misfortune; and he had become a follower of Usibebu holding no position of importance.

The horses of the officials and police and all cattle that happened to be at the fort were carried off. The cattle were the property of friendly natives who had come for protection, amongst whom were the followers of Dinuzulu's uncle Usiwedu. But when Usibebu had been routed and these captures effected the impi conducted itself as if it held the object for which it had set out to have been accomplished. It gradually retired in the direction of Ceza; only a few casual and ineffective shots were fired in the direction of the magistrate's post. Next day this was relieved by a strong force from Inkonjeni, and abandoned, the remnant of Usibebu's men and many other natives retiring under the protection of the troops to the latter place. There Umnyamana and Usibebu, who had so long waged deadly war against each other, had for the time being to regard themselves as "brothers in distress."

Dinuzulu personally accompanied this force; the command of it was, however, in the hands of the old induna Hemulana, who had also commanded at Etshaneni.

Although it has been strongly contended that Usibebu was the sole objective, it seems clear from what subsequently occurred that the officials were also regarded as their enemies by the Usutu party. From Inkonjeni the magistrate beheld the house he had partially built ascending in smoke and flames. The party who burnt it also seized the official safe, and succeeded in wrenching it open.

But the Boers, whose proceedings, and the complaints of the Usutu people in regard to them, had brought the British authorities into the position in which they found themselves, were entirely immune from attack from those people. Indeed, almost immediately after the repulse of the police at Ceza, certain Boer officials employed a portion of Dinuzulu's impi there assembled for the purpose of coercing a chief within their dominions who had threatened to be refractory. Wherever Europeans were found on the British side of the boundary they were killed; on the Boer side the farmers occupied their homes with assured safety.

The situation had become critical. The force available for suppression of the insurrection was small; an increase was necessary to the strength of Imperial troops in the territory. Much depended upon how far the divided sections might be affected, and the nation reunited by the adversity the new rulers had sustained at the hands of their late king's son. Emissaries had been busy since the day of Ceza calling upon chiefs and people in various parts to join him. Two of these, named Unkunzemnyama and Mafukwini, were especially active in the coast districts amongst the tribes of Somkele, Somopo and Bejana, and were producing an effect. About the 28th of June two traders, Knight and White, were attacked by men from the first-named tribe while on their way to Pretorius's magistracy at the Lower Umfolozi, and pursued a great distance, reaching their destination wounded and with great difficulty. They were obliged to abandon their wagon, and a man named Ashby and a native woman who had been unable to leave it were attacked and killed. The magistrate called up the men of the Umtetwa tribe, and a spiritless attack was made upon them at the magistracy on the 30th by a large force composed of men from the three tribes named. Again there arose a question whether the magistrate or Sokwetshata was the object of the attack.

There appears to have been general indefiniteness and indecision on the part of the assailants, and they inflicted little loss and gained no advantage. The Zululand police under Sub-inspector Marshall, behaving with conspicuous

THE STORY OF THE ZULUS 311

gallantry in the face of an enemy overwhelmingly superior in numbers, checked the advance of one of the flanks.

This attack upon the magistracy was not pressed, but an armed party was placed on the road to Eshowe, cutting off communication with the Resident Commissioner. With a view to opening the way a party of Sokwetshata's men were sent out early on the morning of the 5th of July. They marched with a considerable show of bravery as far as to a place called Isikalasemizi, where they found the enemy and opened fire upon them. But as soon as opposition was shown they turned and made what speed they could to the magistracy, being hotly pursued and leaving some forty of their number on the line of retreat.

It transpired later that on the 3rd of the month a trader named Cecil Vivian Tonge, who was quietly travelling in an ox-cart in the direction of the Umhlatuzi River, was overtaken by a party of young men and wantonly stabbed to death by one of their number named Umpikwa, his servants thereupon being pursued and slain by other members of the party. Umpikwa, who was afterwards tried and convicted, could only say in defence of what he had done that it was in compliance with the injunctions of Mafukwini.

The rising had likewise spread in another direction. Tshingana, Dinuzulu's uncle, betook himself with some followers to the fastnesses of the Hlopekulu Mountain on the 4th of June, three days after Ceza. There on the 13th of the same month he was joined by Somhlolo, the acting chief of the Biyela, with a portion of that tribe; the other portion refusing to join him, and subsequently arming on behalf of the Government. According to Tshingana's own account he had nine companies in all with him, these being all under strength, the strongest numbering some thirty men.

Tshingana was one of those whose former kraals fell on the side of the New Republic. Being unable to accept the position of a tenant on a Dutch farm, he had removed into British Zululand and taken up his residence in the White Umfolozi valley, where the principal kraals of the king had been. He had submitted to the new authority and accepted payment of the stipend awarded to him. His reason for joining in the insurrection must remain obscure.

From the Hlopekulu there went forth raiding parties, and the cattle of persons friendly to the Government were taken, and the store of Alfred Moor on the Ulundi plain was looted and burnt down. Tshingana's small endeavour, which is supposed to have been made on behalf of Dinuzulu, must be regarded as having been wanting in definiteness of prospect. His position was within striking distance of the military stationed at Inkonjeni, and so isolated that no succour could reach him in case of attack from the rest of the party he had joined. He and his people collected all their cattle on the mountain, and would appear scarcely to have hoped to accomplish more than the defence of these and themselves.

In the territory previously styled the Reserve, the loyalty of the people to the Government had been well secured. They were generally willing to take up arms in its support; many did so when called upon later, prominent amongst whom were the men under John Dunn and the Basutos of Hlubi.

What presented itself to the authorities as of chief urgency was the necessity to dislodge Tshingana and disperse the men whom he had assembled. This was set about on the early morning of the 2nd of July, just a month after the attempt on Ceza. A native contingent had been brought up from Eshowe numbering some 1000 men; 400 of Umnyamana's men had been enrolled; Major M'Kean of the 6th Dragoons, who had been acting as magistrate at Rorke's Drift, had brought 140 mounted Basutos to the scene; Commandant Mansel commanded 17 mounted and 70 dismounted native police with regular

THE STORY OF THE ZULUS

military training; these forces were "supported" by Captain Pennefather with 5 officers and 129 non-commissioned officers and men of the 6th Dragoons, and 3 officers and 61 non-commissioned officers and men, as mounted infantry, of the 1st North Staffordshire Regiment and Royal Inniskilling Fusiliers under Captain Purdon, altogether a force nearly 2000 strong. Colonel Froome was also to demonstrate from the south of the White Umfolozi River with a squadron of dragoons and some mounted infantry, and two guns of the Royal Artillery under Major Aitchison, together with native levies under Mr. Knight, the magistrate of the Mtonjaneni district, numbering about 500. This force was to co-operate in the attack if necessary, but to guard the road to Empangeni.

The mountain was reached somewhat after eleven o'clock. The mounted Zululand police when ascending a kopje were fired upon by a party of thirty men who had been placed there to guard the approach, twenty of whom were armed with guns. The police retired, their officer, Sub-inspector Osborn, receiving a slight wound. Commandant Mansel then led the infantry against the position. Approaching to within forty yards of it under cover, he ordered his men to charge with fixed bayonets, which they did in a most vigorous style, turning the defenders out of their position and pursuing them beyond all control of their commander. Of the thirty who held the position only ten survived.

The fighting now proceeded in a somewhat promiscuous manner, chiefly between natives and around the cattle. This continued during the greater part of the day, many natives being killed on both sides. The result, which was generally favourable to the attacking force, was rendered conspicuously so by the large number of cattle it captured. One officer of the Inniskilling Fusiliers, Lieutenant Briscoe, was shot through the head from a bush by a native whose presence had not been suspected.

The troops bivouacked on the mountain, and returned to camp next day. Tshingana left during the night and made his way to Dinuzulu at Ceza.

Although this action preceded the affair at Isikalasemizi by three days, it may be described as the determining event of the disturbances. It was soon followed by a general dispersion of armed Usutu. Major M'Kean hastened with a mobile column to the relief of the Lower Umfolozi magistracy, arriving there on the 9th of the month, having encountered no opposition, although John Dunn, who accompanied him with some 2000 men, complained that his rearguard had been molested. Having established a military post at the magistracy, Major M'Kean returned to Eshowe, burning deserted kraals and killing such insurgent stragglers as he happened upon by the way.

The conduct of operations was now in the hands of the officer commanding the regular troops, it having been found that the local police were unequal to the task of restoring order. It was believed to be still necessary to deal with Dinuzulu at Ceza, where his force had become considerable. This threatened to be a difficult matter. An effective attack upon him was rendered impossible by his proximity to the border of the New Republic, and the facility he was afforded in crossing it by the strip of dense bush in rear of his camp. The army which he had gathered there was composed chiefly of men from that State, the Government of which had failed, either through inability or unwillingness, to enforce neutrality. While Mr. Osborn, the Resident Commissioner, declared that these men joined Dinuzulu "without let or hindrance," the Governor believed that the authorities of the New Republic "at all times tried to give effect to the loyal assurances they had constantly given." They had but little force to control the large native population of which they had become the rulers. But a change was in

THE STORY OF THE ZULUS 315

progress. It had apparently not been designed from the first to attempt the maintenance of permanent independence. A treaty of union with the South African Republic was signed as early as the 14th of September 1887, subject to ratification by the Volks Raad. This treaty, which affected the territory defined by the agreement of the 22nd of October 1886, was approved by the High Commissioner and made subject to the provisions of the London Convention of 1884, on the 29th of June 1888. The Government of the South African Republic definitely renounced for ever all claim theretofore advanced to a protectorate over all or any portion of Zululand; and on the 25th (of July 1888) the President telegraphed that the treaty of union had been ratified; that the former President of the New Republic had been appointed Border Commissioner, and "received orders to at once take care of neutrality respecting the Zulu question."

The Imperial troops in the territory now numbered 86 officers and 2163 non-commissioned officers and men, 816 of whom were mounted, including the 6th Dragoons, and large native levies had been organised.

Major M'Kean was the first to undertake an effective movement. With a considerable column he marched along the coast from Eshowe, receiving the surrender of Somkele and several headmen, and reaching Nongoma on the 6th of August without having met with any opposition. A note had been received on the 2nd of the month by the Commanding Officer from a Boer, written on behalf of Dinuzulu, notifying that he did not intend to continue fighting; on the 7th and 9th respectively Undabuko and he evacuated their position at Ceza, burning the shelters which they had constructed and proceeding to what had become the Vrijheid district of the South African Republic. Their surrender was refused by that State on the ground of insufficiency of the law in that respect, but they committed no further acts of aggression. Military posts were established in various parts of the territory, including the vicinity of Umnyamana's Insukazi kraal, Ceza Mountain and the Inhlopenkulu plateau some three miles north of the Nongoma magistracy, which was now reoccupied by the magistrate.

At the last-named military post Undabuko surrendered to the commanding officer (Colonel Martin) on the 16th of September. Dinuzulu, after various movements, causing much speculation as to what he meant to do or attempt, finally proceeded to Pietermaritzburg and surrendered on the 15th of November. Tshingana, having returned to his own kraal, had been arrested on the 6th of the same month.

They and other chiefs and headmen were subsequently indicted before a special Court appointed by legislative proclamation, the members being Mr. Justice Walter Wragg of the Natal Supreme Court, Mr. G. M. Rudolph, and Mr. J. E. Fannin, magistrates of that Colony. They were convicted of treason and public violence, and sentenced to varying but long terms of imprisonment: Dinuzulu, Undabuko, and Tshingana being sent to St. Helena to serve their terms there. Against the common people no proceedings were taken, except in cases where murder had been committed.

A period of peace ensued, during which the house of Zulu had no share in the direction of affairs.

ZULU GENEALOGY

ZULU GENEALOGY

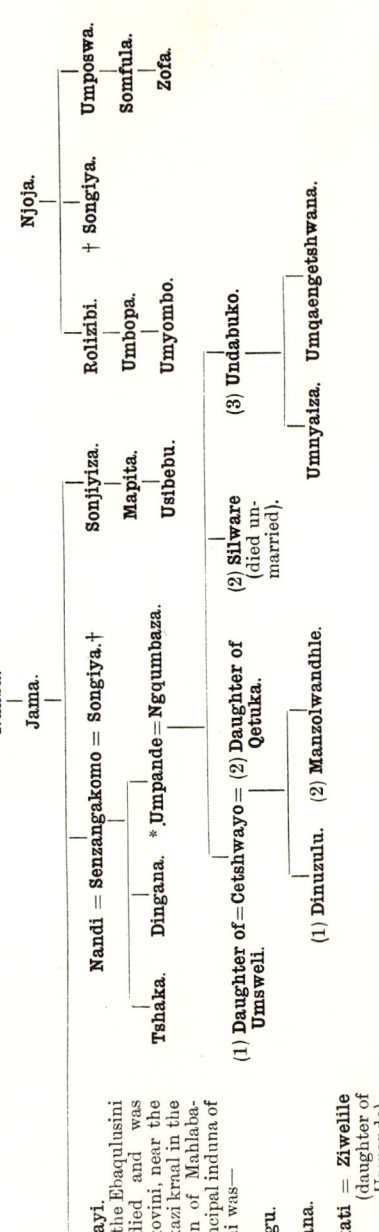

*Umpande = Nomantshali

(4) Umbulaze. (5) Mantantashiya. (6) Umdumba. (7) Umkungu (chief in Eshowe Division). (8) Batonyile (daughter). (9) Poiana (killed about 1856). (10) Umtonga. (11) Umgidhlana.
Killed at Tugela, Dec. 1856.
Prominent in connection with disputes forming events leading to Zulu War.

Other wives = *Umpande. = Other wives.

(12) Sikota. (13) Umsutu. (14) Sukane. (15) Usiwedu = Daughter of Masipula. (16) Dabulamazi. (17) Tshingana. (18) Usiteku. (19) Uhamu.

Mpikanina. Qedicala. Kambi. Madakavana.

*Umpande = other wives.

(20) Mahanana. (21) Tshonkweni (killed at Tugela, 1856). Muntongenankomo.

Mabilwana.

*Umpande = other wives.

(22) Somxawana. (23) Dabulesinge. (24) Magwendu.
Killed at Tugela, 1856.

INDEX

ABANTU, the: migration of, 1; life in, 1687, 2; in 1812, 7–10; population in 1812, 8; records of, in old dwelling-places, 2, 3; cattle pens, 2, 243; stone cairns, 3; huts, construction of, 2, 3; furniture, 4; fire, method of producing by friction, 4; food, 22; work in iron, 5–7; a forge described, 5–6; occupations and interests of, 8–10; tribal fights, 8; hunting, 9–10; law of chase, 9; ambitious of authority, 7; chieftainship, 7; penalty for pretension to functions of chief, 11; principle regarding justification of punishment, 15; vacant annals, 10; illogical, 302. And see under Zulu
Abaqulusi tribe, the, 194, 224, 280; attitude to Uhamu after settlement of Sishweli, 230; dispute with Uhamu, 230–1; defeated at Bivana River, 231, 233, 239; make reprisals, 244
Addison, R. H., 294, 296–7, 308
Aitchison, Major, 313
Ashby, ——, 310

BANTUBENSUMO, chief, 288
Battles and Fights: Bivana River, 231; Ingcome (Blood River), 70–1; Boom-plaats, 117; with John Cane, 69; Congella, 97; Eshowe, siege of, 184, 194–5, 200–2; Estcourt, 69–70; Etshaneni, 271, 309; Gingindhlovu kraal affair, 201; Hlopekulu Mountain, 312–4; Ihlobane Hill, 196–7, 200; Ihlongamvula, 27–28; at the Inkandhla, 269; Intshotshose Stream affair, Prince Imperial killed, 208–9; Inyezane or Iombane, 183–4, 202; Isandhlwana, 173–81, 185–8, 190, 197, 207; Isikalasemizi affair, 310; Itala, 68; Itshana, see Etshaneni; Luneburg, affair near, 195; Majuba, 227, 233; Maqongqo, 86, 88; 'Ndondakusuka, 103–4, 123; Nongoma, 308; Rorke's Drift, 182–3; with Sitimela, 229; Ulundi (Sheet-iron fort), 213, 215; Ulundi, Cetshwayo with Usibebu at, 256–8; Umsebe, 247–9; Weenen, 66; character of native battles, 69, 104, 183, 185, 229, 248–9; and see Zulu War
Bayete, royal salute, 13, 131
Bechuanaland, 286
Bejana, 310
Beje, success of, against Tshaka, 29; subjection of, 33
Beje, raid into Natal, 211–12; trial of, 212
Bekuzulu, a son of Sirayo, 150
Bezuidenhout, Wynand, 61, 66
Biggar, Alexander, 75
Bird's *Annals of Natal*, cited 8, 99
Blood River, 70; conference on Disputed Territory at, 142–3
Boers, the, and native labour, 53, 54; British rule, 54; main motive of great "trek," 54; trek to Delagoa Bay, 1836, 54; the "Commissions" of the voortrekkers, 54; trek to Natal, 55; attacked by Umzilikazi, 55, 112; trek under Retief, 55–7; Dingana's misgivings concerning, 56, 57; Dingana's reply to Retief, 61–2; recover cattle from Sigonyela, 62–3; massacre of Retief and companions, 64–5, 71–2, 87; Weenen, 66–7,

INDEX

87; expedition against Dingana, 67-8; defeat at Itala, 68; fatality of Itala, 68 *n.*; Dingana's Day, 70; decoyed by Bongoza, 72-5; Zulu version of retreat of, 75-6; overtures to Dingana, 76; valour praised by Zulus, 76; attitude to British Government, 77-8; treaty with Dingana, 78-9, 84-5, 95; alliance with Umpande, 82-4; view of Dingana, 83; last campaign against Zulus, 85-9; resolve to depose Dingana, 85; offer reward, 85; arrest Unzobo, 86; feeling regarding Unzobo and Undhlela, 86; trial and execution of Unzobo and Kambazana, 87-8; declare Umpande "King of the Zulus," 89-90; request Umpande to nominate Chief Captains, 83-4; annex major portion of Zululand in satisfaction of debt, 89, 118; relations with Umpande, 98; freedom, 92-3; thefts of stock of, 93-4; raid on the Mabaca, 94-5; practice with Bushmen, 94; and captured native children, 94-5; relations with British, 95-6; alarm at increased native population, 96; set aside Faku's land for native occupation, 96; demand withdrawal of British from Port Natal, 97; repulse Captain Smith, 97; submit to British authority, 97, 98

Potgieter: separation of Potgieter, 69; 112; Potchefstroom founded, 112; antipathy to British, 114; hope of establishing relations with Holland, 114-5; intercourse with Smellekamp, 114-5; proposal to open up trade through Delagoa Bay, 114; new "trek" in 1845 (to Lydenburg district), 115; land purchased from Swazis, 115-6; the Lydenburg Republic, 116, 119

Pretorius: claims in Natal, 116; "trek" from Natal under Pretorius, 116; march on Bloemfontein, 117; defeated at Boom-plaats, 117; Sand River Convention, 117, 118; formation of parties involving dissension and strife, 117-8; the Utrecht district, 118; Cornelius van Rooyen, 118; cession of land by Cetshwayo; the Disputed Territory, 119, 130, 143, 144

Burgers: Burgers elected President, 138-9; condition of life in South African Republic, 138; financial depression, 138; war with Sikukuni, 139-40; Burghers refuse to fight, 140; refuse to pay taxes, 138, 140; loss of confidence in Burgers, 141; resolve to elect Kruger, 141; British annexation of Transvaal, 141-2, 157, 191, 193; demand for retrocession, 142, 191-3, 206, 227, 233; aloofness from Zulu War, 192; insurrection of, 232-3; Lang's Nek Pass, Majuba, 227, 233; condemn Settlement of Zululand, 233; urge release of Cetshwayo, 233; take advantage of the confusion in Zululand, 260, 268; manifest solicitude for Zulus, 268; give assurances of disinterestedness, 269, 270; send assurances to Usibebu, 270; disingenuousness of, 270; aid Dinuzulu at Itshana, 271-2; demand payment for services at Itshana, 273; Dinuzulu declared king by, 275; receive document granting territory signed by Dinuzulu and Grant, 273-4; with right to establish the New Republic, 274; reward repudiated by Dinuzulu, 273, 275-6

New Republic: assumption of sovereignty over Zululand, 275; Volks Raad established at Vrijheid, 276; negotiations with British as to boundary and protectorate, 276-7, 278; treatment of natives, 277; shoot Dabulamanzi, 278; burn Ulundi kraal, 278; abandon claim to protectorate over Zulus, 278, 315; agreement as to boundary, 278-9; proviso "B." 279; Zulu protest against boundary agreement, 279-80, 281; demarcation of boundary, 280-2; immune from attack during Dinuzulu's insurrection, 309-10; employ impi to coerce refractory chief, 310; attitude of New Republic during insurrection, 314; union with South African Republic, 315; refuse surrender of Dinuzulu and Undabuko, 315

Boer War, 1889 and 1901, 68 *note*, 276
Boesman's Randt (Pietermaritzburg), 82

INDEX 323

Bongoza, the Zulu decoy, 72–4, 77, 105
Botha, Louis, 68, *note*
Brass moulding, 51, 52; the "Ingxota" or brass armlet, 51–2, 100
Briscoe, Lieut., 313
British, the (*see also* Natal), at Bay of Natal, 52; and fugitive natives, 52; relations with Dingana, 52, 58–9; view as to land south of Tugela, 53; establish Durban, 53; petition English king to recognise Victoria (Natal), 53; petition refused, 55; effect of British rule on Boer relations with natives, 53–4, 113; alliance with Boers against Dingana, 68; defeat of, by Zulus after Itala, 69; Government concern on account of Boers, 77, 95–6; relations with Boers, 55, 78–9, 95–6; peace with Dingana: troops withdrawn, 79, 84; Faku appeals to, for protection, 95; resume military occupation of Port Natal, 96–7; under Capt. Smith attack Boers, 97; establish administration in Boer territory, 97–8; relations with Umpande, 98; receive cession of St. Lucia Bay, 98; refuse aid to Umbulazi, 103; prevent Boer intercourse with Smellekamp, 114; establish authority at Bloemfontein, 117; sign Sand River Convention, 117; and the "Disputed" territory, 140–4, 151–2, 154, 158–9; view of weakness of Boer Government, 141; and South African Federation, 141; annex Transvaal (1877), 141–2; war with Sikukuni, 145, 168–9; possibility of war with Cetshwayo, 148, 154; territory violated, 149–51, 155–6, 159; hopes of averting war, 157; Ultimatum to Cetshwayo, 159–62, 164–8, 194; complaints of Zulu government, 159–61; require abolition of Zulu military system, 161, 166; forces available for war, 168–70
Zulu War, 171 ff.; *and see that heading*
Government's requirements under settlement of Sishweli, 221, 226; Liberals condemn war, 232; criticism of Transvaal annexation, 232; Boer insurrection, 232–3; abandon Transvaal, 233; Government favours Cetshwayo's release, 234; vacillating policy of, 242; error as to Zulu government, 245; attitude to Zululand and Native Reserve, 253; determination to maintain position in the country, 259; enjoin chiefs to remain quiet, 260, 265; threaten Cetshwayo, 261; efforts to bring about settlement in Zululand, 263–6, 294; intention not to extend sovereignty over Zululand, 268; and Wm. Grant's appointment, 273; Zulus ask intervention in New Republic boundary dispute, 275, 277; negotiations regarding boundary, 276–8; boundary agreement, 278–80, 285; demarcation commission, 280–2; Protectorate suggested to Zulus, 281–3; Protectorate over Eastern Zululand, 283; annex Zululand, 284–7; view of Usibebu's expulsion, 290; restore Usibebu, 291–2; Dinuzulu's insurrection, 301 ff.; *see also under* Bulwer, Frere, Havelock, Osborn.
Bromhead, Lieut., 182, 186
Brownlee, Charles, 204; suggestions as to terms of peace with Cetshwayo, 205, 207
Buller, Major R. (Sir Redvers), 169, 170; at Ihlobane, 196; operations of, quoted, 210–1; reconnaissance to Nodwengu kraal, 212
Bulwer, Sir Henry (Governor of Natal), 144; on the Disputed Territory, 144, 152; precautions against invasion, 154; quoted on Zulu military system, 166–7; views as to war with Zulus, 168; difference with Lord Chelmsford, 206–7; Cetshwayo's restoration, 235–8, 245, 252; Reserved Territory, 242; establishment of Dinuzulu, 264; recommendation after Cetshwayo's death, 267–8; boundary, New Republic, 276–82; otherwise mentioned, 151, 165, 234, 262, 266
Burgers, T. F., 138–42
Bushmen, the, 93–4
Butshelezi, a headman, 305–6

CACHET, F. Lion, quoted, 54, 89–90
Cane, John, 25, 26, 42–3, 44, 56, 69
Cannibalism, 29
Cape Colony, ceded to England (1806), 54; sends aid against Dingana, 70; Kafir wars, 145, 170, 185
Cardew, Col. Frederick, 280
Carey, Capt., 208
Celliers, Sarel, 66
Cetshwayo: meaning of name, 102; his mother, 34, 102–3; and Umbulazi, rival claimants for succession, 103; defeats Umbulazi, 103–4; spares Umpande, 105; orders death of Umpoiyana and Nomantshali, 105, 106; the Fund' u Tulwana campaign, 107; recognition of his title to succession, 108; negotiations for surrender of Umtonga and Umgidhlana, 119, 152; cedes land to Boers, the "Disputed Territory," 119; story of his sending sack of millet to Secretary for Native Affairs,[120; Zulu nation at time of his accession, 121, 130, 132; Dunn procures firearms for, 121; proclaimed king of the Zulus, 124, 128, 241; requests a British representative at his coronation, 122, 160; progress to Mahlabatini, 122–3, 240; jealousy of the northern chiefs, 123–4; promises to adopt modifications of law suggested by Natal Government, 124–7, 149, 159–61; Masipula poisoned, 129; coronation and exhibition of cattle, 129–30; the theft of chlorodyne, 128; and indiscriminate shedding of blood, 125, 159–60; killing without trial usual in his reign, 128, 159, 161, 163; missionary reports as to killing and witchcraft, 153; no case known of killing by, for mere caprice, 154; Zulu statement regarding, 163; military discipline under, 131; the marriage of the Ingcugce, 133–6; 157–8; the fight between two regiments, 135–8; 148, 149; view of British authorities regarding, 137; attitude of, regarding "Disputed Territory," 130, 140, 142–4, 148; reoccupies Luneburg, 155; credited with encouraging hostility to Europeans, 145–6; view that he was head of combination of Kafir races against whites, 157; view of his character, Sir Bartle Frere quoted, 157–58; his unreliability, quoted, 158; attitude of, to missionaries, 147–8, 161–2; determination to assert his rights against whites, 149, 158; European fears regarding: view of his administration, 149, 160, 167; view of proceedings of Mehlokazulu, 151; and award of disputed territory commission, 159; British Ultimatum to, 159–66, 168, 194; action regarding Ultimatum, 165–6; abandons hope of averting hostilities, 166; attitude to invasion of Natal, 182; grants protection to Vijn, 187; *Cetshwayo's Dutchman* cited, 187, 210, 216; attitude of Usibebu to, 189; overtures to the Boers, 192; offers safe conduct to Col. Pearson's column, 195; his attempts to secure cessation of hostilities, 195, 203, 207, 210; conditions of peace, 204–5, 207, 209, 216; reply to Lord Chelmsford, 210; watches battle of Ulundi, 213; flight of, 215–8, 257, 295; orders his people to make peace, 215; reflections of, 215–6; capture of, 217–8; difficulty of suppression of his influence, 218; release of, urged by Boers, 233; his importunity for release, 233; movement in favour of his restoration, 234; taken to England, 235; impression of, in London, 235; opposition to his restoration, 235; landed at Port Durnford, 236, 240; conditions of restoration, 238; restriction of dominion and power, 236–8; feeling of his people and chiefs regarding restoration, 236–44; his misgivings concerning, 240; his reception, 240–1; restoration difficulties, 244; does not reorganise regimental system, 247; his supporters proceed against Usibebu, 247; battle of Umsebe, 247–50; suffers blame for, 250; operations against Uhamu, 251, 254; view of the Reserved Territory, 244, 253, 254, 263; appoints Wm. Grant resident adviser, 253, 262; weakness of his posi-

INDEX

tion, 254; attack upon Usibebu, 254; defeat at Ulundi, 256-8; wounded by Ralijana's men, 257; believed to be dead, 258, 259; a fugitive in the Reserve, 259, 261; evades Mr. Osborn, 259, 261; accusations against British, 259; supposed intercourse with the Boers, 260; demoralisation of his adherents, 260; Mr. Osborn threatens coercion, 261, 262; disregards requests to proceed to Eshowe, 259, 261, 262; begins to realise his hopeless position, 262; persuaded by Mr. Fynn, proceeds to Eshowe, 263; objections to reinstatement of, 263; chiefs throw off his authority, 264-5; his partisans' attack on Umfanawendhlela, and other disturbances, 265; death, 129, 266-7

Zulu impression of his reign, 131; confidence in, 131-2; otherwise mentioned, 51, 221, 223, 230, 276, 290, 291

Chard, Lieut., 182, 186
Charters, Major, 77-8
Chelmsford, Lord, 168; confidence in, 185; forces under, 169-70, 200, 204; plans of, 170-5, 200, 211; retreat after Isandhlwana, 180-1, 183, 186; advance to relieve Eshowe, 200-1; peace negotiations by, 203-4, 207-10, 212; difference with Sir Henry Bulwer, 206; victory at Ulundi, 212-3; withdrawal, 215
Clarke, Sir Marshal, 145
Cloete, The Hon. Henry, 97-9, 118
Colenso, Bishop, *Cetshwayo's Dutchman* cited, 187, 210, 216
Congella, 31; battle of, 97
" Cowards," fate of, under Tshaka, 18-9, 29
Cromwell, Oliver, cited, 257
Cullis, ——, 44

DABULAMANZI, a brother of Cetshwayo, 202, 205, 224, 269; death of, 277-8, 285
Dambuza, *see* Unzobo
Dartnell, Major, 170, 174, 175, 180
Deighton, Mr., a trader, 156, 159
De Jager, fugitive from the Itala battle, 68
Delagoa Bay, 116, 121; trade with, opened by Dingiswayo, 14; Potgieter's attempt to open up a trade with, 114-5
de Lange, Johannes, 54, 74, 82; hunting exploits of, 93; adopts habits of Zulu people, 93
Delegorgue, M. Adulphe, quoted on Umpande, 83, 84, 100, 111
Derby, Earl of, 266
Dilikana, chief of the Amambata, 199, 257
Dingana, assassinates Tshaka, 40-1; slays Mahlangana, 41; assumes chieftainship, 41-2; declares his policy, 42, 45; sends mission to the Cape, 42; Hlambamanzi reports to, on white methods, 42-3; seizes Cane's cattle, 44; massacre of chiefs by, 49; his brothers, 49; Matiwane appeals to his mercy, 49-50; massacres Gowujana and his people, 50; and asylum of fugitive subjects in Natal, 52, 79; expedition against Umzilikazi, 56; misgivings concerning the Boers, 56, 57; relations with the English, 58; attitude to missionaries, 58-60, 147; reply to Retief, 61-2; his cattle recovered from Sigonyela, 62-3; massacres Retief and his party, 64-5; massacre of Weenen, 65-6; alliance of Dutch and English against, 68; battle of Itala, 68-9; unsuccessful attack on Boers, 69-70; Dingana's Day, 70-1; repels Boers, 75-6; retires from Umgungundhlovu, 76-7; distinguishes the young regiment, 77; negotiations of Capt. Jarvis with, 78; desire of, for peace, 78; agreement with British, 78-9; conditions of peace, 79; fails to return Boer cattle, 79, 81, 85; expedition to Swaziland, 79, 81-2;

x

growing discontent with, among Zulus, 79, 246; contemptuous view of Umpande, 88, 105; danger from growing power of Umpande and Mapita, 81, 102; disaffection of Umpande, 82, 84; alarmed by proceedings of Boers and Umpande, 85-6; Boer distrust of, 83; his chief indunas, 86-8, 224; defeated at Maqongqo, 86, 88, 95; executes Undhlela, 87; flight of, 90; meditates descent on Swaziland, 90; death of, 90, 281; his mother, 34

Characteristics, 45, 47, 51; capricious, 46-7; cruel to women, 47; inquisitive, 47; treacherous, 48; vain, 47, 60

State and military strength of, 45; his warlike expeditions unimportant, 45, 50, 56; the Umgungundhlovu Kraal, 42, 45, 76; private apartments of (Isigodhlo), 45-6; the king's women, 46-7; tradition regarding his destruction of his subjects, 48, 79

Otherwise mentioned, 56, 100, 102, 112, 133, 186, 257

Dingiswayo: the wanderings of Godongwana, 11; gains ideas from white people, 12; chief of the Umtetwa, 12; military organisation of, 12-13; conquests of, 13, 15; war song of, 15, 132: wars with Zwidi, 15, 16; opens trade with Delagoa Bay, 14; encouragement to ingenuity, 14; attributes of, 14; death of, 13, 16; influence of, on the tribal condition, 17; otherwise mentioned, 39, 219, 228

Dinuzulu, Cetshwayo's heir, 226, 264, 267; approached by the Boers, 268-70; expels Usibebu, 272, 290; recognised as king, 272-3, 275; Wm. Grant appointed adviser to, 273; signs document rewarding Boers, 273; repudiates document, 275-6; asks for British intervention, 275, 277; complains of Boer treatment, 277-8; protests against boundary agreement, 279-81, 283; refuses British Protectorate, 281-5; attitude to annexation, 285, 287, 289; refuses stipend, 290; fails to comply with magistrate's summons, 288-9; his cattle seized for fine, 288, 300; appeals to Boers, 288; British demand explanation from, 288-90; builds personal kraal in Usibebu's territory, 290; appears before Governor, 292; attitude to repatriation of Usibebu, 292-3, 295-6, 298; representations as to Usibebu's boundary, 299; gathers force at Ceza, 301-2; raids cattle, 302-3; decision to arrest him, 303; engagement with troops at Ceza Mountain, 304-5; raids Butshelezi's kraal, 305-6; attacks Nongoma, 307-9; Boers employ his impi, 310; discrimination between Boer and British territory, 310; attack on Pretorius' magistracy, 310-11; attitude to the New Republic, 314; gives up fighting: shelters in Vrijheid, 315; surrender and exile, 316; otherwise mentioned, 300, 307, 311, 314

Disputed territory, the, 119, 143; Cetshwayo's determined attitude, 130, 140, 148; Zulu claims, 142-4; arbitration, 144, 152; award, 158-9

Drakensberg, the, 118

Dunn, John, 103-4, 121, 123, 223-4, 232; volunteers in Umbulazi's service, 104; quoted on ruling the Zulu, 128; quoted, 130; receives the Ultimatum, 164-5; defection from Cetshwayo, 189; at relief of Eshowe, 201; position under settlement of Sishweli, 223-4, 236; quoted, action against Sitimela, 228-9

Otherwise mentioned, 129, 137, 291, 312, 314

Durban established, 53

Durnford, Lt.-Col. A. W., 144, 170, 172, 175, 176, 177

Dutch, the, *see heading* Boers

ENGLISH, *see under* British

Englishman, Thomas Halstead, the first slain by a Zulu, 65

Escombe, Harry, quoted, 253

Eshowe, division of Zululand, 30

INDEX 327

Eshowe, 81, 293; siege of, 184, 194–5, 202; relief of, 200–1, 211; value of defence, 202; Cetshwayo's offer of safe conduct to garrison, 195, 201
Esselen, D. J., 278
Estcourt, 69
Europeans: Settlers, Farewell's companions, 25; in Dingana's country, 44, 58, 66; views on war with Cetshwayo, 148

FAKU, Pondo chief, 95–6
Faku (occupation of Luneburg), 155, 156
Fannin, J. E., 316
Farewell, Lieut., 21, 24–5, 27, 35, 42
Fingoes, the, 29
Fire: produced by friction, the Uzwati described, 4; preservation of, 4
Frere, Sir Bartle, 141, 144, 205; quoted, on Cetshwayo's incitement of native chiefs against Europeans, 146; on the attitude of the Zulus, 152, 156–7, 166, 169, 233; on the character of Cetshwayo, 157–8; "disputed territory" award by, 158–9; Cetshwayo's coronation promises, 161–2; quoted, conditions for peace, 204; interview with Joubert, 191–2; the Transvaal and Federation, 205–6
Froome, Col., 313
Frontier Light Horse, the, 169, 170, 196, 197
Fugitive natives, 44, 52, 81
Fugitive's Drift, 178
Fynn, Henry Francis, 24–6, 33–7, 44, 242; cited, Dingiswayo, 13; received by Tshaka, 21; views instance of Tshaka's tyranny, 21; quoted, Tshaka's dress, 22–3; on battle with Sikunyana, 27–8; account of Tshaka's death, 40–1
Fynn, Henry Francis (secundus), 242, 245, 246, 254, 256, 262; cited, chiefs slain at Ulundi, 257
Fynney, F. Bernard, quoted, 162–3

GALLOWAY, Mr., quoted, 296
Gallwey, Hon. Michael, H., 144
Gama, Vasco da, 1, 20
Gambusha, Dingana's envoy, 78–9
Gardiner, Capt. Allan, 53, 55; account of Dingana in 1835, 45–7, 49–50; missionary work of, 59
Gardner, Capt., 182
Gidjimi, wife of Zwidi, 15
Gilbert, Lt.-Col., 170
Girls of the Great House, massacre of, by Tshaka, 32; Dingana's "Isigodhlo," 45–7; source of danger to the public, 31, 46
Girls, paternal power over, transferred in exchange for cattle, 32
Gladstone, Mr., 232, 266
Glyn, Col., 174
Godide, son of Undhlela, 88, 211, 224, 257
Godongwana, see Dingiswayo
Gowujana, a brother of Dingana, 49–50
Gququ, a brother of Umpande, 99
Grant, William, 253, 262, 273, 275
Gun running, 121, 132; guns in Usibebu's possession, 258
Gwekwana, an induna, 154

HAIANA, a brother of Usibebu, 245, 257
Halstead, Thomas, 25–6, 63, 65, 68
Harness, Major, 170

INDEX

Havelock, Sir A., annexation of Zululand: appointed Governor, 283–6; attitude to Dinuzulu, 288, 290, 292, 298, 302; Usibebu's repatriation, 291, 297–300; neutrality of the New Republic, 314–5
Hemulana, an induna, 309
Hicks-Beach, Sir Michael, 157, 191
Hlambamanzi, a Cape frontier native, 21, 28, 35, 43, 57
Hlomuza, Usibebu's brother, 290, 296
Hlubi, Basuto chief, 223, 236, 312
Holland, Boer efforts to establish political relations with, 114–5
Hunting, 9–10, 110, 122
Huts, construction of, 2, 3

INDIAN Mutiny cited, 180
Ingcugce, marriage of the, 133–6
Iron, work in, 5–6; the only metal mined by Zulus, 52
Isaacs, Nathaniel, 26, 27, 36; *Travels* cited, 26; testimony as to massacre of women of the Great House, 31–2
Isandhlwana, battle, 173–81, 185–8, 190, 197, 207, and *see* 108; Zulu loss at, 188, 198; Zulu commander, 188, 257
Isivivane, the (stone cairn), 3
Izigqoza, Umbulazi's party, 103–4

JAEL and Sisera, a Zulu type of, 260–1
Jarvis, Capt., 78
Jobe, Umtetwa chief, 11
Johnston, Sir H. H., *Colonization of Africa*, cited, 1
Joubert, Piet, 191–3, 233

KAMBAZANA, companion of Unzobo, 87–8
Kambula, 194, 196; the battle at, 197–9, 213
Kangela, *see* Congella
Ka Qwelebana, wife of Sirayo, 149
Kimberley, 139, 140
Kimberley, Lord, 233
King, Lieut., 26, 27, 33, 35, 36, 42
King, Richard, 97
Knight, John L., 299–300, 313
Knight, ——, trader, 310
Kraals: Banganomo, 270; Bulawayo, 30, 32; Dukuza, 31, 33, 42; Ebaqulusini, 194; Ekuvukeni, 254; Ekushumayeleni (of Umnyamana), 215; Gibigxeku, *see* Bulawayo; Gingindhlovu, 201; Gqikazi, 263; Inkukazi, 316; Inkungwini, 247; Landandhlovu, 109; Mahashini, 307; Mahlabatini, 122; Nobamba, 27; Nodwengu, 212; Nyakamubi, 33; Sixebeni, 99; Ulundi, 130, 246, 256; Umbonambi, 210; Umgungundhlovu (principal seat of Dingana), 42, 45, 76
Kreli, Galeka chief, 145
Kruger, Paul, 141, 191, 192
Kwabiti, Zulu commissioner, 281

LANDMAN, Carl, 74
Langazana, wife of Senzangakona, 71, 99, 105, 106, 293
Limpopo River, 38
Livingstone, Dr., quoted; on Boer licence with natives, 113; on Boer methods of warfare, 113–4
Lobengula, 30
Lonsdale, Commandant, 170, 180–1
Louw, Dirk, storekeeper, 303, 306; Piet Louw, 304; Klaas Louw, 306

INDEX 329

Lucknow, relief of, storming of the Sikandrabagh cited, 180
Luneburg, occupation of by Cetshwayo, 155, 156 ; action at, 195
Lutuli, Martin, 181

MABOKO, son of Masipula, 129, 237, 242, 245, 246, 288
M'Kean, Major, 312, 314, 315
Madumba, a son of Umpande, 105
Mafukwini, chief, 310, 311
Mahanana, uncle of Dinuzulu, 288
Mahlangana, assassin of Tshaka, 40–1
Mahloko, brass worker, 51, 100
Mahu, son of Tokotoko, 245
Majuba, 227
Makosini, the place of kings, 16, 240, 277, 279
Malusi, Ndwandwe chief, 15
Mandhlagazi, the, Usibebu's followers, 255, 272, 302
Mankulumana, son of Somapunga, 265
Mansel, Commt. George (Zulu Carbineers), 243, 269, 294, 304, 312–3
Mantantashiya, a son of Monase, 104
Manyosi, favourite of Dingana, 48
Manzini, a chief, 102
Mapita, cousin of Tshaka, 31, 81, 82, 89, 123
Maqongqo hills, 86
Marshall, Sub-Inspector, 310
Marter, Major, 218
Martin, Col. (Sir Richard), 301
Martineau's *Life of Sir Bartle Frere* cited, 141
Masipula, Umpande's chief induna, 124, 129, 224, 238, 240
Matabeleland, 30
Matiwane, blacksmith, 5, 8
Matiwane, chief, appeals to Dingana's mercy, 49 ; is murdered, 50 ; the Kwa Matiwane (place of execution), 49–50, 65
Matshana, son of Mondise, 108, 172, 173, 223
Matshobana, father of Umzilikazi, 30
Mavumengwana, son of Undhlela, 88, 224
Mawa—The Crossing of Mawa, 99, 107
Mawewe, son of Jobe, 11
Maziyana, native, a border guard, 149–50
Mehlokazulu, Sirayo's chief son, 149–51, 159, 168, 257
Meyer, Conrad, 268
Meyer, L. Johannes, 276, 278
Milne, Lieut. R.N., 176
Missionaries, amongst the Zulus, 58–61, 66, 147, 161 ; Capt. Allan Gardiner, 59 ; American Mission, 60 ; the Rev. F. Owen, Church Missionary Society, 60 ; leave Umpande's country, 100 ; attitude of Cetshwayo to, 147–8, 161–2 ; Cetshwayo's accusations against, 148, 149 ; the Rev. A. Nachtigall quoted, 145 ; accounts of killing under Cetshwayo, 152–3 ; resume work after the war, 225 ; Boers required to guarantee rights of, 276, 278
Monase, Umbulazi's mother, 103, 105
Mondise, 108
Moor, Alfred, 312
Moriarty, Capt., 195
Moselekatse, *see* Umzilikazi
Msimbiti, Jacob, 21, *see* Hlambamanzi
Mtonjaneni Heights, Sanqonqo, 73

330 INDEX

NACHTIGALL, the Rev. A., quoted, 145
Nandi, mother of Tshaka, 17, 34; death of, 24, 33, 34, 42
Napier, Sir George, 94
Natal, in 1687, 1; Bay of, 20; coast lands abandoned by Zulus, 42; Dutch "trek" to, 55; position of Dutch and British in, 95–6, 116–7; military occupation of Port Natal resumed by British, 96–7; British administration established, 97; Umpande cedes territory, 98; asylum of fugitive natives in, 44, 52, 79, 108, 151; native population of, 96, 99, 107, 186; Refugee Regulations issued, 107; Matshana seeks protection from Natal Government, 108; boundaries of, 118; Government sends Mr. Shepstone to Cetshwayo's coronation, 122, 160; endeavours to modify Zulu law, 124–7; Zulu violation of border of, 149–51; fears of invasion in, 154, 236; troops in, 158, 161, 169; feeling in, at commencement of Zulu war, 185; fears of invasion after Isandhlwana, 185–6, 188, 191, 195; sense of security restored, 203; *and see under* Bulwer
Natal, Lieut.-Governor, *see* Bulwer, Sir Henry, *and* Havelock, Sir A.
Natal Mercury cited, 148, 149
Natal Native Contingent, 169, 185–6; Wood's Irregulars, 197
Native life: Natal in 1687, *see* Abantu
Native reserve, 236, 238; main principle in, 242; defence in, 243; position in, at restoration, 239, 243–4, 252–4, 259, 261–3; extension of suggested, 264, 268; conflict with Usutu in, 268–70; official changes in, 293; loyalty in, 312, *and see under* Osborn
Natives' declaration on their treatment by Boers and Matabele contrasted, 113
Newdigate, General, 208
Ngcapayi, chief of the Mabaca people, 93, 94
Ngqengelele, Umnyamana's father, 31
Ngqumbazi, Cetshwayo's mother, 34, 102–3
Nkandhla district, 17
Nkosinkulu, one of Dingana's ancestors, 16, 64
Nomantshali, a wife of Umpande, 105–6, 119
Nombengula, 30
Nompetu, daughter of Zwidi, 30
Nongalaza, Umpande's chief induna, 85, 86
Nongoma magistracy, 72, 249, 293–4; attack by Dinuzulu, 305–9

OFTEBRO, Mr., cited, 153
Ogle, 78
Orange Free State, 207
Osborn, Mr. (Sir Melmoth), 222; appointed British Resident, 222; complaints to, 227, 230–1; Sitimela, 228; duties as Resident end, 241; Resident Commissioner in the Reserve, 254; asks for troops, 259; action regarding Cetshwayo in the Reserve, 261–2; conflict with Dabulamanzi, 269–70; New Republic boundary commission, 280–2; British Protectorate, 282–4; Usibebu's restoration, 291, 300–1, 303, 306; neutrality of New Republic, 314
Otherwise mentioned, 251, 258, 266, 267, *et passim*
Osborn, Sub-Inspector, 300, 308, 313
Ossthuisen, Martenus, 66
Overland traffic opened, 1828, 43
Owen, Rev. F., of the C.M.S., 60–1; quoted on Dingana's appearance, 51

PEARSE, Sub-Inspector, 294, 303
Pearson, Col., 170, 183–4, 194–5
Pennefather, Capt., 303–5, 313
Pietermaritzburg, 82; Zulu War monument in, 214

INDEX 331

Pomeroy-Colley, Sir G., 227
Pondos, the, *see* Faku
Portuguese, 28, 115
Potchefstroom, 112
Potgieter, Hendrik, 69, 112-3; antipathy to British, 114; intercourse with Smellekamp, 114-5; resentment at Volks Raad's decision to purchase land, 115; Lydenburg Republic of, 115-6, 119
Pretorius, Chief Commandant, 77, 89, 94, 97, 116-7, 118; defeated at Boom-plaats, 117
Pretorius's Lower Umfolozi Magistracy, 310, 314
Prince Imperial, circumstances of his death, 208-9, 211, 212
Pulleine, Lieut.-Col., 174, 176
Purdon, Capt., 313

RALIJANA, son of Somfula, 257
Rawana, the stronghold of, 194
Rensburg, Hans von, 54
Resident Commissioner, *see* Osborn, Sir Melmoth
Retief, Pieter, 55; seeks permission to occupy land south of Tugela, 55, 56, 64; Dingana's reply to, 61-2; recovers cattle from Sigonyela, 62-3; massacred, 65; his remains, 71-2
Roberts, Lord, *Forty-one Years in India,* quoted, 180
Robertson, the Rev. R., 147; quoted on the killing under Cetshwayo, 153
Rogers, Major, 170
Roman, ——, escapes from Retief massacre, 65
Rooyen, Cornelius van, 118-9
Rorke's Drift, 175, 182-3, 186, 197; lessons of, 197; Zulu loss at, 198
Rudolph, Mr., quoted, 154, 156
Rudolph, G. M., 316
Russell, Major, 170
Rustenburg District, 112, 115, 117

ST. Lucia Bay, ceded by Umpande, 98, 118
Sambane, a chief, 133
Sandilli, Gaika chief, 145
Sand River Convention, 117, 118
Santinga, Umnyamana's brother, 305
Schlikmann, Capt. von, 140
Scotch, the Highland, cited, 217
Scott, Dr., 266
Scott, Governor, 29
Seketwayo, chief of Umdhlalose tribe, 172, 257
Senzangakona, Tshaka's father, 16-7, 49, 71, 194
Shepstone, Capt. G., 176, 177
Shepstone, Henrique, 291
Shepstone, Hon. John Wesley, 144, 240
Shepstone, Sir Theophilus, cited, 7, 14-5, 141, 148, 149, 240; obtains recognition of Cetshwayo's title to succeed, 108, 122; crowns Cetshwayo, 124, 162; and the disputed territory, 142-3; on Cetshwayo's unreliability, 158; on Zulu settlement, 283-4; recommends Usibebu's restoration, 291
Otherwise mentioned, 127, 128, 241
Sibamu, Zulu councillor, 279
Sigonyela, raids Dingana's cattle, 62-3
Sikukuni, chief of the Bapeda, 115, 139-40, 145, 146, 168
Sikunyuna, chief, Ndwandwe tribe, 26-9
Sikwata, father of Sikukuni, 115, 139

INDEX

Sintwangu, Zulu envoy, 154, 168
Sirayo, Zulu chief, 148, 149, 151, 159, 165, 168, 172, 189, 223, 257
Sishweli, the Settlement of, 218–20 ; *and see sub-heading under* Zulus
Sitimela, pretender to chieftainship of Umtetwa tribe, 228–9
Siziba, Zulu envoy, 277
Smellekamp, 114–5
Smith, Capt., 95, 97 ; cited, on Gququ, 99
Smith, Sir Harry, 116 ; defeats Pretorius at Boom-plaats, 117
Smith, Mr., surveyor, 155, 159, 170
Sobuza, King of the Swazis, 90–1 ; story of Dingana's death, 91
Sokwetshata, chief of the Umtetwa, 260, 272, 292, 310–11
Somhlolo, chief, 311
Somapunga, a son of Zwidi, 26–7, 28, 219, 265
Somfula, chief, Hlabisa tribe, 257, 295, 299
Somkele, a chief, 225, 252, 260, 264, 310, 315
Somopo, 310
Songiya, Umpande's mother, by whose name Zulus swear, 124, 257, 295
Sotobe, Tshaka's envoy, 35–6, 42, 78, 217, 283
Sotshangana, 36
South African Republic, *see under heading* Boers
Special Commissioner, *see* 276, *and under* Bulwer, and Havelock
Spies, R. T., 278
Stavem, Mr., 153
Stuart, Prince Charles Edward, cited, 217
Swazis, the : Zulu campaign against (Fund' u Tulwana), 107 ; send cattle into Transvaal for protection, 107 ; Umswazi and Somcuba cede territory to the Boers, 115–6 ; aid Boers against Sikukuni, 140 ; Umbilini, 194 ; otherwise mentioned, 85, 216, 222, *and see* Sobuza
" Swim-the-water," *see* Hlambamanzi

TENGWANA, a native, 99
Tokotoko, Usibebu's uncle, 245
Tonge, C. V., 311
Transvaal, 108, 141, 145, 205–6, 222, *and see under heading* Boers
Tremlett, Major, 170
Tribal migration, 13, 243
Tribes: Abaqulusi, 194, 224, 230–1, 233, 239, 244, 280 ; Amambata, 199, 257 ; Amandwandwe, 82 ; Amangwane, 49 ; Amatonga, 252 ; Bapeda, 115 ; Biyela, 311 ; Butelezi, 242, 247, 280, 288 ; Gaika, 145 ; Galeka, 145 ; Hlabisa, 217, 237, 245, 257, 294, 295, 299, 306 ; Kumalo, 30 ; Langa, 17 ; Mabaca, 93 ; Ndwandwe, 15–6, 19–20, 24, 29, 219, 224, 237, 265, 308 ; Umdhlalose, 172, 280; Umdhletshe, 237, 245, 306–7 ; Umgazini, 224, 237, 242, 245, 247, 251–2, 280, 288 ; Umpukunyoni, 225, 252, 264, 310; Umtetwa, 11, 13, 219, 225, 228–9, 260, 272, 292, 310 ; peculiarity in language, 13 ; Unzuza, 299 ; Usutu, *see that heading ;* Zungu, 265 ; tribes dispersed from Natal by Tshaka, 29 ; the term "tribe," 296–7
Trichard, Carl Johannes, 54
Tshaka, 16 ; escapes his father, 17 ; serves under Dingiswayo, 17 ; distinguished in valour, 17 ; chief of the Zulu, 17, 39 ; his brothers, 39 ; kills his first sons, 39 ; on Dingiswayo's death reconquers subject tribes, 17, 20 ; enlarges his army, 18 ; experiment with assegai, 18 ; fate of "cowards," 18–9, 29 ; injustice of, 18 ; attacked by Zwidi, 19 ; destroys Ndwandwe tribe, 19–20 ; appearance of white men, 20–1, 26 ; habits of home life of, 22 ; his dress for great occasions, described, 22 ; festivities, 23 ; attempted assassination of, 23–4 ; his tears, 23, 34 ; attitude towards Fynn and Farewell, 24, 25 ; and King, 35 ;

INDEX

campaign against Sikunyana, 27–31; his army on the march, described, 27; submission of Umlotsha, 29; success of Beje against, 29; territories depopulated by, 29; permits Europeans to shelter tribal remnants, 44, 81; expansion of his dominion, 30, 80; assigns territory to Mapita, 31; unmarried, 31; his kraal girls, 32; inhuman disposition evinced in massacre of kraal girls, 32; removes to Dukuza kraal, 33; subjection of Beje, 33; idea of mission to English king, 33, 35; result of mission, 36; death of his mother, 33, 36; massacre and carnage, 34–5; cession of territory to Lieut. King, 35; expedition against Cape natives, 36; Sotobe, 35, 36, 78, 283; expedition against Sotshangana, Balule campaign, 36–8; affects supernatural powers, 37; massacre of women, 37; assassinated, 38, 40–1, 245; burial, 41, 42; translation of spirit, 42; national prosperity following his death, 45; characteristics, 22–3, 37; personality, 39; bloodthirsty tyranny of, 21, 32; Sir Bartle Frere quoted, 158
   Otherwise mentioned, 45, 48, 58, 81, 166, 205, 219, 228, 281; records of, by Farewell and Fynn, 21; by Isaacs, 26
Tshingana, Dinuzulu's uncle, 275, 279, 287, 311–6
Tshambezwe, son of Umnyamana, 288

UHAMU, parentage, 106; attitude to Cetshwayo's coronation, 121, 123–4; chief induna, resents assault on the Tulwana, 136; defection from Cetshwayo, 154–5, 172, 194, 226; hope of securing kingship, 189, 224; position under Sishweli settlement, 224, 226; zeal in enforcing conditions of Sishweli, 226–7; seizure of Umnyamana's cattle, 227, 232; alliance with Usibebu, 230; dispute with the Abaqulusi, 230–1; battle at Bivana River, 231, 233; position of, at the restoration, 239, 242; Abaqulusi make reprisals on, 244; encouraged by victory at Umsebe to resist the king, 251; attacked by Umnyamana, 251, 254; Sir Henry Bulwer's proposal regarding, 264; position of, after Itshana, 272; effect of New Republic boundary, 280; death, 285
   Otherwise mentioned, 241, 262
Umbangulana, chief, 197, 198
Umbilini, Swazi chief, 156, 157, 159, 194, 195–6
Umbomvana, an induna, 104
Umbopa, servant of Tshaka, 40–1; chief of Hlabisa, 237, 245, 257, 294, 295
Umbulazi, 102; applies to British for help against Cetshwayo, 103; defeated by Cetshwayo, 103–4
Umeni, Zulu Commissioner, 281
Umfanawendhlela, 241, 262, 265
Umfinyeli, Xulu chief, 106, 245
Umfokazana, 287
Umgamule, son of Unzobo, 88
Umgidhlana, a son of Nomantshali, 105, 106, 119, 143
Umgojana, a grandson of Zwidi, 219, 224, 237, 308–9
Umkabayi, a sister of Senzangakona, 194
Umkonto, Somfula's son, 299, 306
Umkosana, 287
Umkowana, a headman, 299, 307
Umkumbane stream (Kwa Matiwane—Dingana's slaughtering place), 49
Umkungo, a son of Monase, 105
"Umpakati," the, members of the King's army, 125
Umlandela, Umtetwa chief, 225, 228
Umlotsha, tributary to Zwidi, 29
Umlulwana, a Zulu envoy, 277
Umnyamana, Cetshwayo's prime induna, 31, 142, 197, 210, 215, 226; growing strength of, 109; attitude to Cetshwayo's coronation, 121,

123-4; Disputed territory, 142, 144; and the capture of Cetshwayo, 218; becomes subject to Uhamu, 224, 225; trouble over cattle, 226-8, 251; combines with Undabuko, 226, 230; and the restoration, 241, 242; grievances of, 251; proceeds against Uhamu, 251, 255; precarious position of, after Ulundi fight, 258, 265; and the Boer emissaries, 268-9; and boundary New Republic, 280-1; British Protection, 282-3, 287; the appeal to Boers, 288; secedes from Royal cause, 290, 305, 314; his simile on Usibebu's reinstatement, 302; his cattle raided, 302-3; fears assassination, 303; his domains raided, 305, 309; otherwise mentioned, 199, 205, 216, 249, 264, 273, 279

Umpande, brother of Tshaka, 39, 76, 81; disaffection for Dingana, 82; alliance with the Boers, 82-3; Umpangazita beaten to death, 84; number of his people, 84; expedition with Boers against Dingana, 85; battle of Maqongqo, 86; witnesses against Unzobo and Kambazana, 87-8; Dingana's view of, 88; receives Mapita's submission, 89; declared King of the Zulus, 89; not of Zululand, 90, 92; boundaries of his territory settled, 98; cedes St. Lucia Bay, 98; destroys his brother Gququ and family, 99; life at Sixebeni kraal, 99-100; unaffected by civilised habits of Boers, 100; attitude to missionaries and traders, 100; rigid protection of white property by, 100; Cetshwayo and Umbulazi divide the nation, 103; six of his sons killed in battle, 104; his life spared by Cetshwayo, 105; his authority gone, 105-6; the death of Umpoiyana, 106; takes wives for the spirit of Unzibe, 106; campaign against Swazis, 107; character of his rule, 107-8; length of his reign, 110; death of, 111, 112, 130

Characteristics, the fool of the family, 102; M. Delegorgue quoted, 84, 85, 111; his mother, *see* Songiya

Otherwise mentioned, 34, 109-10, 118, 119, 121-2, 133, 135, 143, 152, 162, 213, 263, 268, 271

Umpangazita (Umpangazowaga), an induna of Dingana, 84
Umpikwa, 311
Umpoiyana. a son of Nomantshali, 105, 106, 119
Umsebe, battle of, 247-9; curious scene: the demented warrior, 249
Umsundusi, a headman, 188
Umsutshwana, chief, Umdhletshe tribe, 237, 245, 306, 307
Umtetwa, the, *see heading* Tribes
Umtonga, a son of Nomantshali, 105-6, 119, 143
Umtshupana, an induna, 279
Umtumbu, son of Umbopa, 294-5, 299-300
Umzilikazi (Moselekatse), chief of Kumalo tribe, 30, 51; attacks "trekkers," 55, 56; despoiled by Dingana, 56, 85; defeated by Boers, 112
Undabuko, Cetshwayo's brother, 175, 225; quoted, 175, 182; the representative of the throne, 226; position under Sishweli settlement, 225; refuses stipend, 290; asks for Cetshwayo's bones, 226; combines with Umnyamana, 226, 230; expelled by Usibebu, 230, 232, 237, 245; applies for Cetshwayo's restoration, 234; regent on Cetshwayo's death, 267, 287; cattle seized for fine, 288, 300; British annexation, 287-9; appeal to Boers, 288; summoned to Eshowe, 292; Usibebu's repatriation, 298, 301; decision to arrest him, 303; shelters in Vrijheid, 315; surrender and exile, 316; otherwise mentioned, 273, 275
Undhlela, a chief induna of Dingana, 85-8, 211, 224, 257; the "tail" of, 90
Undulunga, a son of Umnyamana, 249
Ungowadi, a son of Nandi, 41
Unguazonco, brother of Nandi, 40
Ungungunyana, 28
Unkabonina, brother of Umbopa, 217, 257
Unkunzemnyama, chief, 310

INDEX 335

Untshingwayo, an induna, 188, 257
Unzibe, brother of Tshaka and Umpande, 39 ; Umpande takes wives for spirit of, 106
Unzobo, chief induna to Dingana, 85–8
Usibebu, son of Mapita, 31, 89 ; attitude to Cetshwayo at coronation, 121, 123–4, 241 ; scouting before Isandhlwana, 175 ; resists Cetshwayo, 189 ; attitude to war with English, 189 ; narrow escape of, 189–90 ; territory assigned to under treaty of Sishweli, 225, 297 ; zeal in enforcing conditions, 226, 227 ; alliance with Uhamu, 230, 242, 251, 254, 262, 264 ; expels Undabuko and Usiwedu, 232 ; position at the restoration, 236–9, 245, 297 ; demands submission of Maboko, 246 ; wages war against Cetshwayo, 250, 254 ; battle of Umsebe, 247–51 ; reproved by Special Commissioner, 250 ; difficulties of, with surrounding tribes, 251–2 ; his followers known as the Mandhlagazi, 255 ; wars against Cetshwayo at Ulundi, 254–8 ; assisted by Englishmen, 258, 260 ; becomes a terror, 258, 263 ; seriousness of quarrel with royal party, 267 ; attacks Somkele and instigates attacks by Sokwetshata, 260 ; British injunctions to, 260, 265 ; view of Cetshwayo's position, 262 ; moral support to people in the Reserve, 262, 263 ; objections to recognition of, 263 ; extension of his authority suggested, 264, 268 ; assurances of Boers to, 270 ; appeals to British, 270 ; battle of Itshana, 270–2 ; takes refuge in the Reserve, 272, 290 ; British view of his expulsion, 290 ; pleads for restoration, 290–1 ; restoration urged by officials, 291–2 ; restoration, 292–5 ; his reception, 296 ; necessity of assigning territorial limits to, 297 ; Mr. Addison's settlement, 297–9 ; attitude of Dinuzulu to, 298–9, 301–2 ; presses for removal of Usutu, 299, and Hlabisa, 300 ; attacked by Unzuza tribe, 299 ; raids and reprisals, 305–7 ; defeated by Usutu at Nongoma, 308–9 ; retires to Inkonjeni, 309 ; characteristics of, 123, 246, 255, 295
   Otherwise mentioned, 106, 132, 241, 244, 265, 274, 280
Usigcwelegcwele, an induna, 137
Usikizana, Usibebu's chief induna, 290
Usingananda, chief, 259
Usiteku, a brother of Cetshwayo, 119, 249
Usiwedu, brother of Cetshwayo, 119, 187, 216, 225, 232, 237, 245, 257, 289, 302–3, 309
Usutu party, adherents of Cetshwayo, 103, 242 ; the ultra Usutu, 245 ; commit acts of violence against Usibebu, 246, 247 ; prepare to resist Usibebu, 296 ; complaints against Usibebu, 299 ; general dispersion of armed Usutu, 314, *see* Dabulamanzi, Dinuzulu *et passim*
Utrecht District, 118, 143, 155
Uys, Piet, 67, 68, 69
Uys, Piet (secundus), 170, 193, 196 ; monument to, at Utrecht, 193

VAAL RIVER, the, 118
Vaccination introduced amongst Zulus, 108
Van Staden, Jacobus, 268
Vijn, Cornelius, 187, 209–10, 216–7
Vryheid, 119, 196

WEATHERLEY, Col., 196–7
White, ——, trader, 310
Wolseley, Sir Garnet, 146, 155, 206–7, 215, 218–9, 308
Wood, Gen. Sir Evelyn, 170 ; operations of, 171, 172, 193-7 ; battle of Kambula, 197–8, 208 ; cited, Zulu loss at Kambula, 198 ; arbitrates in disputes with chiefs, 227, 232, 251
Wragg, Justice W., 316

INDEX

XULU family, the, 106
Xwana, Zulu sentinel, 73

ZEYIZE, envoy, 277
Zonyama, 287; nephew of Sotobe, 217
Zulu: *and see heading* Abantu
Administration, 80, 108; governing power and moral restraint, 58–9; aims of, 59; will of the king not absolute, 245; punishment of death too generally applied, 80, 124–5, 159–60, 163; establishment of guilt, 80; sentence, 80; confiscation of property, 80, 162–3; discrimination in dealing with accused persons, 108–10; asylum of fugitives, 44, 52, 80–1, 108, 132, 151; death for failing in military duty, 153; white persons and property, 100, 148; an administration of justice described, 100–1; Natal attempt to modify Zulu law, 124–6, 160–1; under Sishweli settlement, 221; laws, &c., promulgated at annexation, 286; *see sub-head*, Witchcraft

Agriculture: condition of land, 243; primitive method of manuring, 243; first-fruits festival, 135, 144

Army, the: military organisation, 9–10, 160, 166–7; divisions, 177; list of regiments, 110; regimental system, 110, 120; regiments mentioned, 133, 135–6, 177, 182; arms, 9, 18, 174; battle order, 177; signalling, 73, 196; character of native battles, 69, 104, 183, 185, 229, 248–9; advantages and hardships of attachment to, 125, 160, 167, 222; the Umpakati, 125; punishment for failing to discharge military duty, 153; strength at period of Zulu war, 176–7

Asseverations, 116, 124, 257

Bayete, the royal salute, 13, 131

Beliefs: propitiation of ancestral spirits, 61; spiritual life, 61, 106, 132; rites to ensure rain, 132; as to swelling of slain enemies, 180

Characteristics, 46, 64, 181; affections, absence of sympathy for feelings of females, 135; age, reverence for, 135; conservatism, 52; dignity, 209; leisureliness, 209; loyalty, not reliable in adversity, 218; memory, great power of, 164; tears as a warning of danger, 34; wariness, 39–40; circumspection of those in authority, 39–40, 81; clear voices, 73, 196; John Dunn quoted on, 128

Customs and habits, 52; classification according to age, 133; enemies, killing of, 260; girls translated into the families of chiefs, 32; leave to "gather the bones," 81, 226; Kok'umkonto, 227; heroism, celebration of, 260–1; tribute, daughters as consideration for, 32; chiefs, execution by strangulation, 49

Faction fighting, 160, 286, 287

History: absence of written records, 2, 10, 187, 258

Kraals, *see that heading*

Marriage: conjugal infidelity a capital offence, 31, 149; custom of chiefs, 31–2; the women of the Great House, 32; of soldiers, 160, 161, 167, 222

Old men, considered an incumbrance, 32; Zulu reverence for age, 135; and the nation's records, 8, 258

Ornaments, 51; the Ingxota, 51–2; head-rings, 77

Poisons, 129

INDEX 337

Zulu (*continued*):
Proverbs and Metaphors; to "gather the bones" of a person, 81, 226; Kwa Matiwane, 50; Manyosi, 48; the Isigodhlo, 46; the refinement of cruelty, 47

Religion, attitude to Christianity and converts, 60–1, 147, 225, *and see* Beliefs *above*

Tribes, *see that heading*

Weapons, 9, 18

Witchcraft, 126–7, 153–4, 163, 286, 287, 299; witch doctors, 80, 110, 126; baboons in, 126–7, 137

Women: absence of sympathy for feelings of, 135; of the "Great House," 32, 46–7, 238; wives, *see* Marriage; Nandi, first woman to whom greatness is assigned, 34; Songiya, by whose name Zulus swear, 124, 257, 295

Zulu Carbineers, *see* Mansel

Zulu Native Reserve Territory, *see* Native Reserve

Zulu War:
Battles and Fights: Eshowe, siege of, 184, 194–5, 200–2; Gingindhlovu kraal, 201; Ihlobane Hill, 196–7, 200; Intshotshose Stream affair: Prince Imperial killed, 208–9; Inyezane, or Iombane, 183–4, 202
Isandhlwana, 173–81, 185–8, 190, 197, 207; Zulus engaged, 177; impis get out of hand and attack, 177, 180; closing scene described as a butchery, 180; British retreat after, 181; condition of Zulus after, 181
Kambula camp, decisive battle at, 198, 200, 213; strength and condition of Zulus, 197–8
Luneburg, affair near, 195
Rorke's Drift, 182–3; lessons of, 197; persistence of Zulus at, 183
Ulundi, or Nodwengu (sheet-iron fort), 213–15; incidents of march on, 211–12
British: forces engaged in, 168–70, 195, 204; disposition of forces and plans, 170–5; method of causing diversions, 200, 211; Natal Kafirs employed, 211; losses, 195, 213–4; view of Zulu power, 200
Causes of, 142 ff., 236, 257; Zulu ignorance of, 213
End of, 203, 213; destruction of Zulu national system, 203, 218–9
Peace, negotiations, 204, 209, 212; suggestions as to terms of, 205; settlement of Sishweli, 218–20, *and see sub-heading under* Zulu
Zulus: marshalling of forces, 172–3; plans of, 172–3, 175, 186–7, 203; hunger of, 173, 175–6, 181; ignorant drinking by, 181; condition of, before Kambula, 197; sufferings of wounded, 199; losses, 198–9, 213; mourning and wailing for slain, 187–8, 199; ignorance of cause of war, 213; instance of betrayal, 197; view of Boer aloofness, 192; attitude to invasion of Natal, 182

Zulus (*and see under chiefs' names*): the house of Zulu, 16; chiefs, ancestors of Tshaka, 16

Tshaka: campaign against Sikunyana, 27–31; expansion of dominion, 30, 80; Balule campaign, 36–8, 81; death of Nandi, 33–6; Natal coast lands abandoned, 42; thankfulness for death of Tshaka, 42; national prosperity after Tshaka's death, 45

Dingana: expedition against Umzilikazi, 56; defeat Dutch at Itala, 68; defeat English, 69; defeated at Ingcome (Blood River), 71; discontent with Dingana's government, 79; battle of Maqongqo, 86; death of Unzobo, 88

Umpande: land annexed by Boers, 89; life under Umpande, 98–9; the

338 INDEX

Zulus (*continued*):
crossing of Mawa, 99, 107 ; Fund' u Tulwana campaign, 107 ; 'Ndondakusuka battle, 103–4 ; exodus into Natal after battle, 107 ; scourge of small-pox, 108

Cetshwayo : nation at Cetshwayo's accession, 120–1, 130 ; habit of discussing strength in comparison with that of England, 121 ; general arming with guns, 121 ; coronation of the king, 129–30 ; view of Cetshwayo's reign, 131 ; general peace under Cetshwayo, 132 ; the "marriage of the Ingcugce," 133–6 ; fight between regiments, 135–8, 148, 149 ; the Disputed territory, 119, 140–4, 148, 152, 158–9 ; European view of Zulus, 147 ; attitude to missionaries and converts, 147–8, 161 ; violate British territory, 149–51, 159 ; invasion feared by British, 154, 157 ; suspicion of British intentions, 154–6 ; guards seize Smith and Deighton, 155–6, 159, 165 ; attack on Swazi kraals, 156 ; life under Cetshwayo, white view of, 153–4, 159–60 ; Zulu complaint of Cetshwayo, 162–3 ; statement of deputies, 163 ; British Ultimatum to, 159–66, 168, 194 ; action regarding Ultimatum, 165–6 ; discussion of Ultimatum, 167–8 ; view of British strength, 168 ; united against British, 188

Zulu War, *see that heading*

Sishweli, settlement of, 218–20 ; notion of reviving clans, 219 ; feeling after the war, 219, 222–3 ; views of relations to British, 219-20, 222–3 ; country divided and assigned to chiefs, 220–5 ; British Government's requirements, 221, 226 ; submission of people to chiefs, 221–2 ; prepare to pay tax, 222–3 ; frauds by natives, 223 ; administration by the chiefs, 223–5 ; complaints of oppression, 227, 231 ; control passing from chiefs, 230 ; disaffection to chiefs, 234 ; disadvantages of settlement, 231, 296 ; necessity for central authority, 231–2 ; meeting of chiefs at Inhlazatshe, 232

Movement for restoration of Cetshwayo, 234 ; attitude of people and chiefs to restoration, 238–44 ; position in the Reserve, 252–4, 259, 261 ; division and confusion, 252, 258, 263 ; battle of Ulundi, 256–8 ; notables slain, 257–8 ; conditions of a settlement, 264 ; no remedy that would not involve bloodshed, 268 ; receive Boer assurances, 268–70 ; Itshana battle, 271–3 ; territory claimed by Boers, 273–4 ; protectorate over, assumed by Boers, 274 ; repudiate Boer claims, 275 ; ask British intervention, 275, 276, 277 ; made to realise subjection to Boers, 277 ; complaints of Boer treatment, 277 ; and boundary commission, 278 ; tribes deprived under boundary decision, 280 ; protest against boundary decision, 279–81, 283, 285 ; deputation sends letter to Queen Victoria, 280 ; refuse British Protectorate, 281–3 ; laws and traditions as to territory, 283 ; Royal house and interests of the people, 284 ; annexation of Zululand, 283–7 ; position of royal family and chiefs after proclamation, 286 ; appeal to Boer protection, 288 ; attitude to annexation, 286–7, 289, 301–2

Zuya, brass worker, 51

Zwidi, chief Ndwandwe tribe, 15, 19 ; slays Dingiswayo, 16 ; attacks Tshaka, 19 ; defeated by him, 19 ; establishes settlement north of Utrecht, 20, 24 ; death, 20, 26 ; otherwise mentioned, 219

RENEWALS: 691-4574

DATE DUE

FEB 2 5		
MAY 1 0		
NOV 0 3		
~~NOV 2 1~~		
MAY 0 9 2008		

Demco, Inc. 38-293